ADAPTIVE 2019

The Eleventh International Conference on Adaptive and Self-Adaptive Systems and Applications

May 5 - 9, 2019

Venice, Italy

ADAPTIVE 2019 Editors

Nadia Abchiche-Mimouni, University of Evry, France
Sebastian Herold, Karlstad University, Sweden
Mirco Schindler, Technische Universität Clausthal, Germany
Christoph Knieke, Technische Universität Clausthal, Germany
Piotr Malak, University of Wrocław, Poland
Tomasz Walkowiak, Wroclaw University of Science and Technology, Poland

Printed from e-media with permission by:

Curran Associates, Inc.
57 Morehouse Lane
Red Hook, NY 12571

Some format issues inherent in the e-media version may also appear in this print version.

Printed by Curran Associates, Inc. (2019)

International Academy, Research, and Industry Association (IARIA)
412 Derby Way
Wilmington, DE 19810

Phone: (408) 893-6407
Fax: (408) 527-6351

petre@iaria.org

Additional copies of this publication are available from:

Curran Associates, Inc.
57 Morehouse Lane
Red Hook, NY 12571 USA
Phone: 845-758-0400
Fax: 845-758-2633
Email: curran@proceedings.com
Web: www.proceedings.com

Table of Contents

ADAPTIVE 2019

Forward

The Eleventh International Conference on Adaptive and Self-Adaptive Systems and Applications (ADAPTIVE 2019), held between May 5 - 9, 2019 - Venice, Italy, continued a series of events targeting advanced system and application design paradigms driven by adaptiveness and self-adaptiveness. With the current tendencies in developing and deploying complex systems, and under the continuous changes of system and application requirements, adaptation is a key feature. Speed and scalability of changes require self-adaptation for special cases. How to build systems to be easily adaptive and self-adaptive, what constraints and what mechanisms must be used, and how to evaluate a stable state in such systems are challenging duties. Context-aware and user-aware are major situations where environment and user feedback is considered for further adaptation.

The conference had the following tracks:

- Self-adaptation
- Adaptive applications
- Adaptivity in robot systems
- Fundamentals and design of adaptive systems

Similar to the previous edition, this event attracted excellent contributions and active participation from all over the world. We were very pleased to receive top quality contributions.

We take here the opportunity to warmly thank all the members of the ADAPTIVE 2019 technical program committee, as well as the numerous reviewers. The creation of such a high quality conference program would not have been possible without their involvement. We also kindly thank all the authors that dedicated much of their time and effort to contribute to ADAPTIVE 2019. We truly believe that, thanks to all these efforts, the final conference program consisted of top quality contributions.

Also, this event could not have been a reality without the support of many individuals, organizations and sponsors. We also gratefully thank the members of the ADAPTIVE 2019 organizing committee for their help in handling the logistics and for their work that made this professional meeting a success.

We hope ADAPTIVE 2019 was a successful international forum for the exchange of ideas and results between academia and industry and to promote further progress in the area of adaptive and self-adaptive systems and applications. We also hope Venice provided a pleasant environment during the conference and everyone saved some time for exploring this beautiful city.

ADAPTIVE 2019 Chairs

ADAPTIVE 2019 Steering Committee

Roy Sterritt, Ulster University, UK
Constantin Paleologu, University Politehnica of Bucharest, Romania
Claudia Raibulet, University of Milano-Bicocca, Italy
Radu Calinescu, University of York, UK
Po-Hsun Cheng, National Kaohsiung Normal University, Taiwan
Marc-Philippe Huget, Polytech Annecy-Chambery-LISTIC | University of Savoie, France
Ryotaro Kamimura, Tokai Univerisity, Japan
Valerie Camps, Paul Sabatier University - IRIT, Toulouse, France

ADAPTIVE 2019 Industry/Research Advisory Committee

Weirong Jiang, Google, USA
Jessie Y.C. Chen, U.S. Army Research Laboratory, USA
Sherif Abdelwahed, Distributed Analytics and Security Institute (DASI), USA
Marc Kurz, University of Applied Sciences Upper Austria, Faculty for Informatics, Communications and Media, Austria
Habtamu Abie, Norwegian Computing Center/Norsk Regnesentral-Blindern, Norway

ADAPTIVE 2019

Committee

ADAPTIVE 2019 Steering Committee
Roy Sterritt, Ulster University, UK
Constantin Paleologu, University Politehnica of Bucharest, Romania
Claudia Raibulet, University of Milano-Bicocca, Italy
Radu Calinescu, University of York, UK
Po-Hsun Cheng, National Kaohsiung Normal University, Taiwan
Marc-Philippe Huget, Polytech Annecy-Chambery-LISTIC | University of Savoie, France
Ryotaro Kamimura, Tokai Univerisity, Japan
Valerie Camps, Paul Sabatier University - IRIT, Toulouse, France

ADAPTIVE 2019 Industry/Research Advisory Committee
Weirong Jiang, Google, USA
Jessie Y.C. Chen, U.S. Army Research Laboratory, USA
Sherif Abdelwahed, Distributed Analytics and Security Institute (DASI), USA
Marc Kurz, University of Applied Sciences Upper Austria, Faculty for Informatics, Communications and Media, Austria
Habtamu Abie, Norwegian Computing Center/Norsk Regnesentral-Blindern, Norway

ADAPTIVE 2019 Technical Program Committee

Sherif Abdelwahed, Distributed Analytics and Security Institute (DASI), USA
Habtamu Abie, Norwegian Computing Center/Norsk Regnesentral-Blindern, Norway
Nadia Acbchiche-Mimouni, University of Evry, France
Jose M. Alcaraz Calero, University of the West of Scotland, UK
Harvey Alférez, Universidad de Montemorelos, Mexico
Richard Anthony, University of Greenwich, UK
Abdalkarim Awad, University of Erlangen, Germany
Charles K. Ayo, Covenant University, Ogun State, Nigeria
Dirk Bade, University of Hamburg, Germany
Arvind Bansal, Kent State University, USA
Nik Bessis, Edge Hill University, UK
Stefan Bosse, University of Bremen, Germany
Darko Bozhinoski, Gran Sasso Science Institute, Italy
Antonio Brogi, University of Pisa, Italy
Radu Calinescu, University of York, UK
Valerie Camps, Paul Sabatier University - IRIT, Toulouse, France
Carlos Carrascosa, Universidad Politécnica de Valencia, Spain
Jessie Y.C. Chen, U.S. Army Research Laboratory, USA
Po-Hsun Cheng, National Kaohsiung Normal University, Taiwan
Enrique Chirivella Perez, University of the West of Scotland, UK

Maher Chaouachi, University of McGill, Canada
François Charpillet, Inria, France
Jose Alfredo F. Costa, Federal University - UFRN, Brazil
Anderson da Silva Soares, Professor at Federal University of Goiás, Brazil
Baudouin Dafflon, Université de Lyon, Université Lyon 1, France
Angel P. del Pobil, Jaume I University, Spain
Mihaela Dinsoreanu, Technical University of Cluj-Napoca, Romania
Ioanna Dionysiou, University of Nicosia, Cyprus
Holger Eichelberger, University of Hildesheim, Germany
Fairouz Fakhfakh, University of Sfax, Tunisia
Ziny Flikop, Consultant, USA
Francisco J. García-Peñalvo, University of Salamanca, Spain
Giuseppina Gini, Politecnico di Milano, Italy
Thomas Göthel, Technische Universität Berlin, Germany
Hongsheng He, Wichita State University, USA
Alwin Hoffmann, University of Augsburg, Germany
Leszek Holenderski, Philips Lighting Research, Data Science Dept - Eindhoven, The Netherlands
Mohssen Hosseini, KU Leuven, Belgium
Christopher-Eyk Hrabia, Technische Universität Berlin | DAI-Labor, Germany
Marc-Philippe Huget, Polytech Annecy-Chambery-LISTIC | University of Savoie, France
David Inkermann, Technische Universität Braunschweig, Germany
Weirong Jiang, Google, USA
Clarimar José Coelho, Escola de Ciências Exatas e da Computação (ECEC) - Pontifícia Universidade Católica de Goiàs (PUC Goiás), Brazil
Imène Jraidi, University of Montreal, Canada
Ryotaro Kamimura, Tokai Univerisity, Japan
Alexey Kashevnik, SPIIRAS, Russia
Quist-Aphetsi Kester, Ghana Technology University College, Ghana
Hadis Khorasani, Shahid Beheshti University (SBU), Tehran, Iran
Verena Klös, Technische Universität Berlin, Germany
Oliver Kosak, Institut for Software & Systems Engineering - University of Augsburg, Germany
Daniel Kostrzewa, Silesian University of Technology, Poland
Satoshi Kurihara, University of Electro-Communications, Japan
Marc Kurz, University of Applied Sciences Upper Austria, Faculty for Informatics, Communications and Media, Austria
Mikel Larrea, University of the Basque Country UPV/EHU, Spain
Jinoh Lee, Istituto Italiano di Tecnologia (IIT), Italy
Henrique Lopes Cardoso, FEUP/LIACC, Portugal
Maite López-Sánchez, Universitat de Barcelona, Spain
Tamara Lorenz, University of Cincinnati, USA
Piotr Malak, University of Wrocław, Poland
Ricardo Marco Alaez, University of the West of Scotland, UK
Cesar Marin, The University of Manchester, UK
Mieke Massink, CNR-ISTI, Italy
Dalton Matsuo Tavares, Federal University of Goiás, Brazil
René Meier, Lucerne University of Applied Sciences and Arts, Switzerland
Andreas Metzger, paluno (The Ruhr Institute for Software Technology) / University of Duisburg-Essen, Germany

Copyright Information

Coalition-based Multi-agent Approach for Implementing Ethics

An assistive application case-study

Nadia Abchiche-Mimouni
IBISC, Univ Evry, Université Paris-Saclay,
91025, Evry, France
email: nadia.abchichemimouni@univ-evry.fr

Etienne Colle
IBISC, Univ Evry, Université Paris-Saclay,
91025, Evry, France
email: etienne.colle@univ-evry.fr

Abstract— **This paper presents an adaptive multi-agent approach based on coalitions for ambient assisted living applications. Adaptation is crucial because the challenge is to deal with a dynamic environment in order to provide adequate services to an elderly or a sick person at home. Moreover, it is necessary to take into account constraints such as degree of urgency of the service, intrusion level of the system and person's privacy. Ethical dimension is then important for the acceptability of such applications. The evolution of the degree of intrusion based on the degree of urgency and the availability of the communication devices of the ambient environment are particularly targeted by considering ethical dimension. The results show that not only ethics consideration allows better acceptability of the system, but also the performances are improved.**

Keywords-adaptation; agents coalitions; ethics.

I. Introduction

Adaptivity is widely studied as a capability that makes a system able to exhibit intelligent behavior. Moreover, software increasingly has to deal with ubiquity, so that it can apply a certain degree of intelligence. Our specific context is to assist an elderly or a sick person in loss of autonomy at home by providing assistive applications based on cooperation among a robot and Communication Objects (CO). Maintaining such people at home is not only beneficial to their psychological conditions but helps to reduce the costs of hospitalizations. Ambient assistive robotics can be defined as an extension of ambient intelligence, which integrates a mobile and autonomous robot and its embedded sensors and the CO present in the house. The interaction among the components in such systems is fundamental. Arnand & al. [2] the authors presented a coalition-based multi-agent system (MAS) for implementing an ambient assistive living framework that takes advantage of an Ambient Environment (AE): a robot and its embedded sensors, cooperating with a network of COs. The aim is to provide a service to the person in an adaptive way. A coalition of agents proposes a set of data and the way of combining these data in order to offer the desired service. Adaptation is needed because the context is dynamic and difficult to predict. Depending on the context, the same service can be achieved by different combination of the data. A MAS reifies the sensors, the CO and the robot, allowing the cooperation by means of coalitions formation. The agents combine the data according to their availability and the relevance. Moreover, the system has to deal with privacy and intrusion level so that one minimizes causing inconvenience. This work is based on our previous system COALAA (Coalitions for Ambient Assisted living applications), which is a coalition-based approach for implementing ambient assisted applications [1]. An improvement is proposed by: (1) embedding a Rule-Based Reasoning (RBR) module in the agents in order to reason about the coalition formation criteria, and (2) extending the scope of the adaptiveness to ethical, functional... The new approach can be considered as a general approach for implementing adaptation in ambient assisted applications. New CO can be added in a dynamic way and the way of forming the coalitions can be tuned by the user by introducing new rules in the system.

The rest of the paper is organized as follows: Section II presents an ambient assisted living approach based on multi-agent coalitions. Section III presents a generalized approach which deals with ethical dimension. Section IV highlights its benefits and shows the results validation. Section V concludes with some improvements and perspectives.

II. Coalition-based approach ambient

The principle of coalitions aims at temporarily putting together agents for reaching a common goal. The works [6][8][9] illustrate the relevance of coalition-based approaches for adaptiveness. The methods are various: either incremental, random or centralized. But, all of them proceed in two stages: (1) the formation of agent coalitions according to their ability to be involved in achieving a goal and (2) the negotiation stage among the coalitions in order to choose the one that provides the closest solution to the goal. The interests of the coalition-based formation protocols are the flexibility with which coalitions are formed and straightforwardness of the coalition formation process itself. The coalitions can get rid of dynamically reorganize with local and simple rules defined in the agents.

A. COALAA

COALAA is MAS-based on a coalition-based approach for ambient agents. Each agent in COALAA encapsulates a CO and decides in a local and proactive way when and how to contribute to the required service to the person. A more general notion than a service, called an *effect* has been introduced. An effect can be a particular lighting at a precise place of the residence or the localization of a robot. The MAS configures itself for providing a solution according to the availability of the CO and the respect of criteria. Note that the goal is not to find the optimal solution but a solution close to the required effect. In the coalition formation protocol, the obligation to obtain the required effect and an intrusion level depending on the urgency of the situation, are the most important considered criteria. They are also used during the agent reorganization while trying to achieve a desired effect. The effect obligation criteria is used in priority while the level of intrusion is modified only if needed, i.e., to acquire new data and thus to activate the sensors likely to cause discomfort to the person.

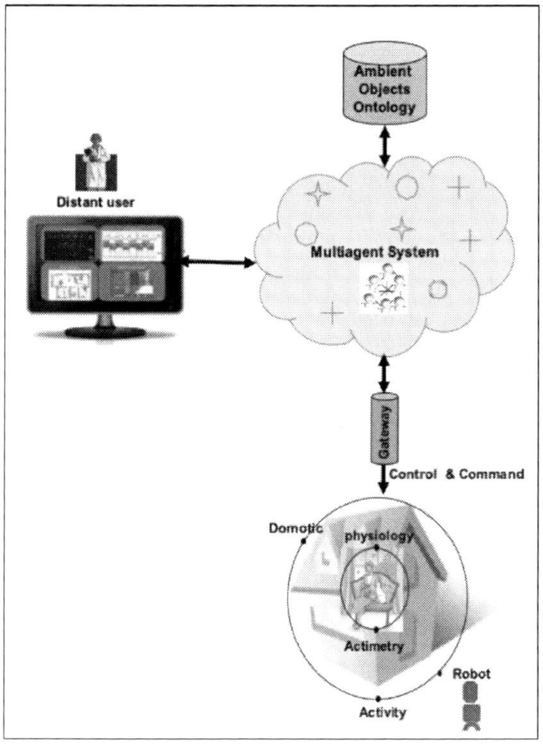

Figure 1. Architecture of COALAA

As shown in Figure 1, several kinds of components are necessary to deal with the complexity of COALAA. An effect is modelled in the form of a triple <t;c;f> where:

-t ∈ T, c ∈ C

-T a set of task labels: localization, enlightening...

-C a set of criteria: accuracy, efficiency, neighbourhood

-F a list of factors: intrusion level, urgency degree...

The designer of the system statically assigns the criteria, while the influencing factors are assigned by the end-user.

The information handled by the system is classified into two types. This so-called persistent information, related to the application domain, puts together data about the structure of the residence and the features of the CO. The second type concerns volatile data mainly the measures provided by the sensors and the orders sent to actuators. The volatile data are distributed in each agent, while persistent data are stored in an ontology named AA (Ambient Assistance) [5][4]. The AA ontology contains four categories of information related to the application domain: The Home category for defining the structure of the environment, the CO category for knowing their characteristics and their operating mode, the User category for defining the user profile and the Task category that puts together the tasks and Services achieved by the system.

The Gateway is a module for the standardization of information exchanged between the ambient environment and the MAS. Its role is to make the agents manipulating the common information format. This standardization is necessary because of the heterogeneity of protocols from different manufacturers.

B. *Agent internal architecture*

The agents of the MAS are created according to the ontologies concepts. Each agent is assigned an internal architecture able to take in charge the agent adaption and reactivity by using three main parameters that are: neighborhood, history, and ability. The neighborhood sets the list of agents that are close to this agent at a given time, according to the topological distance. The history stores previous perceived information that comes from the sensors. This is a simple succession of perceived data, which helps to consider the timescale during the process of coalition formation. The ability identifies the skills of the agent, which are directly related to the encapsulated CO.

C. *Agent behaviors*

In the process of the coalition formation, an agent may be either initiator or candidate. Any agent whose ability can partially meet the desired effect can be a coalition initiator. The initiator exchanges messages with other agents, potential members of the coalition, called candidate agents. The communication is based on exchanges of messages between the initiator agent and candidate agents. As soon as the overall ability of the coalition is close to the desired effect, the initiator agent is pending the negotiation phase. At the end of the coalition formation, each initiator agent that is the referent of a coalition is negotiating with other initiators agents to select the winning coalition. The coalition whose ability is the closest to the desired effect is the winning one. The concept of ability is generic. In the localization application example, it is instantiated by the measure precision. The principle is simple. Each initiator agent sends a message that contains the ability obtained by its coalition. On receipt of this message, each initiator agent compares the ability of the coalition it received to its own one. If its ability is lower than that received, the coalition will be no more considered, otherwise, it is a winning coalition up to receiving a new message. Apart from the desired effect, the formation of coalitions uses other criteria such as the topological neighborhood to reduce the response time or the obsolescence of a measure when the desired effect depends on sensor data. Thus, the first step is the identification of candidate neighbors according to its own location in the environment (defined by the topological distance) and the desired effect. The aim of this strategy is to ensure that a result will be provided. For that purpose, the first selection criteria considered is the topological distance. Once all candidate agents are known, each initiating agent continues the selection of candidates based on the recent measures criteria. When no coalition is able to meet the desired effect, a new search for a successful coalition is restarted after having relaxed the constraints on certain criteria. Indeed, it is possible to increase the level of intrusion of the system despite of the tranquility of the person at home. This authorization to increase the level of intrusion allows, for example, operating a pan-tilt camera of the robot in order to acquire new measures and restart the process of searching for a winning coalition. This point is sensitive because there is a risk of violating the person's privacy. The protocol of coalition formation is composed of two distinct steps. The first step consists in forming coalitions of agents according to their ability. The second step is a negotiation and refining phase so that the best one, in satisfying the desired effect criteria, is chosen. Figure 2 summarizes the agents' behaviors. The baseline algorithm proceeds in three steps. After initialization, the exchanges among agents follow three main actions: formation of all possible coalitions for each referent, selection of the best coalition according to the coalition precision, deployment of the winning coalition.

The agents' interaction semantic is based on speech act theory [11], allowing the agents to assign a semantic to each message by defining a message a type. The most important types are: Request, Response, Initiate, Acknowledge, Accept and Negotiate.

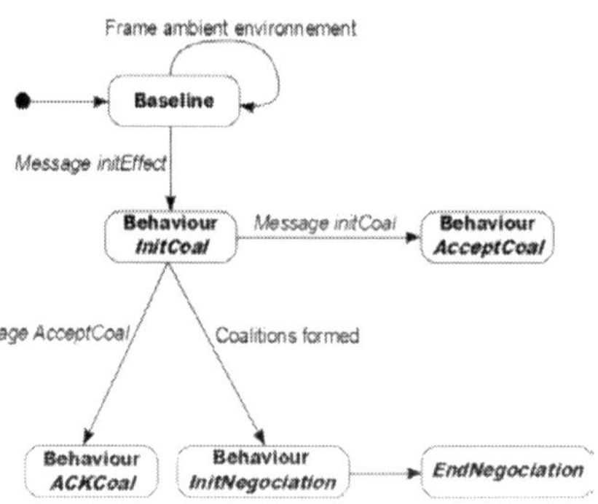

Figure 2: Agent behaviors

D. *Discussion*

COALAA shows the feasibility and the relevance of coalition-based MAS for ambient assisted scenario. It also shows that it is possible to deal with privacy criteria while building the coalitions. This is due to the high degree of adaptability of the coalition formation algorithms. To fit the obligation for the system to give a result, COALAA required the user for manually assign a priority to the criteria and the bounds for the values of the criteria. The next section illustrates this weakness and shows a generalized way of solving this problem.

III. A GENERALIZED CRITERIA MANAGEMENT COALITION FORMATION (COALAA-GEN)

Figure 3 shows an example scenario. A robot in the person's home; the patient has fallen. To move towards her/him and to guide its camera to the remote caregiver, the robot has to be located first. A visual contact will then help the remote caregiver to perform a correct diagnosis of the situation. Depending if the robot is the room P1 or the room P2, the CO required are different.

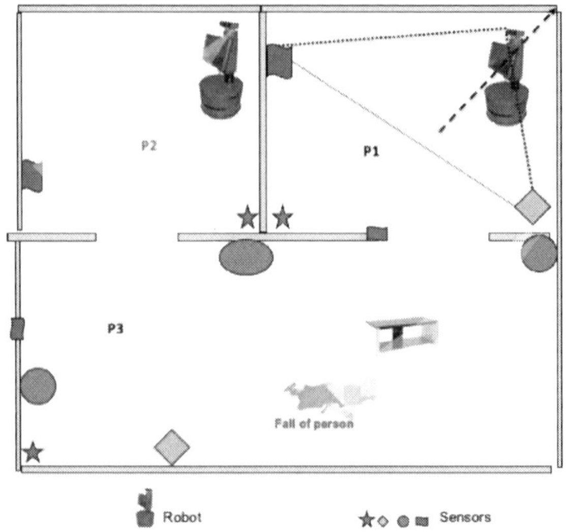

Figure 3: Fall detection scenario

Figure 4 illustrates how the MAS solving this problem. More details can found in [3]. Three kinds of CO are involved: a robot pan-tilt camera, a fixed camera and a presence detection sensor. Three respective ambient agents encapsulate these three CO: a Presence Detector Agent (APD), a Fixed Camera Agent (AFC) and a Pan-Tilt Camera Agent (APTC). Visual markers like Data matrix are associated with each camera. Following the fall of the patient, a request for a localization effect is generated in the form of a triple <t;c;f> where t is a localization task which matches with the desired effect, c matches with a singleton containing the precision criterion needed for the localization task and f matches with a set containing two influencing factors that are the intrusion level and level of urgency. In the considered scenario, we have considered a precision equal to 0.1, a level of urgency equals to 3 (three levels of urgency are considered: low=1, medium=2, high=3) and an intrusion level initialized to 0 (the less intrusion level). So, the triple becomes: <Locate;f0:1g;f3;0g>. The Interface agent (AI) has received the desired effect and then broadcasts the request InitCoal (<Locate;0:1g;f3;0g>) to all the agents of the MAS. As soon as each agent receives the desired effect, it checks its ability. As all sensors in the environment have a precision that is not better than the desired effect, each agent initiates a coalition with immediate neighborhood. In this figure, only interactions with APD agent are shown. Assuming that all agents are topologically close, APD broadcast a coalition formation request by sending an

InitCoal message. Each agent receiving the initialization message checks if its ability is adequate with the request of coalition formation. If yes, it sends an acceptance message labelled AcceptCoal to be a candidate. Such a message contains the precision of the agent. APD adds progressively answer acceptance, and accumulates the abilities, which are the precision in the considered localization task. By this way, it calculates the overall ability of the coalition until it reaches that of the desired effect. Then, it sends ACKCoal acceptance to confirm the membership of the candidate to the formed coalition. The next step is to activate the coalition. The robot moves to the place designated by the coalition and guides its pan-tilt-camera to the remote caregiver. First of all, the distant user has to verify that the person is in his field of vision, so it can perform a correct diagnosis of the situation and adopt an adequate action. Conversely, if the person is not well located the system restarts searching for a new result, after having increased the intrusion level. This allows the cameras to be moved randomly so that the chances of getting a visual marker are increased. The consequence will be improving the precision of the result.

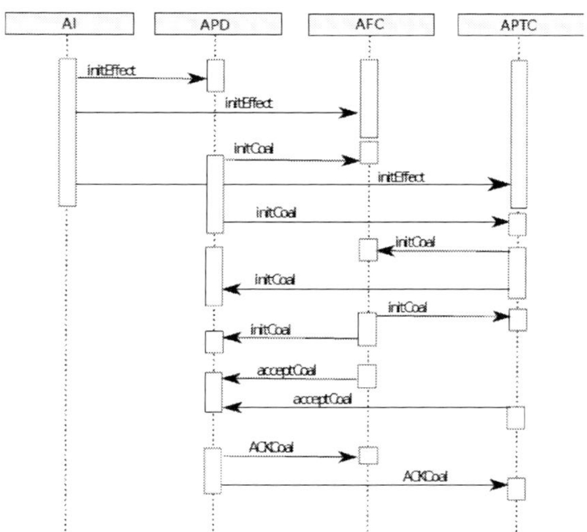

Figure 4: Interaction diagram

A. Agent rule-based reasoning module

The previous scenario shows that criteria management is critical. Indeed, obtaining a successful coalition depends on the order in which the criteria have been considered. In the above scenario, if the first considered criterion was the level of intrusion (instead of the precision), then the first result would have been the correct one. Then, the question could be the following: why can one not have a management criteria step integrated in the coalition formation process? This is the main contribution of this work. We have introduced into each agent of COALAA a Rule-Based Reasoning (RBR) module responsible of determining a priority of the criteria to consider according to the context. The RBR is also responsible of assigning and adjusting the criteria values. The RBR is used for interleaving the execution of the behaviors in a dynamic way.

The RBR is composed of a Knowledge Base (KB) and an inference engine. The KB contains a set of rules and a set of facts. The rules are given in the form of implications. The facts describe the state of the world. The inference engine is a special interpreter that controls the triggering of the rules according to the KB. The form of a rule is: *IF <antecedent> THEN <consequent>*, *<antecedent>* is the condition that must be satisfied to trigger the rule, *<consequent>* is the performed action when the rule is triggered. Antecedent is satisfied if the condition matches the facts in the KB.

Instead of having a procedural control, each behavior is modelled by a production rule whose activation condition is precisely the context of its execution. The behaviors of the agents are associated with trigger conditions. These conditions represent the context that makes behaviors possible to be executed. Explicit chaining between the behaviors is no more needed since the inference engine triggers the rules. For example, the AcceptCoal behavior is chained with the InitCoal behavior. So, the InitCoal behavior is executed once the AcceptCoal behavior is terminated. The rules below express in Jess syntax [12] that if an agent has in its working memory an InitCoal message and if the agent has an ability ?x, so the rule can be triggered. In this case, the core of the behavior associated with the rule is executed.

```
(defrule check-ability"accepts to join coalition if required ability"
(Message InitCoal ?x)(Ability ?x)=>(assert (Behavior AcceptCoal ?x)))
(defrule perform-ability"Create an accept message" (Behavior
AcceptCoal ?y) => (bind ?m (createMessage (AcceptCoal ?y)))
```

As said earlier, agent architecture is endowed with a RBR module responsible of a declarative reasoning process. It consists in an inference engine that implements a decision module. The facts represent the knowledge that have been extracted from the ontology, the perceived data and the exchanged messages among the agents. For that purpose, a set of rules is defined to determine, depending on the context, the most relevant criteria to consider first at each step of the coalition formation process. When the coalition proposed by the system is not a correct one, the RBR is in charge of determining the most relevant criteria to relax or to modify. The involved rules in this case are some kinds of heuristics that guide the coalition process in managing the criterion. For example, if a coalition does not include a CO whose precision is sufficient, it is advisable to relax the intrusion level. This increases the degree of freedom of the system regarding to its actions allowing the cameras to be activated or lights to be switched on. Another use of the RBR for the management criteria concerns the addition of new criterion such as data freshness. It is sometimes more relevant to consider not sufficiently precise data if they are very recent. For example, a presence detector can only inform that the person is situated in a particular room. Suppose that a particular presence detector "informs" that the person is in the room R1 and a camera "shows" that the person is in the right corner of the room R2. Obviously, the information given by the camera is more accurate, but if it is too old it should be obsolete and will not help correctly locating the person. It is suggested here to consider the date of perceived information for determining the priority of the criteria.

Note that exception handling is not provided in the current version of the system.

IV. ADAPTIVENESS MULTI-DIMENSIONALITY

The results are obtained in a real environment composed of heterogeneous sensors and markers. The platform includes several sensors of the market and dedicated sensors developed in our laboratory. The environment is composed of three rooms equipped with a set of sensors and the robot with its own sensors. The localization is based on goniometric measurements provided by robot on-board sensors and environment sensors. These can provide localization information allowing the localization of the robot in its environment using real-time data either from the robot on-board sensors or from the sensors in the environment. COALAA-GEN has been implemented using the Jade multiagent platform [5], where each agent embeds an instance of Jess. The production rules are given as a text file input parameter to the agents.

A. Computational adaptiveness

COALAA-GEN and COALAA have been compared to the well-known CNP protocol [7]. The Figures below shows the obtained results. The tests have been performed with a dozen scenarios. Each scenario has been executed with CNP, COALAA and COALAA-GEN. For COALAA and CNP, different values for the criteria have been experimented. COALAA-GEN has been tested with the same collected data, without any user intervention for criteria management. The figures below summarize the results.

Figure 5 shows the number of formed coalitions depending on the number of agents present in the MAS. The preferred strategy in our approach is to obtain a maximum number of coalitions that meet the selection criterion. The goal is to maximize the number of solutions to meet the request to increase the chances of securing a result. The number of coalitions is less than or equal to the number of initiators. In terms of the number of formed coalitions, the Contract Net protocol is less efficient than COALAA. COALAA-GEN gives the result with fewer numbers of agents. This can be interpreted by the fact that "intelligent" criteria management helps the agents to be more relevant for coalition formation. The response times are compared (see Figure 6). This time corresponds to the time spent in calculating the coalitions, including the message exchanges. The fact that the number of coalitions that the CNP can form is lower than the number of initiators has a direct effect on the response time. It also impacts the number of exchanged messages (Figure 7). The curve representing the number of exchanged messages follows the same rate for CNP, COALAA and COALAA-GEN. However, COALAA-GEN shows a higher number of exchanged messages. Unlike the CNP, COALAA and COALAA-GEN avoid system crashes, by a progressive coalition formation, which in contrast increases the number of exchanged messages. In terms of time response COALAA, COALAA-GEN and CNP are almost similar; CNP is slightly better in terms of response time. But in terms of obtained COALAA-GEN is the best. Indeed, a failure can be catastrophic and thus the few milliseconds delay in the response time may be insignificant, if success to complete the task is assured. This is explained by the fact that COALAA-GEN continues reorganizing until a solution is found (even with deteriorated criteria).

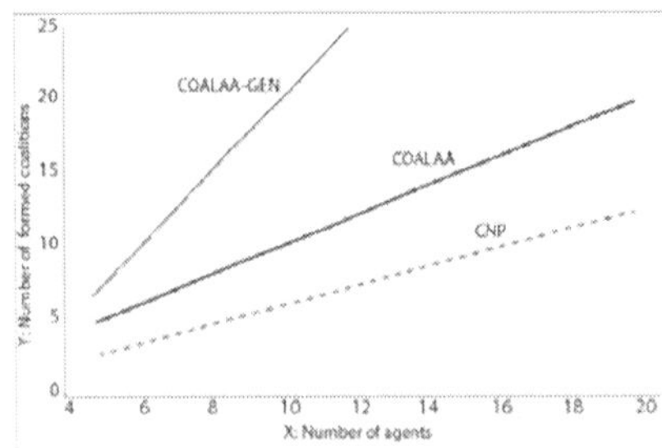

Figure 5. Formed Coalitions

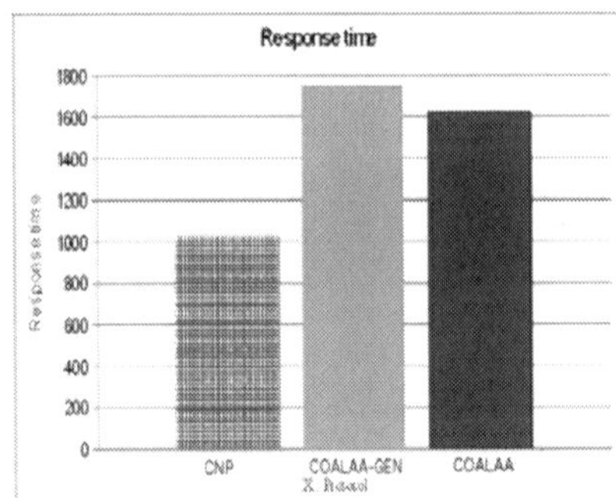

Figure 6. Response time

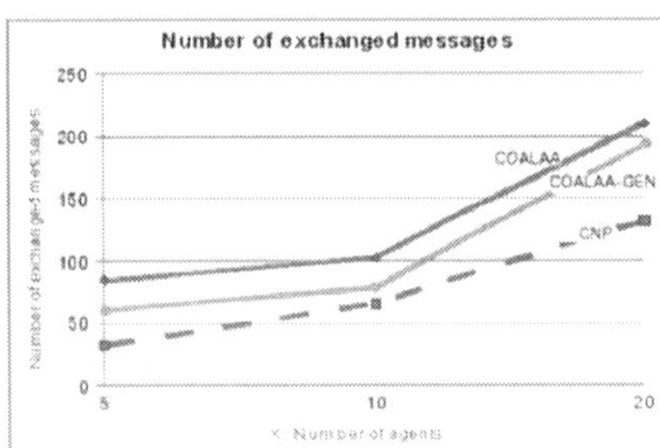

Figure 7. Exchanged messages

B. Methodological and functional adaptiveness

The genesis of the MAS is done automatically in COALAA-GEN. This is a very important feature of the system. In fact, modifying the AE, by adding or suppressing CO, automatically updates the ontology and triggers automatic MAS reconfiguration. In case of such modifications, the user does not need to do any specification to make the system adapting its architecture to AE dynamic updating. This ability is qualified by methodological adaptiveness. We refer to functional adaptiveness while dealing with services that the system can offer to the user. The description of the ability of the CO used by the agents to construct services according to the "effect description" is included in the "task" ontology part. This allows the agents to perform an automatic detection of their ability to perform an effect.

C. *Ethical adaptiveness*

An original specificity of our system is that it deals with ethical dimension in an adaptive way. Adding ethical values as criteria for forming the coalitions ensures this specificity. The level of intrusion of the system is modelled in such a way that it is upgraded only in case of emergency and if the user wishes to. Moreover, the personal data are stored in the equipment of the house and are uploaded only if needed by the distant caregiver and if the user has agreed. The degree of intrusion of each CO is modelled in the ontology as an attribute associated to the CO concept. The personal data are kept locally in the agent and are not stored in the distant ontology. But if the distant caregiver needs it (in case of emergency), the private data are uploaded, with a special status that is, volatile. This means that they are deleted from the distant storage as soon as they have been used. In the presented scenario, only two ethical criteria have been considered: the level of intrusion and the data privacy. They have been modelled as criteria for coalition formation. Adding new criteria is performed by adding new rules:

```
(defrule crit-manag-001"add new criteria" (Crit ?type ?name)
=>(assert (Coal Crit ?name)))
(defrule crit-manag-002"assign new criteria for coalition formation"
=>(modify (Coal Crit ?name)))
```

D. *Control adaptiveness*

The fact that an inference engine has been employed instead of a procedural algorithm has a direct effect on the intelligence of the system. The behaviors are involved only when their associated rules are triggered, which are themselves triggered when some declarative conditions are met. Since the conditions of the rules can be modified without any procedural modification, the control of the execution of the behaviors is completely adaptive. The user can control and modify the execution of the behaviors even at run time. Furthermore, the system is also able to detect missing information that is able to lead to the execution of a particular behavior. This is ensured by backward chaining rules. The engine seeks steps to activate rules (when necessary) whose preconditions are not met. This is illustrated by the given below:

```
(defrule ctrl-001"alarm occurred, but no behavior to trigger"
(Alarm ?x ?y)(not (Behavior ?z ?t))
=> (assert (Backward ?z ?t)))
```

More generic the rules are, more the system intelligence can be improved.

V. Conclusion and Perspectives

We have introduced a new general approach for improving adaptiveness in ambient assistive applications by adding ethical dimension. A RBR module has been embedded in the agent architecture to dynamically assign the criterion to consider during the coalition formation process and we proposed to deal with the adaptation at different levels. The adaptiveness has been considered according to four dimensions: (1) computational dimension: during the coalition formation process, (2) functional and methodological dimension: while service modelling, (3) ethical dimension: associating the intrusion level to the degree of emergency, (4) control dimension: for behaviors triggering and criteria management. We have compared the obtained results with those previously obtained without the RBR, and we have observed that the adaptiveness has been improved without any performance degradation. The feasibility of this general approach has been showed on a usage scenario to remove the doubt of a false alarm in fall detection. The first results are promising. Current and future work concerns modelling of ethical criteria in the ontology so that one can deal with various situations and contexts. Indeed, recent works [5][10] links ethics and automated reasoning in autonomous systems and artificial intelligence.

References

[1] A. Andriatrimoson., N. Abchiche-Mimouni, E. Colle, and S. Galerne, "An adaptive multi-agent system for ambient assisted living," in ADAPTIVE 2012, Copyright (c) IARIA, 2012. ISBN: 978-1-61208-219-6 ThinkMind, July, pp. 85–92, http://www.thinkmind.org/

[2] R. Anand, E. M. Robert, H. C. Roy, M. and Dennis, "Use of ontologies in a pervasive computing environment," in Knowledge Engineering Review, vol. 18, 2003, pp. 209–220.

[3] F.L. Bellifemine, G. Caire, D. Greenwood, Developing Multi-Agent Systems with JADE. Wiley Eds. 2007.

[4] V. Bonnemains, C. Saurel, C. Tessier, "Embedded ethics: some technical and ethical challenges," Ethics and Information Technology. SSN: 1388-1957 (Print) 1572-8439 (Online) 10.1007/s10676-018-9444-x, 2018, pp. 41–58.

[5] A. Kivela and E. Hyvonen, "Ontological theories for the semantic web,". in Semantic Web. Finland, May, 2002, pp. 111–136.

[6] M. Sims., C. Goldman, and V. Lesser, "Self organization through bottom up coalition formation," Proc. of the 2nd international joint conference on Autonomous agents and multiagent systems, 2003, pp. 867-874.

[7] R. Smith, "The contract net protocol: High-Level Communication and Control in a Distributed Problem Solver," Journal IEEE Transactions on computers, Volume 29 Issue 12, December 1980, pp. 1104–1113.

[8] L.-K. Soh and C. Tsatsoulis, "Reflective negotiating agents for real-time multisensor target tracking," IJCAI'01, 2001, pp. 1121-1127.

[9] L. Soh and C. Tsatsoulis, "Allocation algorithms in dynamic negotiation-based coalition formation," AAMAS02 Workshop 7 "Teamwork and coalition formation", pp. 16–23.

[10] Y. Han, S. Zhiqi, M. Chunyan, C. Leung, V. R. Lesser and Q. Yang, "Building Ethics into Artificial Intelligence," in Proc. of the Twenty-Seventh International Joint Conference on Artificial Intelligence (IJCAI-18), 2018, pp..

[11] J. Searle, "Speech acts. an essay in the philosophy of language," Cambridge University Press, 1969. 5527-5533

[12] E. Friedman-Hill, Jess in Action: Java Rule-Based Systems (In Action series) Paperback – July, 2003 by Ernest Friedman-Hill.

A Multi-Agent Approach for Self-adaptive MRI Segmentation

Mohamed T. Bennai*†, Smaine Mazouzi‡, Zahia Guessoum†§,
Mohamed Mezghiche* and Stéphane Cormier†
* LIMOSE Laboratory, University M'Hamed Bougara, Boumerdès, Algeria
† CReSTIC, Reims Champagne Ardenne University, Riems, France
‡ Department of Computer Science, University of Skikda, Skikda, Algeria
§LIP6, Sorbonne University, Paris, France
email: m.bennai@univ-boumerdes.dz

***Abstract*—Medical image processing provides an important help for establishing diagnoses for several pathologies. In medical imagery, image segmentation is crucial for several applications such as lesion detection and delimitation, and tracking of disease evolution. Different image segmentation approaches have been proposed. However, the segmentation parameters are beforehand adjusted in most of those approaches. The latter do not allow the segmentation process to handle all the situations that can be found in the images. The goal of this paper is to introduce a new multi-agent approach for self-adaptive segmentation of Magnetic Resonance Image (MRI) data. Our approach is based on situated agents that interact together, and where each agent can perform discontinuity detection or similarity detection. Each agent parameters rely on its location in the image. That approach was implemented and tested on MRI data, and the first results are promising.**

Keywords–Image processing, image segmentation, multi-agent systems, Self-adaptation.

I. INTRODUCTION

In the last decades, medical image processing was one of the most active research fields in computer science. Segmentation is the most important and critical stage of the image processing. The high diversity of images and the inhomogeneity of artefacts' distribution within the images, such as noise and Intensity Non-Uniformity (INU) in Magnetic Resonance Image (MRI), require the segmentation process to be adaptive so that it can handle both the expected situations and unexpected ones.

Segmentation consists in partitioning a digital image into a set of separated regions, and it is mainly used to extract objects of interest present in an image. Several image segmentation methods were published in the literature. Those segmentation methods are mainly classified as follows [1]:

- Edge-based segmentation: Edge-based methods aim to find the places of rapid transition from one to other regions of different brightness or color value [2]. The edge is determined by the extreme of the first order derivative or a zero crossing in the second order derivative of the pixels' intensity function [3]. One of the first and most efficient techniques, in this approach, is the Canny edge detection algorithm [4].
- Region-based segmentation: Region based segmentation methods use a set of predefined criteria [3] to decompose an image into regions that contain connected pixels with similar properties. Most of the existing solutions use spatial information (pixel positions) with brightness information in the classification process of pixels. One of the most effective techniques is the region growing algorithm [5].
- Other techniques: Some of the segmentation methods described in the literature cannot be classified in the two previous categories. Most of them were borrowed from other disciplines and applied to image segmentation problem (genetic algorithm [6], graph theory [7], neural networks [8], etc.), or multi-agent systems (ant colonies, particle swarm optimization).

Multi-agent systems offer a set of properties that allow making image segmentation adaptive. They take into account several unexpected situations within the same image, or for a set of images. In recent years, many works have been published on image segmentation using multi-agent systems (for further details see [9]). Even if they are able to successfully achieve the image segmentation task, most of those multi-agent approaches are based on centralized agents and do not exploit the full advantages of multi-agent systems such as coordination mechanisms.

This paper introduce a new multi-agent approach for image segmentation and its application to MRI data. The system built with that approach is composed of two types of agents: Discontinuity agents and Similarity agents. Discontinuity agents use image gradient for boundaries detection. Similarity agents generate then homogeneous regions in an iterative and adaptive aggregation process. This process uses the results provided by the discontinuity agents that work on gray level intensity of pixels. Each agent self-adapts to the image data by tuning the best parameters according to the part of the image where it is located.

The paper is organized as follows. Section 2 describes and analyses existing multi-agent image segmentation approaches to show that the adaptation in such approaches is an open issue. Section 3 introduces the proposed multi-agent approach and we show how agents self-adapt according to the content of the image where they are located. Section 4 presents the implementation and the experimental results. Finally, Section 5 summarizes the contribution and describes some perspectives of this work.

II. RELATED WORK

Image segmentation is a very active field of computer science. Several approaches have thus been proposed (see [10]). To improve the efficiency of those segmentation approaches and to explore new ideas, recent works have proposed to use multi-agent systems to distribute the segmentation process, allowing adaptive processing in several cases. This section describes and analyses those multi-agent segmentation approaches.

Liu and Tang [11] introduced the first adaptive approach for image segmentation. They developed a multi-agent system based on a set of reactive agents operating in a 2D image. Agents select their behavior (breeding, moving and vanishing) according to local stimuli of the environment. Each agent explores the environment searching for a pixel of a homogeneous segment. After detecting this pixel, the agent breeds offspring agents in their neighborhood aiming to find the rest of the segment. Such behaviors is a kind of adaptation to the image content.

For the approach presented by Duchesnay *et al.* [12], the segmentation is performed in two steps:

- a pre-segmentation (using a quadtree for region detection and an edge detection algorithm for contour detection),
- and a merging process (using agents interaction).

In the first step, the system generates a set of regions and contours. They are then used to create a society of agents that are organized as an irregular pyramid and interact to make merging decisions. This process is repeated until the stabilization of the system. Agent self-organization, throw the merge process, can be considered as a self-adaptation of the organization according to the extracted segments of the image.

In [13], Germond *et al.* presented a framework for MRI image segmentation based on the cooperation of three different modules (a multi-agent system, a deformable model and an edge detector). The multi-agent system is composed of two different types of agents (region agents and edge agents). Those agents use information provided by the deformable model and the edge detector. Agents, in this system, adapt their processing according to the results provided by the previous modules.

The approach presented by Bourjot *et al.* [14] uses a swarm mechanism inspired by the collective web weaving behavior of social spiders for 2D grayscale image segmentation. The approach is modeled as a multi-agent system where reactive agents represent spiders exploring their environment, namely the input image. During this exploration and according to their behavior, agents interact together, select one of the three different actions (move, fix silk and return to web) to weave webs. Self-switching between behaviors according to the image data is also a kind of adaptation of agents to different situations.

Recently Arbai and Allioui [15] proposed a multi-agent system for the detection of Alzheimer lesions in MRI images. The system is divided into three main parts: the data, the knowledge, and the agents. In this configuration, three different sorts of agents (supervisor agent, analysis agent and segmentation agent) use the knowledge part to perform the segmentation of the MRI image according to the data part. This data represents the input image in addition to some information extracted with pre-treatment.This approach is based on the cooperation of agents using different segmentation methods.

Generally, MAS-based image segmentation relies on classical image segmentation algorithms. They encapsulate those algorithms in agents. They then endow those agents with interaction and coordination mechanisms to reach the global goal which is the partition of an image into its structural parts. However, in most of the published works, authors proceed by a fixed (off line) parameter tuning for all the parts of the image where agents process. So, agents perform segmentation task uniformly in the whole image. Such an approach does not allow processing images where artefacts are not uniformly distributed, such as MRI data.

In this work, we introduce a novel approach that allows agents to self-adapt to the image data, so the processing will be specific to each part of the image where an agent operates.

III. A NEW MAS APPROACH

In the proposed multi-agent based approach, segmentation is based on the collaboration of different types of agents. The latter are situated in an environment, which is a two dimension MRI image. Those agents interact to achieve the image segmentation. Two kinds of agents are used and are built aiming to get benefits on the discontinuity and the similarity properties of pixels. The discontinuity allows finding boundary pixels of regions, while the similarity allows the agglomeration of all pixels sharing a similar gray level intensity. The two populations of agents cooperate to accomplish their goal: partitioning the image into homogeneous regions. The segmentation process is described in Figure 1. The two main phases of the system are: discontinuities detection and similarities detection.

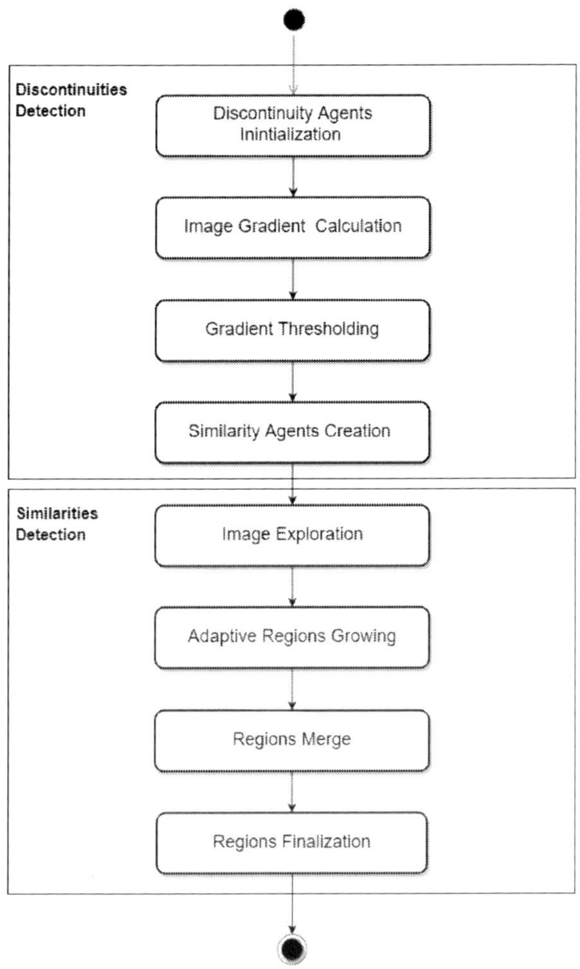

Figure 1. The two stages of image segmentation.

We show, in the following subsection, that similarity agents are self-adaptive and perform region growing according to the sub-region where they are situated. Each agent calculates the used parameters according to the artefacts in the part of the image where it operates, namely the noise and the Intensity Non-Uniformity (INU).

A. Discontinuity detection

Discontinuity agents (DAgents) are created and uniformly dispersed on the image. The image is decomposed in areas, where each one is associated with a DAgent. DAgents are thus situated; they execute their behavior without moving from their positions. They first calculate the standard-deviation of the image data at the pixels in their respective areas. If the calculated standard-deviation is bellow a given threshold, each agent labels all the pixels of its area as probably region pixels (Class 1). Otherwise, the agent estimates the gradient of the pixels included in its area using a Sobel Filter [16]. The gradient is then used to perform a *k*-mean clustering. Pixels with high gradient are labeled as boundary pixels (Class 2), pixels with low gradient are labeled as region pixels (Class 1). Finally, DAgent chooses in its area the pixel (labeled C1) with the lowest gradient and creates a Similarity Agent (SAgent) on that position, and provides it the pixel similarity threshold (PST) which is set to the standard-deviation of its area.

B. Similarities detection

SAgents are mobile agents exploring the image, seeking homogeneous regions to detect and to delimit. The agent behavior and parameters are defined so that the regions of the image can be extracted despite the alterations it contains, which are the INU and the noise. After their creation, the agents start their activity using the following behavior:

1) Exploration: A SAgent explores its environment searching for a seed pixel. A seed pixel is a Class 1 pixel with no Class 2 pixels in its neighborhood. The size of the neighborhood can be set manualy according to the content nature of the processed images. It is low (3 x 3) for images that contain a lot of details such as outdoor images, and it is higher for images with vast homogeneous regions such in several medical images. When encountering a seed pixel, the SAgent switches to the next behavior.
2) Region Growing: The method used in this step was partially inspired by the work of Pohle and Toennies [17]. Firstly, starting from its initial position, a SAgent uses a random walk to self-adapt to the homogeneous region in which it is moving, and estimates its features. During this walk, the SAgent considers all the encountered $Class1$ pixels with a similar gray level, up to the threshold PST. The latter depends on the SAgent, and it was communicated by the DAgent. Its value depends on the intensity of the pixels forming the neighborhood of the seed. Secondly, the SAgent uses the set of explored pixels to calculate the features of its region (i). The used features are the gray level mean E_i and the standard derivation σ_i. Finally, these features are used to perform a standard region growing. The SAgent, starting from its seed pixel, iteratively adds to its region, all the surrounding pixels satisfying the assimilation predicate P and then, updates its region.

$$P(Pixel) = \begin{cases} true & if\ I(P) \in [E_i \pm (\sigma_i \times \alpha)] \\ false & otherwise \end{cases}$$

where $I(P)$ is the intensity of the pixel P, and α is an adjustment parameter. This processing is iterated until no more adjacent pixels can be added. The result of this step is generally an over-segmented image with too many regions. This over-segmentation has to be refined using a merge operation.
3) Region Merge: In this step, The SAgents interact together to expand their regions by merging with those of their neighbors. Two SAgents are considered as neighbor if they have adjacent region borders. During their interaction, the SAgents use the contract net protocol [18] to evaluate the relevance of the merge of their two regions. Each SAgent evaluates the benefits of a merge by comparing the standard-derivation of its region before and after the merge. All possible merges are considered, and the SAgent selects the one that minimizes the resulting standard derivation. Then, the SAgent performs the merge of its region and the chosen one. Lastly, the agent that has performed the merge updates its list of neighbors and starts looking for another merge, while the other agent (involved in the merge) will be deactivated. The process is repeated wwhile a merge is possible between two neighbors.
4) Region Finalization: the purpose of this step is to calculate the final borders of the detected regions. It also allows the smoothing of the obtained regions. Each SAgent browses the pixels situated inside its region that were initially excluded during the region growing step. The SAgent then assimilates all the pixels that satisfy the assimilation condition according to the new region assimilation parameters.

When no more agents are active, the system stops and the set of the non-overlapping obtained regions are displayed. Similarity agents self-adapt to the levels of the artefacts in their respective sub-regions by calculating and using suitable parameters. In classical methods for MRI segmentation, a first stage for INU elimination must be performed, where it is not always successful and it is time-consuming because of its iterative nature

IV. Implementation and Experiments

For the implementation of our approach, we choose to start from scratch instead of using an existing platform such as JADE or MADKIT. Our Multi-agent system is composed of reactive agents with simple behavior and very low communication. Thus, we use the $CSharp$ language and Microsoft .Net Framework to implement our agents as generic classes. We believe that this implementation allows us to keep full control of the system and allows optimizing its performance. C Sharp has already been used in multi-agent simulations [19] and it provides an efficient, reliable, and easy to program agent framework for the development agent-based applications [20].

To validate the efficiency of the implemented approach, some MR images from the Brain Web dataset are used.

Experiments are performed on a PC with an I7 1.9 GHz processor and 8 GB RAM.

For our experiments, we choose the Brainweb phantom database that it is a MRI dataset produced by McConnell Brain Imaging Center at Montreal Neurological Institute [21]. It provides different simulated brain phantom volumes, with different simulation options among which values of noise and intensity non-uniformity. In our experiments, we use bi-dimensional slices extracted from T1 MRI with an image size 181x217, and a pixel size of 1mm x 1mm. Those images are generated in 9 versions by varying the level of noise (5%, 7%, 9%) the level of intensity non-uniformity (0%, 20%, 40%) called INU. The image shown in Figure 2a is a slice of an MRI. It is an image with a high level of noise. It is provided to the implemented multi-agent segmentation system as an input image. The system uses then the approach described in the previous section. First, we show, in Figure 2b, the different regions forming the brain tissues by averaging the intensities within the slice. Figure 2c represents a binary image of the contours that are generated at the first step of the segmentation process by the population of DAgents. Figure 2d introduces the region corresponding to the white matter tissue of the brain at this slice. We can notice that despite the high level on the artefacts, the region was well delimited.

Figure 3 and Figure 4 introduce the results with two MRI from the same dataset, with higher levels of INU (respectively 20% and 40%) and the high level of noise (5%). We can note that despite such high level of deformation (Figures 3a,4a), the obtained region contours, and the extracted white matter region, introduced respectively in Figures 3c, 4c and Figures 3d, 4d were correctly computed.

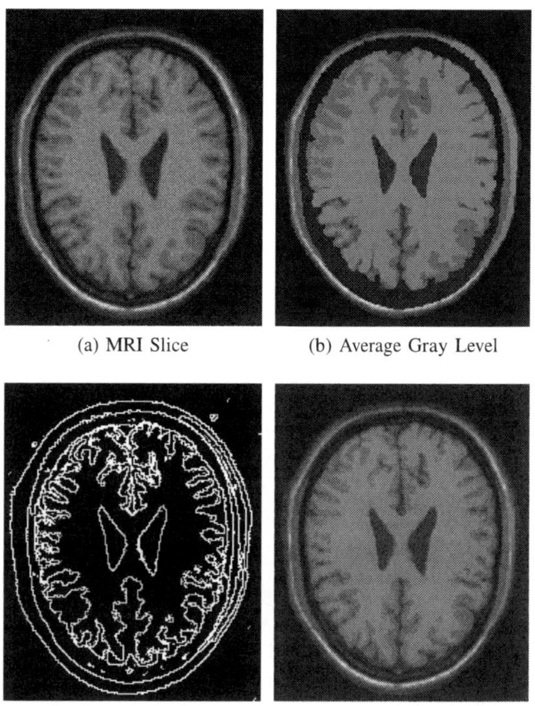

(a) MRI Slice (b) Average Gray Level

(c) Detected Edges (d) WM Region

Figure 2. Segmentation example of a MRI slice with 5% of noise level and 0% INU.

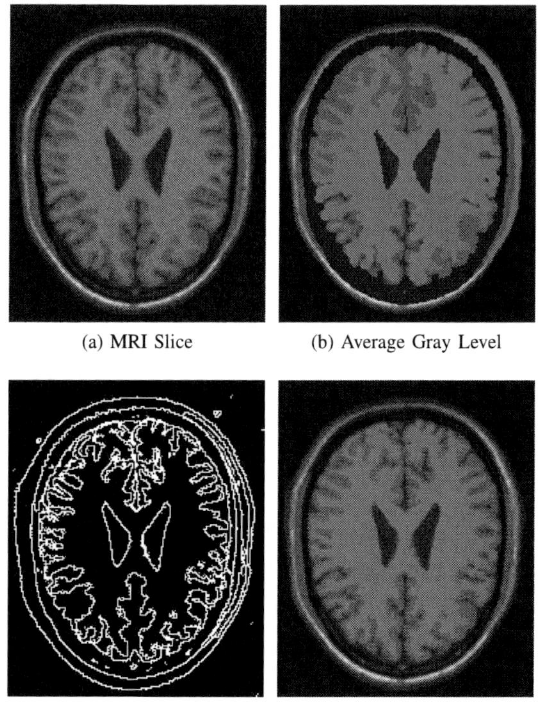

(a) MRI Slice (b) Average Gray Level

(c) Detected Edges (d) WM Region

Figure 3. Segmentation example of a MRI slice with 5% of noise level and 20% INU.

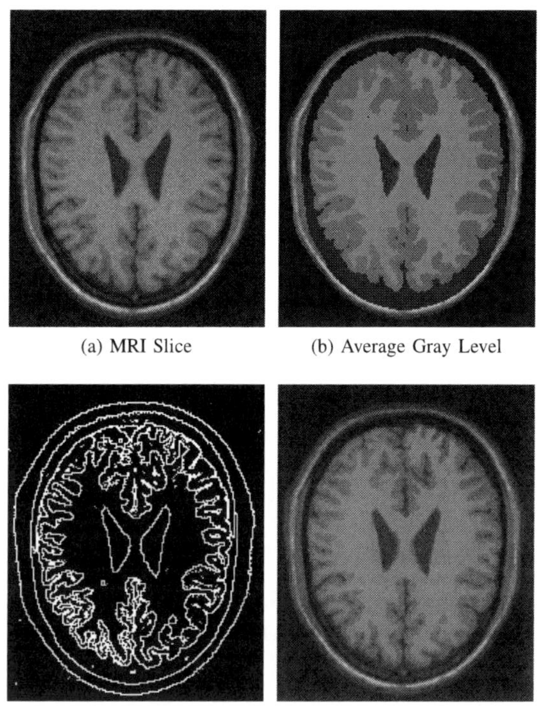

(a) MRI Slice (b) Average Gray Level

(c) Detected Edges (d) WM Region

Figure 4. Segmentation example of a MRI slice with 5% of noise level and 40% INU.

According to the visual results, we can note the potential of our approach to segment MRI data, by considering the whole volume, slice per slice. In particular, we have faced the INU problem in MRI by making agents self-adapt to their respective sub-regions, so the artefact was efficiently treated. To quantitatively evaluate our approach, we conducted a set of tests using the κ-coefficient (kappa), also known as Dice similarity coefficient as the evaluation metric for the White Matter region extraction. This coefficient is commonly used in the medical image processing to evaluate the performance of segmentation algorithms which has a predefined ground truth information or dataset. It is calculated using the following formula [22]:

$$\kappa = \frac{2 * TP}{(2 * TP) + FP + FN} \quad (1)$$

where TP, FP and FN are the numbers respectively of True Positive, False Positive and False Negative instances of pixel labeling. The value of the κ coefficient well expresses the segmentation quality.

The results of our experiments are presented in Table I:

TABLE I. κ Coefficient calculated for white matter extraction with different noise and INU levels

	INU levels		
Noise levels	0%	20%	40%
κ for 5%	93,4	94,9	94,7
κ for 7%	91,5	90,4	92,0
κ for 9%	91,2	89,5	90,5,

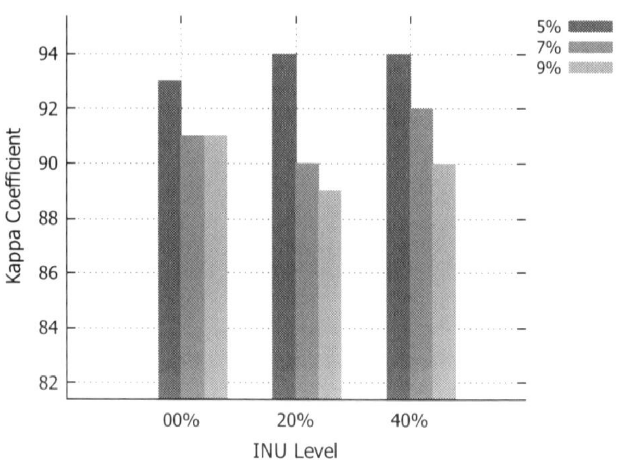

Figure 5. κ coefficient evolution for White Matter extraction with different noise and INU levels

Table I and Figure 5 show the effectiveness of our approach for the White Mater despite the increase in artefact levels occurring in the processed image. The obtained results show that the increase in noise level has an impact on the quality of the extraction, which is acceptable at such levels (5%, 7% and 9%). This incidence is still minor compared to the level of image degradation. Figure 5 also illustrates the robustness of the approach against the INU artefact of the segmented image. It thus reflects the adaptation that our system can demonstrate in the execution of its task.

In addition to the intrinsic evaluation, we evaluate the quality of our results by comparing them to the ones obtained from other segmentation methods published in the literature. For this purpose, we used the comparison data provided by Yazdani et al. [23]. The results introduced in [23] concern volumic data, while ours are obtained from 2D slices. Nevertheless, this does not significantly affect the κ coefficient in our case because it is based on ratios of large sets of pixels or voxels.

TABLE II. κ Coefficient calculated for white matter extraction with different noise levels and 20% INU level

	Noise level		
Approches	5%	7%	9%
Our System	92,0	94,0	93,0
EM	92,2	90,1	86,4
SPM 5	93,6	90,2	86,3
HMC	93,9	92,3	91,7
Fast	94,8	94,3	91,9
FCM	92,0	88,0	84,0
NL-FCM	91,5	89,8	83,2
UFBSMRI	94,9	94,4	92,2

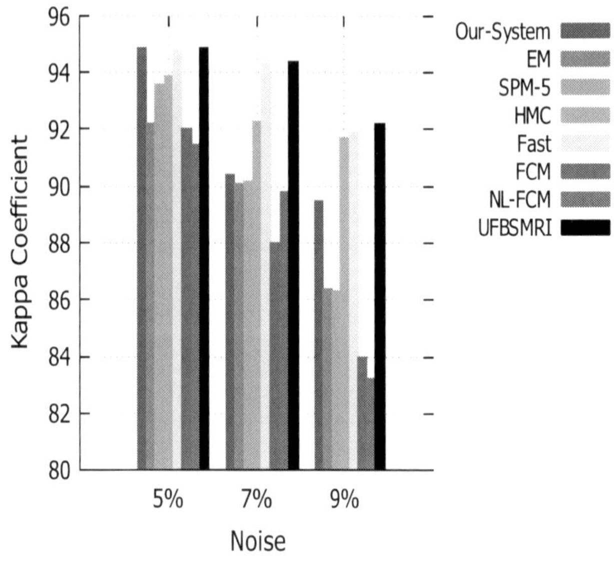

Figure 6. κ coefficient evolution for White Matter extraction with different noise levels and 20% INU level with different approaches

In Table II and Figure 6, we can note that our multi-agent system has acceptable results and has a good robustness against increasing noise, compared to the methods involved in the comparison. Due to the absence of data concerning the other approaches for various INU levels, we were only able to compare our results according to only 20% INU level.

With these results, we can assume that due to their capability of self-adaptation to their respective regions, the agents of our approach do not need training data. Such a feature allows the method to be usable for different images with several artefact levels, without previous training. Also, agents are weakly coupled, so they permit the physical distribution of the method.

V. Conclusion and Future Works

In this paper, we proposed a new multi-agent approach for MRI segmentation. That approach is based on two different populations of agents: Discontinuity Agents (DAgents) and Similarity Agents (SAgents). These different agents interact in an environment, namely the image, to perform its segmentation. DAgents use image gradient and k-means classification to distinguish boundary pixels from region ones. SAgents use then the resulting classification during the region detection process. SAgents start with an adaptive region growing algorithm, where agents are competing to expand their regions. When no more expansion is possible, SAgents collaborate the merge their regions.

The proposed multi-agent approach does not require any human interaction during the image segmentation. It also self-adapts to different levels of image artefacts. Other advantages of our approach are its capability of detecting many regions in parallel during the segmentation process and its robustness to noise and INU. Our approach gives promising issues for the segmentation of different kinds of images. However, this approach still suffers from some limitations such as the setting of some parameters. Moreover, Other self-adaptive agent strategies, such as social utility, will be considered in future works.

References

[1] D. D. Patil and S. G. Deore, "Medical image segmentation: a review," International Journal of Computer Science and Mobile Computing, vol. 2, no. 1, 2013, pp. 22–27.

[2] S. Dantulwar and R. Krishna, "Performance analysis using single seeded region growing algorithm," International Journal of Innovative Research in Advanced Engineering, vol. 1, no. 6, 2014, pp. 2349–2163.

[3] G. E. Suji, Y. V. S. Lakshimi, and G. W. Jiji, "Image segmentation algorithms on mr brain images," International Journal of Computer Applications, vol. 67, no. 16, April 2013, pp. 18–20.

[4] J. Canny, "A computational approach to edge detection," IEEE Transactions on pattern analysis and machine intelligence, no. 6, 1986, pp. 679–698.

[5] R. Adams and L. Bischof, "Seeded region growing," IEEE Transactions on pattern analysis and machine intelligence, vol. 16, no. 6, 1994, pp. 641–647.

[6] B. Bhanu, S. Lee, and J. Ming, "Adaptive image segmentation using a genetic algorithm," IEEE Trans. Systems, Man, and Cybernetics, vol. 25, no. 12, 1995, pp. 1543–1567.

[7] Z. Wu and R. Leahy, "An optimal graph theoretic approach to data clustering: Theory and its application to image segmentation," IEEE transactions on pattern analysis and machine intelligence, vol. 15, no. 11, 1993, pp. 1101–1113.

[8] A. N. Skourikhine, L. Prasad, and B. R. Schlei, "Neural network for image segmentation," in Applications and Science of Neural Networks, Fuzzy Systems, and Evolutionary Computation III, vol. 4120. International Society for Optics and Photonics, 2000, pp. 28–36.

[9] M. Amahrir, M. A. Sabri, and A. Aarab, "A review on image segmentation based on multi-agent systems," in Intelligent Systems Conference (IntelliSys), 2017. IEEE, 2017, pp. 614–621.

[10] N. M. Zaitoun and M. J. Aqel, "Survey on image segmentation techniques," Procedia Computer Science, vol. 65, 2015, pp. 797–806.

[11] J. Liu and Y. Y. Tang, "Adaptive image segmentation with distributed behavior-based agents," IEEE Transactions on Pattern Analysis and Machine Intelligence, vol. 21, no. 6, 2002, pp. 544–551.

[12] E. Duchesnay, J.-J. Montois, and Y. Jacquelet, "Cooperative agents society organized as an irregular pyramid: A mammography segmentation application," Pattern Recognition Letters, vol. 24, no. 14, 2003, pp. 2435–2445.

[13] L. Germond, M. Dojat, C. Taylor, and C. Garbay, "A cooperative framework for segmentation of mri brain scans," Artificial Intelligence in Medicine, vol. 20, no. 1, 2000, pp. 77–93.

[14] C. Bourjot, V. Chevrier, and V. Thomas, "A new swarm mechanism based on social spiders colonies: from web weaving to region detection," Web Intelligence and Agent Systems: An International Journal, vol. 1, no. 1, 2003, pp. 47–64.

[15] K. Arbai and H. Allioui, "Mri images segmentation for alzheimer detection using multi-agent systems," in Advanced Intelligent Systems for Sustainable Development (AI2SD'2018), M. Ezziyyani, Ed. Cham: Springer International Publishing, 2019, pp. 298–313.

[16] I. Sobel and G. Feldman, "A 3x3 isotropic gradient operator for image processing," a talk at the Stanford Artificial Project in, 1968, pp. 271–272.

[17] R. Pohle and K. D. Toennies, "Segmentation of medical images using adaptive region growing," in Medical Imaging. International Society for Optics and Photonics, 2001, pp. 1337–1346.

[18] R. G. Smith, "The contract net protocol: High-level communication and control in a distributed problem solver," IEEE Trans. Computers, vol. 29, no. 12, 1980, pp. 1104–1113.

[19] R. Nourjou and M. Hatayama, "Simulation of an organization of spatial intelligent agents in the visual c# .net framework," International Journal of Computer Theory and Engineering, IJCTE, vol. 6, no. 5, 2014, pp. 426–431.

[20] A. Grosso, A. Gozzi, M. Coccoli, and A. Boccalatte, "An agent programming framework based on the c# language and the cli," in 1st Int. Workshop on C# and .NET Technologies on Algorithms, Computer Graphics, Visualization, Computer Vision and Distributed Computing, Plzen, Czech Republic, vol. 1, no. 1-3, 2003, pp. 13–20.

[21] D. L. Collins et al., "Design and construction of a realistic digital brain phantom," IEEE transactions on medical imaging, vol. 17, no. 3, 1998, pp. 463–468.

[22] M. T. Bennai, Z. Guessoum, S. Mazouzi, S. Cormier, and M. Mezghiche, "Towards a generic multi-agent approach for medical image segmentation," in International Conference on Principles and Practice of Multi-Agent Systems. Springer, 2017, pp. 198–211.

[23] S. Yazdani, R. Yusof, A. Karimian, A. H. Riazi, and M. Bennamoun, "A unified framework for brain segmentation in mr images," Computational and mathematical methods in medicine, vol. 2015, 2015, Article ID: 829893, URL: https://www.hindawi.com/journals/cmmm/2015/829893/ [accessed: 2019-04-08].

Implementing Ethics in e-Health Applications through Adaptation: reflection and challenges

Nadia Abchiche-Mimouni
IBISC, Univ Evry, Université Paris-Saclay
91025, Evry, France
email: nadia.abchichemimouni@univ-evry.fr

Abstract—**The present contribution opens a reflection on what can adaptation mechanisms, inherent to multi-agent systems, bring for the implementation of ethical principles during the design and the implementation of e-health applications. Several works propose ethics approaches. But, since ethics values differ from one culture to another, it is not possible to have a general approach which can be used every time. The intuition is that adaptation capabilities is a good start. This aim of this paper is to raise ethics challenges in eHealth and discuss across interdisciplinary debate questions such as: which ethics to adopt for eHealth applications? How to implement ethics in eHealth applications? How can adaptation features help implementing the identified ethics challenges and questions?**

Keywords-ethics; e-Healtn; adaptation.

I. INTRODUCTION

The development of e-health, particularly thanks to machine learning methods and the use of Big Data places this type of application in the field of complex systems. In addition to the distributed aspect of the data and their heterogeneity, care units also require to be modeled as a complex system. The ethical issues inherent to the use of patients' personal data on the one hand, and the need to treat patients in an individualized and transparent way in the other hand, suggest that adaptation of paramount importance. Indeed, ethics requirements differ greatly between jurisdictions, institutions and cultures, while technological infrastructure is increasingly global and connected.

Multi-agent system paradigm provides instruments to represent and manage distributed and/or heterogeneous entities characterized by autonomy, interaction, cooperation and proaction. So, adaptation characterizes such systems which are suitable for modelling complex systems. We think that Multi-agent systems provide a good omen as a tool for the design and implementation of ethic in eHealth applications.

The aim of this paper is to raise ethics challenges in eHealth and discuss across interdisciplinary debate questions such as:

- Which ethics to adopt for eHealth applications?
- How to implement ethics in eHealth applications?
- How can adaptation features help implementing the identified ethics challenges and questions?

The next section illustrates why adaptation is needed in healthcare applications. Section III gives definition of ethics. Section IV gives a summary of existing computational approaches about ethics. The paper concludes by open issues.

II. E-HEALTH

E-health applications have been developed in many aspects of health. This concerns areas such as telemedicine, prevention, home care, remote chronic disease monitoring (diabetes, hypertension, heart failure, etc.) or electronic medical records. It is seen as a solution to major challenges such as the aging of the population and the management of dependence, universal access to quality care and the significant increase in expenditure and the explosion of chronic diseases. Therefore, many challenges await researchers and application developers in this area. The diversity of situations and the need to propose solutions adapted to individuals, populations and hospital practitioners opens the question of the adaptability and ethics that must be implemented [12].

III. DEFINITION OF ETHICS

Ethics requirements differ greatly between jurisdictions and institutions, while technological infrastructure is increasingly global and connected. Moreover, ethics is not simply about compliance, but requires active reflection during the design process, especially for e-health applications.

We adopt the definition of Cointe and his colleagues [5] because it explicitly states the ethics in a formal and easy way to implement when most authors remain vague.

According to Cointe and his colleagues, ethics is a normative practical philosophical discipline of how one should act towards others. It encompasses three dimensions:

1. Consequentialist ethics: an agent is ethical if and only if it weighs the consequences of each choice and chooses the option which has the most moral outcomes. It is also known as utilitarian ethics as the resulting decisions often aim to produce the best aggregate consequences.
2. Deontological ethics: an agent is ethical if and only if it respects obligations, duties and rights related to given situations. Agents with deontological ethics (also known as duty ethics or obligation ethics) act in accordance to established social norms.
3. Virtue ethics: an agent is ethical if and only if it acts

and thinks according to some moral values (e.g., bravery, justice, etc.). Agents with virtue ethics should exhibit an inner drive to be perceived favorably by others.

IV. IMPLEMENTING ETHICS AND ADAPTATION

Almost all papers referring to the implementation of ethics in Artificial Intelligence (AI) focus on societal and legal aspect of the challenges. Very few works are done for implementing ethics values in AI. In [14], the authors have performed a survey from AAAI (Association for the Advancementof Artificial Intelligence) conférence on AI, AAMAS (International Conference on Autonomous Agents and Multiagent Systems), ECAI (European Conference on Artificial Intelligence) and IJCAI (International Joint Conference on Artificial Intelligence), as well as articles from well-known journals. They propose a taxonomy which divides the field into four areas:

1. Exploring Ethical Dilemmas: technical systems enabling the AI research community to understand human preferences on various ethical dilemmas [1][4][9];
2. Individual Ethical Decision Frameworks: generalizable decision-making mechanisms enabling individual agents to judge the ethics of its own actions and the actions of other agents under given contexts [3][6][7];
3. Collective Ethical Decision Frameworks: generalizable decision-making mechanisms enabling multiple agents to reach a collective decision that is ethical [8][10][11];
4. Ethics in Human-AI Interactions: frameworks that incorporate ethical considerations into agents which are designed to influence human behaviors [2][13].

This study offers an interesting overview of recent works on ethics. However, the adaptation dimension is not addressed when it is essential, especially for individualizing eHealth approaches.

V. CONCLUSION AND PERSPECTIVES

This article has outlined the elements that will help to draw some challenges and questions that could be raised about ethics, adaptation in healthcare domain. The state of the art in the domain of ethics in AI reveals that adaptation has not been addressed. Future works will concern the questions and scientific issues, such as adaptation mechanisms, raised at all the stages of the modeling, development, testing and deployment of e-health applications, in particular in multi-agent system domain.

REFERENCES

[1] M. Anderson and S. Leigh Anderson, "GenEth: A general ethical dilemma analyzer," In In AAAI, pp. 253–261, 2014.

[2] C. Battaglino and R. Damiano, "Coping with moral emotions," In AAMAS, pages 1669–1670, 2015.

[3] Joseph A. Blass and Kenneth D. Forbus, "Moral decision-making by analogy: Generalizations versus exemplars," In AAAI, pp. 501–507, 2015.

[4] J.F. Bonnefon, A. Shariff, and I. Rahwan, "The social dilemma of autonomous vehicles," In Science, 352(6293):1573–1576, 2016.

[5] N. Cointe, G. Bonnet, and O. Boissier, "Ethical judgment of agents' behaviors in multi-agent systems," In AAMAS, pp. 1106–1114, 2016.

[6] M. Dehghani, E. Tomai, K. D. Forbus, and M. Klenk, "An integrated reasoning approach to moral decision-making," In AAAI, pp. 1280–1286, 2008.

[7] A. Loreggia, N. Mattei, F. Rossi, and K. B. Venable, "Preferences and ethical principles in decision making," In The 2018 AAAI Spring Symposium Series, pp. 54–60, 2018.

[8] R. Noothigattu et al., "A voting-based system for ethical decision making. In AAAI," pp. 1587–1594, 2018.

[9] A. Sharif, J-F. Bonnefon, and I. Rahwan, "Psychological roadblocks to the adoption of selfdriving vehicles," In Nat. Hum. Behav., 1:694–696, 2017.

[10] M. P. Singh, "Norms as a basis for governing sociotechnical systems," In ACM Trans. Intell. Syst. Technol.,5(1):21:1–21:23, 2014.

[11] M. P. Singh, "Norms as a basis for governing sociotechnical systems," In IJCAI, pp. 4207–4211, 2015.

[12] D. F Sittig, A. Wright, E. Coiera, F. Magrabi and R. Ratwani, "Current challenges in healthinformation technology– related patient safety,"In Health Informatics Journal (Special Issue Article) pp. 1–9, 2018.

[13] H. Yu, C. Miao, C. Leung, and T. J. White, "Towards AI-powered personalization," In MOOC learning. npj Sci. Learn., 2(15):doi:10.1038/s41539–017–0016–3, 2017.

[14] H. Yu et al.,. "Building Ethics into Artificial Intelligence," In IJCAI, pp 5527–5533, 2018.

Regulated Walking for Multipod Robots

Jörg Roth
Nuremberg Institute of Technology
Faculty of Computer Science
Nuremberg, Germany
e-mail: Joerg.Roth@th-nuernberg.de

Abstract— **Following a computed path is a fundamental task for robot motion. The goal is to compensate error effects, such as slippage and create a movement that minimizes the difference between planned and real positions. This problem becomes even more difficult in case we have legged mobile robots instead of wheeled robots. In this paper, we present an approach to regulate paths for multipods. It is based on explicit slippage detection and re-uses a trajectory planning component to compute regulation trajectories. The approach is implemented and tested on the Bugbot hexapod robot.**

Keywords – Multipods; Hexapod; Autonomous Walking; Path-Following; Trajectory Regulation.

I. INTRODUCTION

Multipod robots are robots with multiple legs, inspired by insects. Their main advantage is that they can walk over rough terrain or go over small obstacles. In contrast to bipedal robots, multipods have a stable footprint, thus the control does not have to consider dynamics or balancing issues.

In the context of task execution, a robot must follow a planned path to a target. Walking usually is slower than driving, but we have to face new problems: walking is much more imprecise. In addition, we have the concept of *gaits* – we first have to plan sequences of leg movements (i.e., servo commands) to move the whole robot. Even though we may consider multipods as holonomic vehicles, we get non-holonomic constraints as a result of gait execution capabilities. Certain sensor configurations may cause further restrictions. For example, a sensor that prevents falling downstairs ideally points in front, thus we may prefer forward walking.

Our approach is based on the following ideas:

- We introduce the concept of *virtual odometry* to abstract from complex walking gaits.
- We measure and compensate slippage as main source of disturbance.
- We compute regulation trajectories to a pose ahead on the formerly planned path.

To compute regulation trajectories we use the same approach as for the global path planning. However, as the regulation trajectories are much shorter, the planning is much faster.

In section 2, we present related work. In section 3, we present our regulation approach. Experiments are presented in section 4. Section 5 concludes the paper.

II. RELATED WORK

Research on path following and trajectory tracking has a long tradition in control theory [4][11][18]. The basic goal is to provide a formal representation of the so-called *control law* [1]. Both, the vehicle and trajectories are strongly formalized in order to derive quality statements, in particular regarding the controller's stability [2].

Model Predictive Control (*MPC*) [9][12] is based on a finite-horizon continuous time minimization of predicted tracking errors. At each sampling time, the controller generates an optimal control sequence by solving an optimization problem. The first element of this sequence is applied to the system. The problem is solved again at the next sampling time using the updated process measurements and a shifted horizon.

Sliding Mode Control (*SMC*) is a nonlinear controller that drives system states onto a sliding surface in the state space [15][20]. Once the sliding surface is reached, sliding mode control keeps the states on the close neighborhood of the sliding surface. Its benefits are accuracy, robustness, easy tuning and easy implementation.

The *Line-of-Sight* path following principle leads a robot towards a point ahead on the desired path. It is often used for vessels [6] or underwater vehicles [19]. The approaches differ how to reach the point ahead. Examples are arcs, straight lines or Dubins paths.

Another approach explicitly measures and predicts slippage, in particular of wheeled robots. As this is often a main source of disturbance to follow a path, it is reasonable to model it explicitly. In [10], effects on motors are measured for this. [16] uses GPS and inertial sensors and applies a Kalman filter to estimate slippage.

The majority of vehicles that are considered for the path following problem are wheeled robots because their behavior can formalized easily. Multipods are only rarely taken into account. [5] presents trajectory planning and control for a hexapod that mainly keeps the robot balanced in rough terrain.

Pure Pursuit describes a class of algorithms that project a position ahead on the planned trajectory and create a regulation path to reach this position (e.g., an arc). Early work about Pure Pursuit is [17]. The basic version only tries to reach a position ahead without considering the robot's orientation [3]. Improvements dynamically adapt the look-ahead distance [8].

III. The Regulation Approach

In contrast to easy to formalize wheeled robots, we have to face issues that make it difficult to apply a traditional approach based on control theory. First, walking is in general more error-prone than driving. As a result, we cannot execute regulation trajectories as precisely as expected. Second, as multipods may be different in the capabilities to execute certain gaits, we want to consider the set of possible walking commands as black box. As a consequence, it is not useful to integrate kinematic properties into the model. Finally, our regulation mechanism should directly consider obstacles and an arbitrary cost function, again given as black boxes. A certain regulation trajectory may not only be based on regulation parameters, but also on the environment.

Our approach was inspired by the pure pursuit idea. We project the current position ahead to the target and try to get there. We extend the basic idea in two ways:

- We try to reach a planned *configuration*, i.e., position *and* orientation.
- We are not restricted to a certain primitive trajectory (e.g., arc) to reach the configuration ahead, but execute a full trajectory planning step.

We re-use the trajectory planning both to compute a full plan to the final target, as well as for the regulation approach. As a benefit, both components produce output that can directly be used as walking command by the motion system. In particular, the motion capabilities are modeled in one place in the system. But we have to face two issues:

- As the regulation component permanently calls a trajectory planning, we have to consider execution time. In our approach, we thus apply an efficient trajectory planning approach [13].
- As we do not explicitly model a control law, we have to consider sources of disturbance, foremost the slippage effect.

The regulation is embedded into a data flow as presented in Figure 1. We have the following major components:

Navigation provides a point-to-point route planning in the workspace (i.e., without dealing with the robot's orientation). This component does *not* consider non-holonomic constraints. It computes a line string of minimal costs that in particular avoids obstacles. This component is useful to segment the overall path planning task.

Trajectory Planning computes a walkable sequence of trajectories and considers non-holonomic constraints.

Trajectory Regulation permanently tries to hold the planned trajectories, even if the position drifts off.

Simultaneous Localization and Mapping (*SLAM*) constantly observes the environment and computes the most probable own location and location of obstacles by motion feedback and sensors (e.g., Lidar or camera). The current error-corrected configuration is passed to all planning components. Observed and error-corrected obstacle positions are stored in an *Obstacle Map* for further planning tasks.

The *Evaluator* computes costs of routes and trajectories based on the obstacle map and the desired properties. Cost values may take into account the path length, expected energy consumption or the amount of turn-in-place operations. Also, the distance to obstacles could be considered, if, e.g., we want the robot to keep a safety distance where possible.

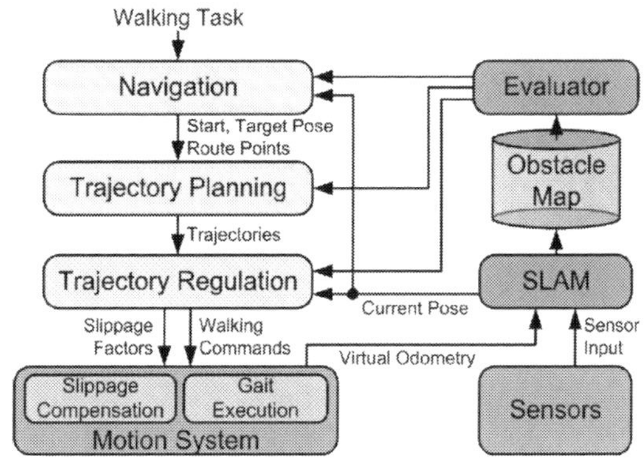

Figure 1. Data flow to execute walking tasks

The *Motion System* is able to execute and supervise walking commands by formalized gaits. It also considers slippage and provides *Virtual Odometry*. These concepts are described in the following sections.

In this paper, we assume *Navigation*, *Trajectory Planning* and *SLAM* already exist. We may use an approach as described in [13] for this. We here focus on *Trajectory Regulation*.

A. Gaits

Multipods can walk in different ways. First, we can look at the actual trajectory, e.g., straight forward, sideways (i.e., crab gait), arc or turn in place. Second, we can distinguish the *gait* that defines the time sequence of legs on the ground (*stance phase*) or swing in moving direction (*swing phase*). An important observation: we can deal with trajectory and time sequence independently. This means, the respective trajectory shape is *not* influenced by the sequence pattern.

Figure 2 shows the two phases for a specific leg. Let (f_{xi}, f_{yi}) denote neutral foot position. It marks the center of a stance movement from $(f_{xi}, f_{yi})+(s_{xi}, s_{yi})$ to $(f_{xi}, f_{yi})-(s_{xi}, s_{yi})$ in local robot coordinates. In world coordinates, the foot remains on the ground at the same position (in the absence of slippage). We assume the stance movement is linear or can at least be linearly approximated.

In the swing phase, the leg is lifted and moved in walking direction. The gaits define the cooperation of legs in the respective phases. Many gaits are known, e.g., *Tripod*, *Wave*, *Ripple* that differ in stability and propulsion [14]. We assume gait execution and the choice for a certain gait is encapsulated in the Motion System component.

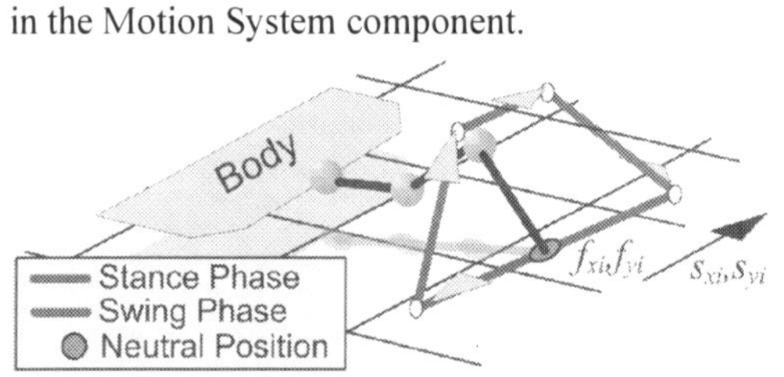

Figure 2. Gait movement phases

B. Virtual Odometry

Leg movement with a complex timing pattern is difficult to handle in the context of trajectory planning and regulation. For geometric computations the model of turning wheels is more convenient. This leads to the idea of *virtual odometry*: We transform walking to corresponding wheeled movement. We could think of roller-skates attached to the multipod's legs while the legs remain in neutral position. To fully describe gait movement with the help of virtual odometry we need

- the neutral position (f_{xi}, f_{yi}),
- the stance vector (s_{xi}, s_{yi}) for each leg i,
- the time t_{st} that the gait resides in stance phase for a complete step of one stance and one swing phase.

Note that t_{st} depends on the respective gait (e.g., Tripod or Wave). For a small time Δt, a foot of leg i moves along the vector

$$2 \cdot \frac{\Delta t}{t_{st}} \begin{pmatrix} s_{xi} \\ s_{yi} \end{pmatrix} \tag{1}$$

in local robot coordinates. We derivate over time. Not necessarily all legs move along the same vector, thus the robot's pose changes over time by

$$\begin{pmatrix} \Delta_x \\ \Delta_y \\ \Delta_\theta \end{pmatrix} = \Psi\left(\begin{pmatrix} f_{xi} \\ f_{yi} \end{pmatrix}, \begin{pmatrix} f_{xi} \\ f_{yi} \end{pmatrix} + \frac{2}{t_{st}} \begin{pmatrix} s_{xi} \\ s_{yi} \end{pmatrix} \right) \tag{2}$$

Here, Ψ denotes a function that computes a roto-translation which maps all positions of the first list to positions of a second list, meanwhile minimizing the mean square error. There exists an approach based on Gibbs vectors [7] to set up and solve a linear equation system for Ψ.

For $\Delta_\theta \neq 0$, the robot walks along an arc with center

$$\begin{pmatrix} c_x \\ c_y \end{pmatrix} = \frac{1}{2} \begin{pmatrix} 1 & -1/\tan(\Delta_\theta/2) \\ 1/\tan(\Delta_\theta/2) & 1 \end{pmatrix} \begin{pmatrix} \Delta_x \\ \Delta_y \end{pmatrix} \tag{3}$$

and curve angle Δ_θ. For $\Delta_\theta = 0$, the robot walks along a straight line with direction (Δ_x, Δ_y). Considering both cases, the moving distance for a leg i over time Δt is

$$\ell_i(\Delta t) = \Delta t \cdot \begin{cases} |\Delta_\theta| \sqrt{(f_{xi} - c_x)^2 + (f_{yi} - c_y)^2} & \text{if } \Delta_\theta \neq 0 \\ \sqrt{\Delta_x^2 + \Delta_y^2} & \text{if } \Delta_\theta = 0 \end{cases} \tag{4}$$

Note that a turn in place is considered as arc movement with arc center in the robot's center.

We call $\ell_i(\Delta t)$ the *virtual odometry*. It represents the *expected* portion of the overall moving distance of each foot when walking.

C. Slippage Detection and Compensation

In contrast to the expected walking distances, we now compute the real distances. We assume sensors (e.g., Lidar) and respective SLAM mechanisms that permanently measure the robot's real position. We consider these mechanisms as black box, but expect they detect the real pose change (Δ_x', Δ_y', Δ_α') after walking a time Δt. We assume during Δt, only a single movement pattern is executed. This obviously is wrong, if there is a change in the trajectory (e.g., changing from arc to straight). However, for small Δt, we can model both patterns by a single ('average') pattern, thus expect only small errors.

For given (Δ_x', Δ_y', Δ_α') we can apply formulas (3) and (4) to get the *real* walking distances $\ell_i'(\Delta t)$. We define

$$S_i = \frac{\ell_i(\Delta t)}{\ell_i'(\Delta t)} \tag{5}$$

as the *leg-specific slippage factors* and

$$S = \frac{1}{L} \sum_i S_i \tag{6}$$

as the *general slippage factor*, where L is the number of legs. Obviously $S \geq 1$ in reality. S describes the slippage property of the current bottom's pavement. E.g., $S=2$ means, the robot walks half as far as expected when executing a certain trajectory. The S_i describe slippage *per leg* and could indicate malfunctions in leg servos or feet that do not properly touch the ground.

We are able to compensate slippage in two ways:

- Only compensate the general slippage.
- Also consider leg-specific slippage.

The assumption is: what we measured recently is a good estimation for the nearer future. E.g., if we walk on a slippery floor, we can consider the respective slippage factor to execute next trajectories because it is likely to reside on the same floor for a certain time.

To consider the general slippage factor, we have to extend the respective trajectory by the discovered factor, e.g.:

- Walking straight over a certain distance, we have to multiply the planned distance by S.
- Walking on an arc, we have to multiply the planned arc angle by S.

To consider the leg-specific slippage is more difficult. The problem: these factors do not only affect the trajectory length, but also its shape. E.g., if we want to walk straight with different factors S_i for left and right legs, the robot effectively walks on an arc instead. A first approach would be to extend the respective stance vectors. E.g., if for a specific leg we get $S_i=2$ (i.e., leg produces only half of the expected propulsion), we could multiply (s_{xi}, s_{yi}) by 2 to compensate this effect. This however is not always possible because the stance vector length is limited – either by the mechanics, or because neighbor legs should not collide during walking. We usually are only able to shorten the stance vectors. Our approach is thus to compute

$$S_{\max} = \max(S_i)\ ,\ \widetilde{S}_i = S_i / S_{\max} \tag{7}$$

We use S_{max} as the general factor to extend the trajectory and multiply each leg's stance vector by $\widetilde{S}_i$. Note that $\widetilde{S}_i \leq 1$, thus a stance vector only can get smaller.

It depends on the respective scenario, whether the compensation only should consider the general slippage or apply a leg-specific compensation. The latter is only reasonable, if we actually expect a leg-specific slippage that may be result of malfunctioned legs.

D. Regulation Trajectories

When walking on a planned trajectory, the real position differs from the planned position. This is because the execution of walking commands is never absolutely accurate due to slippage and minimal mechanical impreciseness. The task is to compensate the differences during walking and to meet the planned trajectories. This problem is related to control theory, where a system tries to produce a desired output with the help of controllable input values. In the case of trajectory regulation, however, the desired output is a pose that usually cannot directly be achieved by adapting single values or by a primitive walking operation. Due to non-holonomic constraints a *sequence* of trajectories usually is required.

Even though a certain multipod may support holonomic locomotion, not all trajectories may be suitable to get to the planned trajectory. E.g., we may have a cost function that considers a safety distance to obstacles, or we expect an ultrasonic sensor to always point in walking direction. To compute a regulation trajectory we thus need an additional planning step that (similar to the navigation and trajectory planning) minimizes a certain cost function.

To explain our approach, we need some definitions. First, we need a function *TP* that provides a trajectory planning from start pose *s* to target pose *t*.

$$(T_i) = TP\big((s_x, s_y, s_\theta), (t_x, t_y, t_\theta)\big) \tag{8}$$

The result (T_i) is a sequence of primitive trajectories, i.e., expressible by simple walking commands (e.g., arc or straight). *TP* takes into account the route points from the navigation, the cost function and the obstacle map. We can consider *TP* as black box, but solutions are widely known. We, e.g., may use *Rapidly-exploring Random Trees* (RRT). Our implementation is based on sets of *maneuvers* that are combined using a Viterbi approach [13].

We further need to identify an *expected* pose *e* of a current pose *c*.

$$(e_x, e_y, e_\theta) = E\big((T_i), (c_x, c_y, c_\theta)\big) \tag{9}$$

Expected means: the intended pose for a pose that is *not* on the planned path. If the multipod remains on the trajectory sequence, *c* and *e* are equal. But if the current pose leaves the planned trajectory, we have to introduce a notion of '*nearest pose on the trajectory*', whereas we may have different definitions for this. The function *E* may be *stateful* or *stateless*. A stateful implementation observes the current walking task and identifies the expected pose based on walking time or virtual odometry. As an example: we could measure the walking distance since the start of walking on (T_i) and identify the pose that has the respective distance from the start. A stateless implementation only identifies the nearest trajectory point based geometric distance computation.

We finally need a function *A* that projects the current expected pose *ahead*.

$$(a_x, a_y, a_\theta) = A\big((T_i), e, d\big) \tag{10}$$

Here, *d* describes, how much the current expected pose is projected ahead in target direction. Figure 3 illustrates the idea.

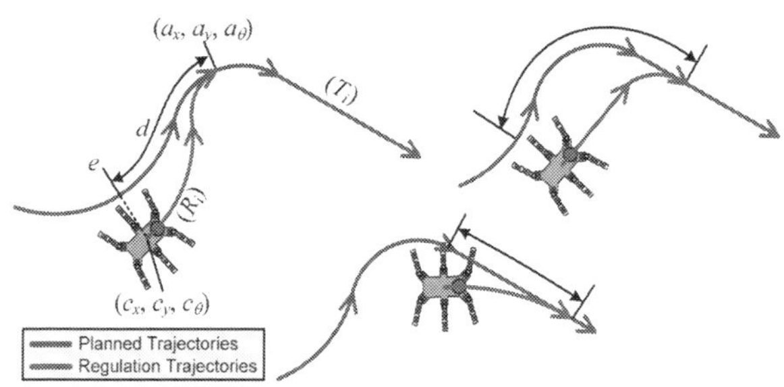

Figure 3. Idea of regulation-ahead

We now compute a trajectory sequence (R_i) that brings the robot back to the originally planned trajectory. Our approach is to compute

$$(R_i) = TP\Big((c_x, c_y, c_\theta), A\big((T_i), E\big((T_i), (c_x, c_y, c_\theta)\big), d\big)\Big) \tag{11}$$

The major benefit: we do not have to introduce a new approach to plan regulation trajectories, but re-use the function *TP*. One could suggest to bypass regulation trajectories and directly compute *TP*(*c*, *t*). However, the pose ahead is much closer to the current pose, thus a planning much more efficient. Furthermore, we do not expect obstacles between current and ahead pose, as the original path already is planned to be obstacle-free. In reality, we can compute (R_i) periodically, e.g., twice a second, without noticeable delay.

We finally have to think about *d*:

- For a small *d*, we force the robot to walk on sharp turns to restore the planned trajectory sequence.
- For a large *d*, the robot walks a long time parallel to the planned trajectory before it reaches the meeting point.

Both lead to higher costs – either because the path gets significantly longer or because the robot walks on positions with higher costs, besides the planned trajectory. Figure 4 illustrates these effects. In this example, we planned a linear

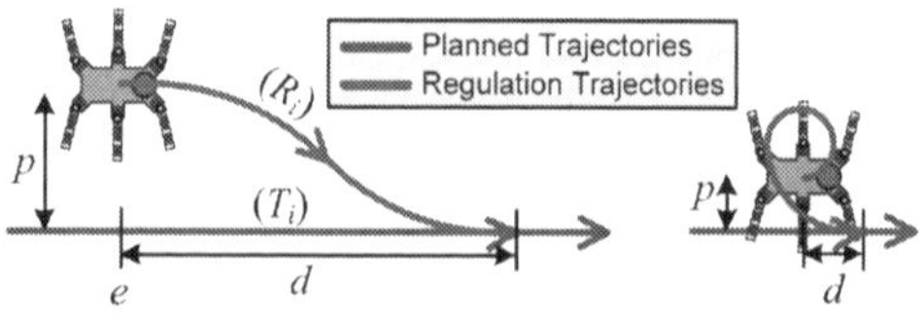

Figure 4. Effects of large and small d, p

trajectory and the real position is besides the linear trajectory with distance p, but with correct orientation angle.

If both p and d are large, usual regulation trajectories contain two arcs. If p and d are small, the regulation trajectory may be a spiral that starts in opposite direction, because arcs cannot be unlimited tight. This situation is unwanted, as the regulation first enlarges the distance to the planned trajectory.

We want to investigate this effect. As a first observation, it heavily depends on the walking capabilities, in particular the set of primitive trajectories and minimal arc radii, in addition the cost function. We thus cannot give a general specification of a 'good' d. However, we can provide an idea to discover d for a respective scenario.

Let $|(R_i)|$ be the length of the regulation trajectories. We define

$$q = \frac{|(R_i)|}{d} \tag{12}$$

as the *stretch factor*. It specifies how much longer the regulation path is compared to the planned path. Figure 5 shows typical curves of q. We used the trajectory planning of the Bugbot [13] for this chart. We planned only forward walking and penalized a turn in place with high costs.

Due to the effect presented in Figure 4 (right), small d result in high q. At a certain point (here at d=40 cm) q is close to 1.0. For d>40 cm, we get only minor improvements of q. As a result, d=40 cm is a good choice for our setting.

This is only an example for a certain scenario. If we want to discover an appropriate d for other scenarios, we have to consider the range of expected position errors (here p), but also the expected orientation errors.

IV. Experiments

We implemented our trajectory regulation approach on

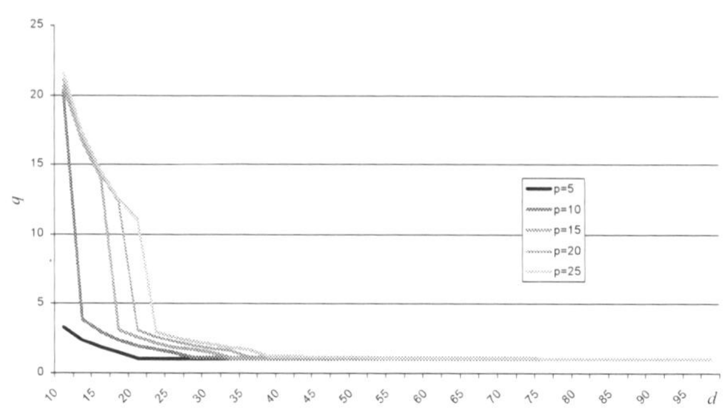

Figure 5. Typical stretch factors (d, p in cm)

Figure 6. The Bugbot

the *Bugbot* (Figure 6). Bugbot is an 18-DOF hexapod based on the Trossen PhantomX Mark III platform. We added a Lidar device and further sensors for collision detection. A Raspberry PI 3B is used for main computations, e.g., route and trajectory planning, SLAM and trajectory regulation. As described in [13], the trajectory planning function TP in equation (8) can efficiently compute a first trajectory in less than 1 ms, even on the Raspberry PI. TP already considers obstacle avoidance and can integrate arbitrary cost functions.

Even though we fully tested the approach on this platform, it was difficult to create a huge number of different experiments in reality. E.g., it is costly to test the slippage detection for different floors and different slippage factors. It is also a problem to adjust leg-specific slippage in reality in a fine-grained manner. We thus created a simulation environment that simulates the Bugbot on hardware- and physical level. A physical simulation component is able to compute gravitation, slippage and collision effects. The control software is the same as on the real hardware, i.e., the simulator's Bugbot model is able to create sensor values and carries out native servo commands.

Figure 7 shows an example to illustrate the effects of

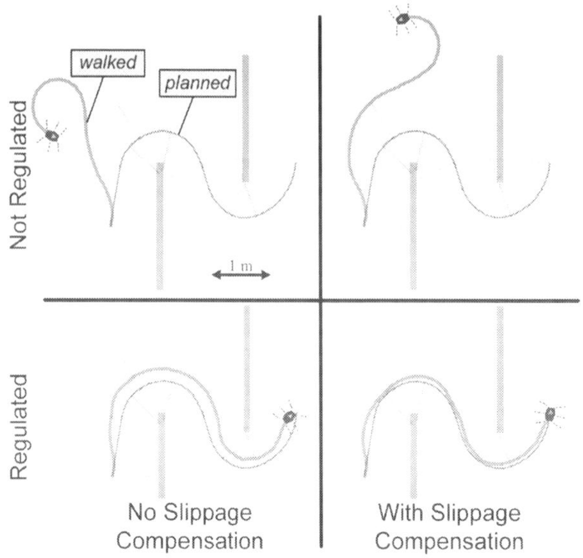

Figure 7. Simple walking scenario

slippage compensation and regulation. We artificially assigned a leg-specific slippage of 2.0 for the three left legs. This means, without any compensation, the robot walks a left arc when planned to walk right (Figure 7 top, left). With slippage detection and compensation, the shape of the planned path is mainly represented. But because the compensation is applied not before a small learning phase, the shape is rotated at the beginning (Figure 7 top, right).

Figure 7 bottom shows the regulation. On the left we see an effect when the regulation tries to meet the planned path. Because the regulation trajectories are not executed properly, we see a constant offset. On the right, we finally see both mechanisms – after a learning phase, the planned trajectory is reproduced very precisely.

Figure 8 shows a more complex example. Here we assigned again a leg-specific slippage of 2.0 and in addition a general slippage of 2.0. This represents a very difficult scenario. In the execution, both mechanisms were applied. We can see a great congruence of planned and walked path.

V. CONCLUSIONS

This paper presented an approach to the path following problem for multipods. We formalized gaits and introduced virtual odometry to abstract from the respective leg configuration. Slippage detection and compensation is used to map planned trajectories to movement commands that are executed more precisely. We compute regulation trajectories with the help of efficient trajectory planning already used for long-range path planning to the final target.

The look-ahead distance currently is based on the developer's experience. Whereas small distances may lead to instabilities, larger distances only increase the time to meet the planned path and increase the cost value, thus are less critical. However, in the future we also want to make the ahead-distance as part of the controllable state.

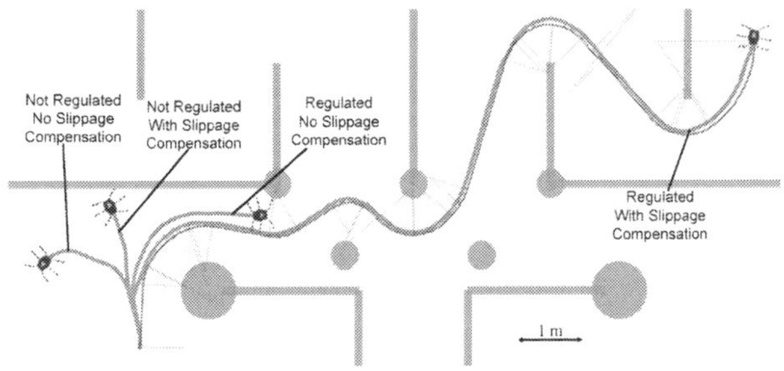

Figure 8. Complex walking scenario

REFERENCES

[1] S. Blažič, "A novel trajectory-tracking control law for wheeled mobile robots", Robotics and Autonomous Systems 59, 2011, pp. 1001–1007

[2] R. W. Brockett, "Asymptotic stability and feedback stabilization", in R. W. Brockett, R. S. Millman, and H. J. Sussmann, (eds.), Differential geometric control theory, Birkhauser, Boston, 1983, pp. 181–191

[3] S. Choi, J. Y. Lee, and W. Yu, "Comparison between Position and Posture Recovery in Path Following", 6th Intern. Conf. on Ubiquitous Robots and Ambient Intelligence (URAI), 2009

[4] D. Dacic, D. Nesic, and P. Kokotovic, "Path-following for nonlinear systems with unstable zero dynamics", IEEE Trans. Autom. Control, Vol. 52, No. 3, 2007, pp. 481–487

[5] H. Deng, G. Xin, G. Zhong, and M. Mistry, "Gait and trajectory rolling planning and control of hexapod robots for disaster rescue applications", Robotics and Autonomous Systems, 2017, pp. 13–24

[6] T. I. Fossen, K. Y. Pettersen, and R. Galeazzi, "Line-of-Sight Path Following for Dubins Paths With Adaptive Sideslip Compensation of Drift Forces", IEEE Trans. on Control Systems Technology, Vol. 23, No. 2, March 2015

[7] J. W. Gibbs, "Elements of Vector Analysis", New Haven, 1884

[8] T. M. Howard, R. A. Knepper, and A. Kelly, "Constrained Optimization Path Following of Wheeled Robots in Natural Terrain", in O. Khatib, V. Kumar, and D. Rus (eds.) Experimental Robotics. Springer Tracts in Advanced Robotics, Vol 39. Springer, 2008

[9] K. Kanjanawanishkul, M. Hofmeister, and A. Zell, "Path Following with an Optimal Forward Velocity for a Mobile Robot", Elsevier IFAC Proceedings Volumes, Vol. 43, No. 16, 2010, pp. 19–24

[10] L. Ojeda, D. Cruz, G. Reina, and J. Borenstein, "Current-Based Slippage Detection and Odometry Correction for Mobile, Robots and Planetary Rovers", IEEE Trans. on Robotics, Vol. 22, No. 2, April 2006

[11] A. Morro, A. Sgorbissa, and R. Zaccaria, "Path following for unicycle robots with an arbitrary path curvature", IEEE Trans. Robot., Vol. 27, No. 5, 2011, pp. 1016–1023

[12] J. E. Normey-Rico, J. Gómez-Ortega, and E. F. Camacho, "A Smith-predictor-based generalised predictive controller for mobile robot path-tracking", Control Engineering Practice 7(6), 1999, pp. 729–740

[13] J. Roth, "A Viterbi-like Approach for Trajectory Planning with Different Maneuvers", 15th International Conference on Intelligent Autonomous Systems (IAS-15), June 11-15, 2018, Baden-Baden, Germany, pp. 3–14

[14] J. Roth, "Systematic and Complete Enumeration of Statically Stable Multipod Gaits", to be published

[15] J. J. E. Slotine, "Sliding controller design for nonlinear systems", Int. J. Control, 40, 1984, pp. 421–434

[16] C. C. Ward and K. Iagnemma, "Model-Based Wheel Slip Detection for Outdoor Mobile Robots", IEEE Intern. Conf. on Robotics and Automation Rome, Italy, April 10-14 2007

[17] R. Wallace, A. Stentz, C. E. Thorpe, H. Moravec, W. Whittaker, and T. Kanade, "First results in robot road-following", Proc. of the 9th Intern. Joint Confe. on Artificial Intelligence (IJCAI '85), Vol. 1 , Los Angeles, Calif, USA, Aug. 1985, pp. 66–71

[18] P. Walters, R. Kamalapurkar, L. Andrews, and W. E. Dixon, "Online Approximate Optimal Path-Following for a Mobile Robot", 53rd IEEE Conference on Decision and Control December 15-17, 2014. Los Angeles, California, USA

[19] M. S. Wiig, W. Caharija, T. R. Krogstad, and K. Y. Pettersen, "Integral Line-of-Sight Guidance of Underwater Vehicles Without Neutral Buoyancy", Elsevier, IFAC-Papers Online, Vol. 49, No. 23, 2016, pp. 590–597

[20] J.-M. Yang and J.-H. Kim, "Sliding Mode Control for Trajectory Tracking of Nonholonomic Wheeled Mobile Robots", Proc. 1998 IEEE International Conference on Robotics and Automation

Evolving Swarm Behavior for Simulated Spiderino Robots

Midhat Jdeed, Arthur Pitman, and Wilfried Elmenreich
Institute for Networked and Embedded Systems / Lakeside Labs
Alpen-Adria-Universität Klagenfurt
Klagenfurt, Austria
Email: *firstname.lastname*@aau.at

***Abstract*—In swarm robotics research, simulation is often used to avoid the difficulties of designing swarm behavior in the real world. However, designing the controller of swarm members remains a non-trivial task due to the complex interactions between members and the emerging behavior itself. In this paper, FRamework for EVOlutionary design (FREVO) is used as tool for the design, simulation and optimization of swarm behavior for a given problem. This paper demonstrates how FREVO can be used to develop and optimize the behavior of the entire swarm simultaneously by applying an evolutionary algorithm. A case study consisting of twenty robots given the task of gathering near a light source while keeping a minimum distance from each other based solely on local information from simplistic sensors is presented. Considering the need of a fitness function to guide any evolutionary process which is a problem-specific function, the robots' controller is evolved according to a fitness function depending on two factors: the robots' proximity to the light source and the ability to keep a minimum distance between the robots. We examine in particular how the problem can be modeled and how evolution can be applied to create a suitable controller for the swarm members.**

Keywords–Swarm robotics; Spiderino; Evolutionary optimization;.

I. Introduction

Inspired by the fascinating collective behavior of fish, birds, ants and bees, swarm robotics have gained an increasing interest in the research community. The defining characteristic of these groups is that the emerging swarm behavior is significantly more complex than that of any individual member [1][2].

Research in swarm robotics can be classified into two main groups. The first one is concerned with hardware and considers aspects, such as locomotion, size, communication and cost [3]. Examples for such hardware platforms for swarm research are Kilobot [4], Colias [5], e-Puck [6], Jasmine [7] and the Spiderino platform [8]. The second group deals with swarm design using software simulation. The behavior and the interactions among swarm members remain a complex topic [9] especially in environments where dynamic interactions occur. In particular, it is often difficult to derive the requirements for an individual robot within a swarm from the desired global behavior. This work focuses on modeling and designing swarm behavior using the FREVO [10] software and tackles the challenge of constructing robot behavior using evolutionary principles which try to develop an optimal solution based on a fitness function.

In the evolutionary process, the main challenge is defining an objective (or fitness) function that is designed to reward a desired behaviour of a swarm, which is highly based on each problem individually. The applicability and performance of a fitness function depends on the employed optimizer, thus, there are no universally suitable fitness functions [11]. Nevertheless, many studies in the field of evolutionary optimization have considered generic methods for fitness function design [12][13]. The author in [13] categorized such methods into a three-dimensional fitness space: *Functional vs. behavioural, Global vs. local, and Explicit vs. implicit*. For instance, an explicit function rewards the way in which a certain goal is achieved, while implicit fitness is focused on how much the goal is reached (e.g., a distance).

Furthermore, in the evolutionary process, moving the evolved controller from simulation to real robots is still a big challenge due to differences between the simulation environment and the real world, an issue is known as the reality gap [14]. Within this paper the reality gap is partially addressed by evolving behavior that can be run as code on real robots, and by the definition of a fitness function that can be also evaluated in an experiment with real robots. Further techniques for addressing this problem include intermittently involving real robots in the evolution process [15] and developing accurate models for sensors and actuators [8]. However, a particular assessment of real hardware behavior is outside the scope of this paper.

Designing swarm behaviour by using evolution is mostly an automatic design method that creates an intended swarm behaviour as a result of a bottom up process starting from interactions between very small components. The process gradually modifies potential solutions until a satisfying result is achieved. Such an evolutionary design approach is based on evolutionary computation techniques and can be done either on individual or on a swarm level. In [16], six components are presented for consideration while designing swarm robotics using evolution:

1) The task description: A highly abstract vision of the problem should be created.
2) The simulation setup: The task description must be transformed into an abstracted problem model.
3) The interaction interface: This interface defines the interaction among agents, i.e., the swarm, as well as their interaction with the environment.
4) The evolvable decision unit: The representation of the system or the agent controller, for example an artificial neural network or finite state machine.
5) The search algorithm: In this task, an optimization method will be applied to the results from the above steps like evolutionary algorithms.
6) The objective function: A problem-specific function, often known as a *fitness function*, that guides the search algorithm to a (semi) optimal solution.

Our approach in this paper is to evolve a controller for a swarm consisting of 20 robots using evolutionary design that follow the six mentioned tasks above. The task is to move within a threshold distance of a light source guided only by simplistic sensors. The process is done in a simulated environment using FREVO. Thus, the main contribution of this paper is to demonstrate our approach using FREVO and how it may be applied to solve tasks related to swarm robotics.

The paper is organized as follows: The next section provides a review of related work. Section III outlines the architecture of Spiderino platform, and FREVO tool is introduced in Section IV. Sections V and VI describe the case study, the implementation process and discuss the results. Conclusions are drawn in Section VII, together with an outline of future work.

II. Related Work

Swarm robotics draws inspiration from nature and seeks to offer novel capabilities, such as self-organization, self-learning and self-reassembly [17]. Much research has been conducted to study different behaviours that can be performed using swarm robotics, such as aggregation, flocking, dispersion, foraging, object clustering and sorting, navigation, path formation, deployment, collective transport of objects [18]–[20]. For example, in [21], the authors present a higher multi-robot organism that is capable of autonomous aggregation and disaggregation. Consequently, evolutionary methods gained an increased interest in the research community as it is an approach to deal with design problem in swarm robotics [22]. Nevertheless, the main challenges remain to overcome open issues, such as scaling in complexity, and having a smooth transition from simulation to the real world [23].

There are several software and frameworks supporting evolutionary design in swarm robotics. AutoMoDe [23] is a software for automatic design which generates modular control software in the form of a probabilistic finite state machine. JBotEvolvern is a Java-based versatile open-source platform for education and research-driven experiments in evolutionary robotics [24], which has been used in many studies [25]–[27]. FREVO, a tool for creating and evaluating swarm behaviour, has been used in several studies as an evolution tool including robotics [28] and pattern generation [29]. In [9], a simulated robot soccer game was implemented to evaluate the capabilities of evolutionary algorithms and artificial neural networks. Moreover, a comparison of two different evolvable controller models based on their performance for a simple robotic problem was presented in [30], where a robot has to find a light source using two luminance sensors. The paper compared the relative advantages of Mealy machines, a type of finite state machine, and a fully meshed artificial neural network.

Nevertheless, several works have been succeeded in exploring the use of evolutionary design for generating a robot controller to perform a task. For example, the authors in [31] introduced an evolutionary approach that demonstrates emergent collective in a swarm of simulated Kilobots. The task was to evolve behaviors of phototaxis and clustering. Also, in [32], an embodied evolution method was introduced and it was shown that using evolved controllers can outperform a hand-designed controller in applications like phototaxis from a random location in an environment. Similar works have been carried out to perform phototaxis using evolution processes [33]–[35].

III. Spiderino Platform

This section describes the Spiderino platform in terms of hardware following by the corresponding software framework to develop a controller using simulated evolution:

A. *Hardware*

Spiderino is a low-cost research robot based on the smaller variant of the Hexbug Spider toy [36]. Figure 1 depicts the Spiderino robot [8], used for the simulation presented in this work. The main aim of designing Spiderino is to be used in swarm research and education. To provide space for sensors, a larger battery, and a Printed Circuit Board (PCB) with Arduino microcontroller, Wi-Fi module, and motor controller, the toy's head was replaced with a 3D-printed adapter. In terms of locomotion, Spiderino has two degrees of freedom: It may turn its head left or right, with a full turn requiring approximately 3 seconds, and it can move forward or backward relative to the direction it is facing by cycling its legs at 0.06 m/s.

Each Spiderino has 6 four-pin interfaces that generically support a variety of sensors. For the experiments in this paper, we assume that each Spiderino is equipped with 3 CNY70 reflective optical sensors [37], positioned at 45°offsets, each consisting of an infrared emitter and a photo-transistor. By turning on and off the infrared LEDs, a Spiderino may distinguish between light sources and obstacles, such as other Spiderinos or walls.

Each robot is equipped with a lithium polymer battery with a capacity of 750 mAh. Spiderino robots consume between 6 mA and 60 mA, with walking being the most expensive operation. Further details of energy consumption are provided in [8].

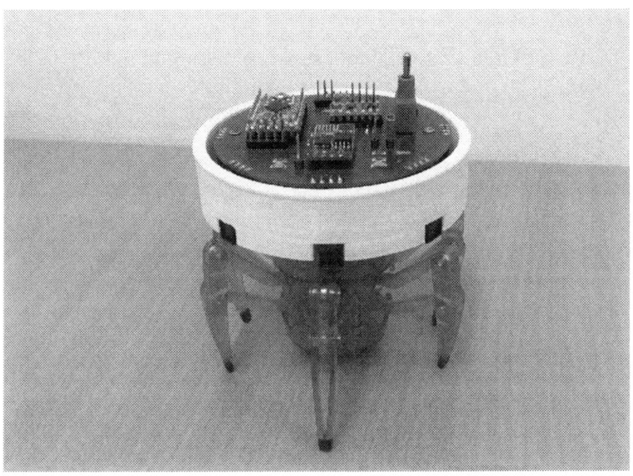

Figure 1. Spiderino robots equipped with CNY70 sensors

B. *Software model*

We created a software framework for the Spiderino platform to allow the robot's controller to be developed using simulated evolution. Attention was paid to modeling the robot

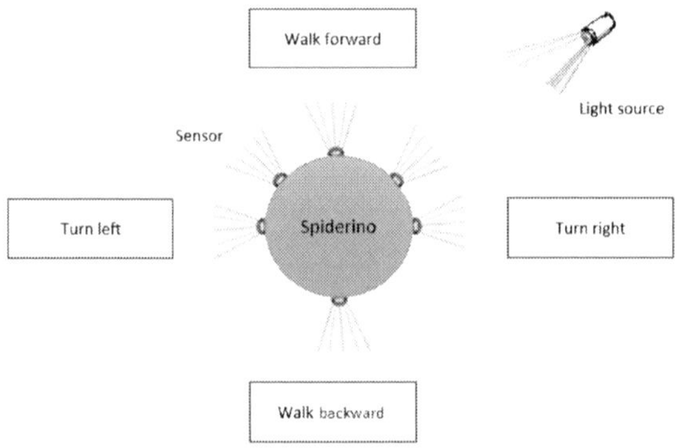

Figure 2. An illustrations model of the sensing phase in Spiderino

accurately to allow validation of the simulation results using actual hardware.

In simulation, each Spiderino is modeled as a solid circular object of radius *spiderinoRadius* (0.06m) moving on a walled flat plane of dimensions *worldWidth* and *worldHeight*. After consideration of the robot's size, weight and locomotion, both friction and momentum were neglected. As outlined in Figure 2, simulation proceeds through *maximumSteps* iterations carried out in two phases:

1) Sense phase: By tracing rays emitted from each of the Spiderino's sensors, the simulator calculates values for both modes of each of the CNY70 sensors.
2) Locomotion phase: Based on the sensor values, a controller may move a Spiderino's head left or right, or walk forwards or backwards. Each movement occurs at speeds given by *spiderinoWalkSpeed* (0.06 m/s) and *spiderinoTurnSpeed* (120°/s) for a period of *stepTime* milliseconds.

To construct a model of the CNY70 sensors, we used the sensor's datasheet [37] as a reference point and gathered empirical evidence about its effectiveness as both a light and proximity sensor. When acting as light sensor, light sources may be detected within a range of few meters depending on factors, such as the light's intensity and ambient light levels (see Figure 3a). When acting as a proximity sensor, the sensor's value is proportional to distance to the closest object (see Figure 3b). Objects may be sensed within a more limited range of approximately 3 cm. If pointed at a light source while measuring proximity, the sensor functions as a light sensor. Objects off-axis up 60° produce amplified readings as described in Figure 3c. For each of the two modes, each sensor value was calculated as the minimum of the values determined for each ray.

IV. FREVO Architecture

FREVO is a tool for creating and evaluating systems using evolutionary methods. In order for it to develop a solution, FREVO needs an input consisting of several components as illustrated in Figure 4. First, it is necessary to define the problem where the evaluation context of the agent has to be implemented. Second, a controller representation should be selected that describes the structure of a possible solution. Third, the optimization method must be selected to optimize the chosen controller representation to maximize the fitness returned from the problem definition. Finally, the ranking module is configured to evaluate all agents in a problem and return a ranking of the candidates based on their fitness.

Two types of problem may be modeled in FREVO. The first, a so called *SingleProblem*, where a single candidate controller is evolved, is used in this paper and requires implementations for three functions:

- *evaluateCandidate()* typically utilizes a simulator to evaluate a candidate controller a returns a fitness value that is used to rank the candidate within the population of the generation.
- *replyWithVisualization()* it is called to replay an evaluation with visualization.
- *getMaximumFitness()* specifies the maximum fitness value that can be achieved.

The second type, a *MultiProblem*, evaluates multiple candidates simultaneously, for example, two soccer teams playing against each other as described in [9]. Additional details about using FREVO and constructing a simple simulation are presented in the project's official online tutorial [38].

V. Case Study

To perform the case study, a problem component named *SpiderinoSim* has been implemented in FREVO. It is written in Java and models an area where the Spiderinos can move around, a light source, some obstacles and multiple Spiderino robots. The light source can be placed in a specified position, either in the center of a world or at a random location. Spiderinos are placed randomly. *SpiderinoSim* has been modeled as a *SingleProblem* in FREVO, which means that the performance of a Spiderino team is evaluated by an absolute fitness value. In the experiment presented in this paper, twenty Spiderinos, initially placed at random locations, were given the task of keeping a distance of 2 cm from each other and approaching a light source (diameter 0.3 m) in a random location in a walled rectangular world of 3 by 2 meters with obstacles. Each simulation consisted of 1500 steps of 100 milliseconds and, thus, lasted 200 seconds and tested the ability of a candidate controller to guide the Spiderinos to the light source.

To rank various candidates during the evolution process, FREVO requires a fitness function. The designed fitness function in this case study depends on three components:

- Final distance to the light source: Candidate controllers were rewarded for getting closer to the light.
- Distance between each other: Candidate controllers were rewarded for keeping a distance of 0.02m between each other and penalized for violating such a distance.

The controller produces two outputs, corresponding to driving one motors for moving forward/backward and turning left or right. A diagram of the Spiderino architecture is given in Figure 5. The inputs of the ANN are twelve values from the six CNY70 sensors, each of them giving a proximity and luminance value.

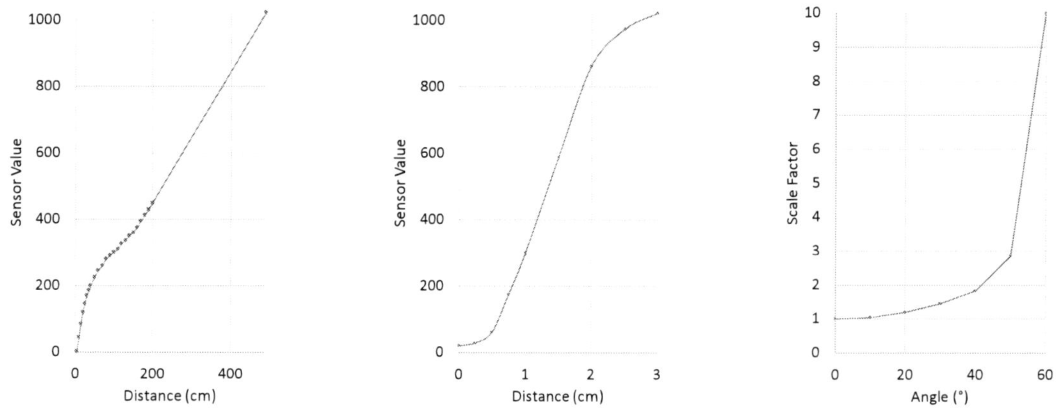

(a) Light sensitivity (b) Object sensitivity (c) Off-axis sensitivity

Figure 3. CNY70 responsiveness

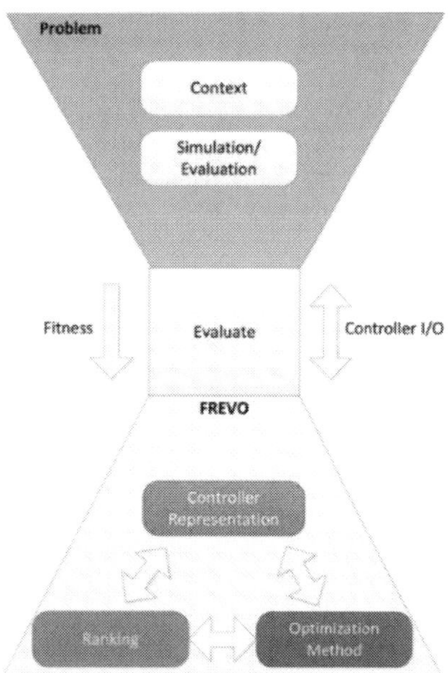

Figure 4. FREVO architecture [10]

FREVO offers many evolutionary and representation methods as documented in [10]. ANNs were used as the basis of the controller in all instances. In particular, we utilized FREVO's Fully Meshed Network component with 6 hidden nodes and 2 iterations. Furthermore, in this work we used Cellular Evolutionary Algorithm with two-dimensional Population (CEA2D), a 2-dimensional cellular evolution algorithm, for optimization.

VI. Results and Discussion

Figure 6 illustrates the performance of the Spiderino swarm in after different number of generations. Case 1 shows the initial position, Case 2 shows a partial successfully results where only about half of Spiderinos reach the goal. Case 3 and 4 (Figure 6c and 6d) show a are more successful behavior where eventually all Spiderinos get to the goal. Figure 7 shows the improvement of performance, expressed by the fitness function value over several generations. Evolving 300 generations took about 12 hours on an 8-core machine. While the result, as shown in Figure 6d is satisfactory, there were still small improvements in the achievable fitness after 300+ generations, which is most likely reflecting in small adjustments in robot distribution. Most importantly, the results obtained support that notion that it is possible to evolve a controller for the task using evolution.

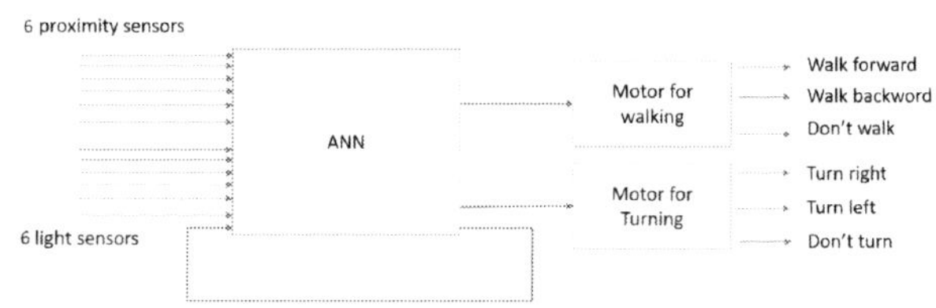

Figure 5. High-level model of a Spiderino in the case study

VII. Conclusion

In this paper, we have described a method for designing swarm behavior using evolution. In the case study, a swarm of twenty robots evolved the skills required to gather at a light source while keepeing a distance from each other. More specifically, the neural network learnt to interpret its twelve sensory inputs to control its motors. While the task introduced in this paper is rather simplistic it is analogous to the homing task in swarm robotics. Moreover, the evolutionary approach may be applied to a wide variety of problems that may be expressed through a fitness function. In a simulated environment, we evolved controllers for 20 robots to approach a light source by utilizing a fitness function depending on three factors: distance from the light source as well as the number of walk and turn steps a robot utilizes.

In future work, we hope to cross the reality gap and apply the evolved controllers to real hardware. To extend the case study, we intend to compare the performance of

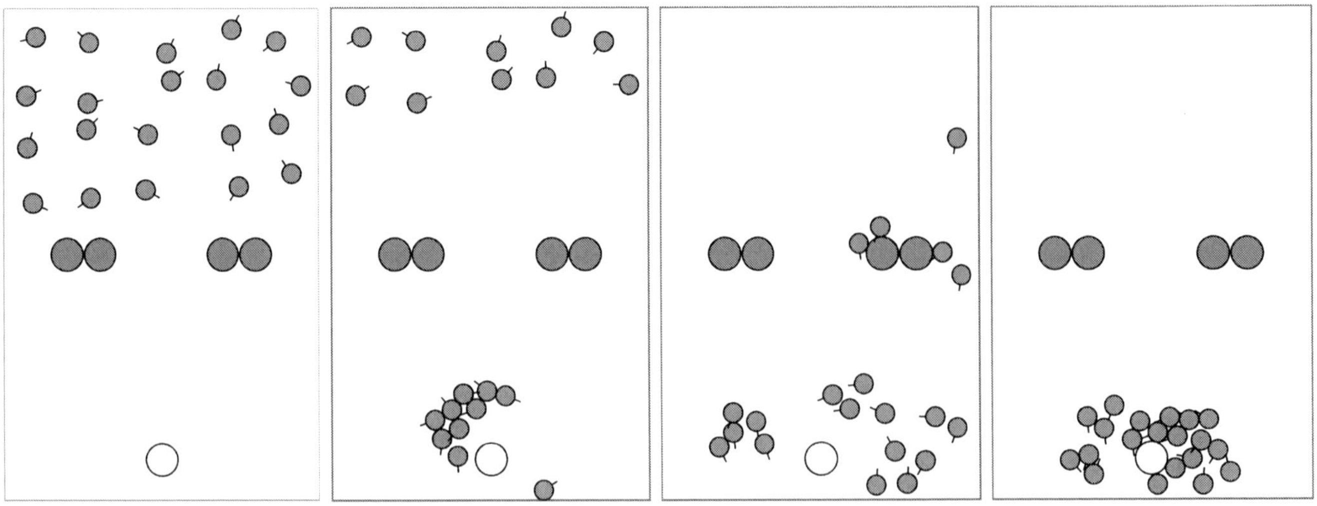

(a) Case 1: Before Running The Evolution, Initial Positions (b) Case 2: After 118 Generations, 1500 Steps, Fitness 57.7 (c) Case 3: After 307 Generations, 750 Steps (d) Case 4: After 307 Generations, 1500 Steps, Fitness 69.5

Figure 6. Sample final simulation states

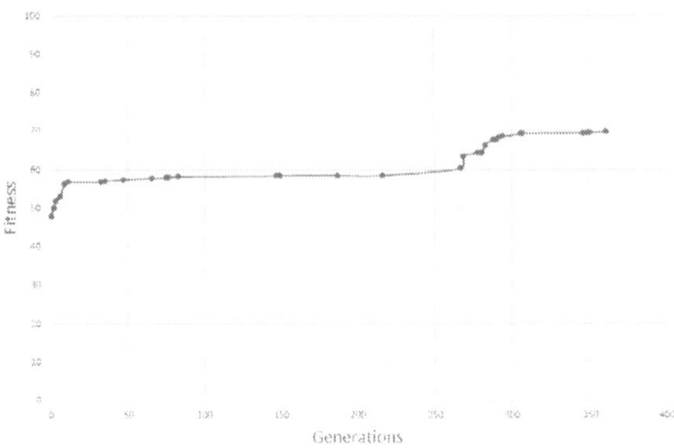

Figure 7. Fitness function values over 361 generation

such controllers with hand-written algorithms and consider factors, such as the time required to reach the light, as well as key swarm properties, such as flexibility and robustness. Another potential work is to rank various candidates during the evolution process using different fitness functions, such as, implementing a multiple-objective function that also takes the energy consumption resulting from locomotion into account.

Acknowledgments

We would like to thank our colleagues Elnaz Khatmi, Markus Müller, Sabrina Huber, and the anonymous reviewers for their constructive comments on an earlier version of this paper. This work was partially supported by Lakeside Labs via the Smart Microgrid Lab and by the Self-Organizing Systems cluster of University of Klagenfurt. The research leading to these results has received funding from the European Union Horizon 2020 research and innovation program under grant agreement No 731946 (Project CPSwarm).

References

[1] Y. Tan, "A survey on swarm robotics," Handbook of Research on Design, Control, and Modeling of Swarm Robotics, vol. 1, 2015, pp. 1–41, DOI: 10.4018/978-1-4666-9572-6.ch001.

[2] H. Hamann, Swarm Robotics: A Formal Approach. Springer, 2018, DOI: 10.1007/978-3-319-74528-2_5.

[3] M. Patil, T. Abukhalil, S. Patel, and T. Sobh, "Hardware architecture review of swarm robotics system: Self reconfigurability, self reassembly and self replication," in Innovations and Advances in Computing, Informatics, Systems Sciences, Networking and Engineering. Springer, 2015, pp. 433–444, DOI: 10.1007/978-3-319-06773-5_58.

[4] M. Rubenstein, C. Ahler, and R. Nagpal, "Kilobot: A low cost scalable robot system for collective behaviors," in Robotics and Automation (ICRA), 2012 IEEE International Conference on. IEEE, 2012, pp. 3293–3298, DOI: 10.1109/ICRA.2012.6224638.

[5] F. Arvin, J. Murray, C. Zhang, and S. Yue, "Colias: An autonomous micro robot for swarm robotic applications," International Journal of Advanced Robotic Systems, vol. 11, no. 7, 2014, p. 113, DOI: 10.5772/58730.

[6] F. Mondada, M. Bonani, X. Raemy, J. Pugh, C. Cianci, A. Klaptocz, S. Magnenat, J.-C. Zufferey, D. Floreano, and A. Martinoli, "The e-puck, a robot designed for education in engineering," in Proceedings of the 9th conference on autonomous robot systems and competitions, vol. 1, no. LIS-CONF-2009-004. IPCB: Instituto Politécnico de Castelo Branco, 2009, pp. 59–65, DOI: 10.7717/peerj-cs.82/fig-5.

[7] S. Kernbach, R. Thenius, O. Kernbach, and T. Schmickl, "Re-embodiment of honeybee aggregation behavior in an artificial micro-robotic system," Adaptive Behavior, vol. 17, no. 3, 2009, pp. 237–259, DOI: 10.1177/1059712309104966.

[8] M. Jdeed, S. Zhevzhyk, F. Steinkellner, and W. Elmenreich, "Spiderino-a low-cost robot for swarm research and educational purposes," in Intelligent Solutions in Embedded Systems (WISES), 2017 13th Workshop on. IEEE, 2017, pp. 35–39, DOI: 10.1109/wises.2017.7986929.

[9] I. Fehérvári and W. Elmenreich, "Evolving neural network controllers for a team of self-organizing robots," Journal of Robotics, vol. 2010, 2010, pp. 1–10, DOI: 10.1155/2010/841286.

[10] A. Sobe, I. Fehérvári, and W. Elmenreich, "FREVO: A tool for evolving and evaluating self-organizing systems," in Self-Adaptive and Self-Organizing Systems Workshops (SASOW), 2012 IEEE Sixth International Conference on. IEEE, 2012, pp. 105–110, DOI: 10.1109/sasow.2012.27.

[11] A. J. Lockett, "Insights from adversarial fitness functions," in Proceedings of the 2015 ACM Conference on Foundations of Genetic Algorithms XIII. ACM, 2015, pp. 25–39, DOI: 10.1145/2725494.2725501.

[12] D. Floreano and J. Urzelai, "Evolutionary robots with on-line self-organization and behavioral fitness," Neural Networks, vol. 13, no. 4-5, 2000, pp. 431–443, DOI: 10.1016/s0893-6080(00)00032-0.

[13] I. Fehérvári, "On evolving self-organizing technical systems," Ph.D. dissertation, Alpen-Adria-Universität Klagenfurt, Nov. 2013.

[14] J.-B. Mouret and K. Chatzilygeroudis, "20 years of reality gap: a few thoughts about simulators in evolutionary robotics," in Proceedings of the Genetic and Evolutionary Computation Conference Companion. ACM, 2017, pp. 1121–1124, DOI: 10.1145/3067695.3082052.

[15] S. Koos, J.-B. Mouret, and S. Doncieux, "The transferability approach: Crossing the reality gap in evolutionary robotics," IEEE Transactions on Evolutionary Computation, vol. 17, no. 1, 2013, pp. 122–145, DOI: 10.1109/tevc.2012.2185849.

[16] I. Fehérvári and W. Elmenreich, "Evolution as a tool to design self-organizing systems," in International Workshop on Self-Organizing Systems. Springer, 2014, pp. 139–144, DOI: 10.1007/978-3-642-54140-7_12.

[17] M. Patil, T. Abukhalil, S. Patel, and T. Sobh, "Ub robot swarmdesign, implementation, and power management," in Control and Automation (ICCA), 2016 12th IEEE International Conference on. IEEE, 2016, pp. 577–582, DOI: 10.1109/icca.2016.7505339.

[18] I. Navarro and F. Matía, "An introduction to swarm robotics," Isrn robotics, vol. 2013, 2012, pp. 1–10, DOI: 10.5402/2013/608164.

[19] L. Bayındır, "A review of swarm robotics tasks," Neurocomputing, vol. 172, 2016, pp. 292–321, DOI: 10.1016/j.neucom.2015.05.116.

[20] Y. Tan and Z.-y. Zheng, "Research advance in swarm robotics," Defence Technology, vol. 9, no. 1, 2013, pp. 18–39, DOI: 10.1016/j.dt.2013.03.001.

[21] S. Kornienko, O. Kornienko, A. Nagarathinam, and P. Levi, "From real robot swarm to evolutionary multi-robot organism," in Evolutionary Computation, 2007. CEC 2007. IEEE Congress on. IEEE, 2007, pp. 1483–1490, DOI: 10.1109/cec.2007.4424647.

[22] V. Trianni, "Evolutionary robotics for self-organising behaviours," Evolutionary Swarm Robotics: Evolving Self-Organising Behaviours in Groups of Autonomous Robots, 2008, pp. 47–59, DOI: 10.1007/978-3-540-77612-3_4.

[23] G. Francesca, M. Brambilla, A. Brutschy, V. Trianni, and M. Birattari, "Automode: A novel approach to the automatic design of control software for robot swarms," Swarm Intelligence, vol. 8, no. 2, 2014, pp. 89–112, DOI: 10.1007/s11721-014-0092-4.

[24] M. Duarte, F. Silva, T. Rodrigues, S. M. Oliveira, and A. L. Christensen, "Jbotevolver: A versatile simulation platform for evolutionary robotics," in Proceedings of the 14th International Conference on the Synthesis & Simulation of Living Systems. MIT Press, Cambridge, MA, 2014, pp. 210–211, DOI: 10.7551/978-0-262-32621-6-ch035.

[25] M. Duarte, A. L. Christensen, and S. Oliveira, "Towards artificial evolution of complex behaviors observed in insect colonies," in Portuguese Conference on Artificial Intelligence. Springer, 2011, pp. 153–167, DOI: 10.1007/978-3-642-24769-9_12.

[26] J. Gomes, P. Urbano, and A. L. Christensen, "Evolution of swarm robotics systems with novelty search," Swarm Intelligence, vol. 7, no. 2-3, 2013, pp. 115–144, DOI: 10.1007/s11721-013-0081-z.

[27] T. Rodrigues, M. Duarte, S. Oliveira, and A. L. Christensen, "What you choose to see is what you get: an experiment with learnt sensory modulation in a robotic foraging task," in European Conference on the Applications of Evolutionary Computation. Springer, 2014, pp. 789–801, DOI: 10.1007/978-3-662-45523-4_64.

[28] W. Elmenreich, R. D'Souza, C. Bettstetter, and H. de Meer, "A survey of models and design methods for self-organizing networked systems," in Proceedings of the Fourth International Workshop on Self-Organizing Systems, vol. LNCS 5918. Springer Verlag, 2009, pp. 37–49, DOI: 10.1007/978-3-642-10865-5_4.

[29] W. Elmenreich and I. Fehérvári, "Evolving self-organizing cellular automata based on neural network genotypes," in International Workshop on Self-Organizing Systems. Springer, 2011, pp. 16–25, DOI: 10.1007/978-3-642-19167-1_2.

[30] A. Pintér-Bartha, A. Sobe, and W. Elmenreich, "Towards the light-comparing evolved neural network controllers and finite state machine controllers," in Intelligent Solutions in Embedded Systems (WISES), 2012 Proceedings of the Tenth Workshop on. IEEE, 2012, pp. 83–87, Electronic ISBN: 978-3-902463-09-8.

[31] J. Holland, J. Griffith, and C. O'Riordan, "Evolving collective behaviours in simulated kilobots," in Proceedings of the 33rd Annual ACM Symposium on Applied Computing. Association for Computing Machinery, 2018, pp. 824–831, DOI: 10.1145/3167132.3167223.

[32] R. A. Watson, S. G. Ficici, and J. B. Pollack, "Embodied evolution: Distributing an evolutionary algorithm in a population of robots," Robotics and Autonomous Systems, vol. 39, no. 1, 2002, pp. 1–18, DOI: 10.1016/s0921-8890(02)00170-7.

[33] F. Silva, P. Urbano, L. Correia, and A. L. Christensen, "odneat: An algorithm for decentralised online evolution of robotic controllers," Evolutionary Computation, vol. 23, no. 3, 2015, pp. 421–449, DOI: 10.1162/evco_a_001417.

[34] F. Silva, L. Correia, and A. L. Christensen, "Leveraging online racing and population cloning in evolutionary multirobot systems," in European Conference on the Applications of Evolutionary Computation. Springer, 2016, pp. 165–180, DOI: 10.1007/978-3-319-31153-1_12.

[35] E. Di Paolo, "Spike-timing dependent plasticity for evolved robots," Adaptive Behavior, vol. 10, no. 3-4, 2002, pp. 243–263, DOI: 10.1177/1059712302010003006.

[36] HEXBUG Micro Robotic Creatures, accessed: 26.3.2019. [Online]. Available: https://www.hexbug.com

[37] CNY70 Datasheet, accessed: 26.3.2019. [Online]. Available: https://datasheet.octopart.com/CNY70-Vishay-datasheet-5434663.pdf

[38] FREVO Tutorial, accessed: 26.3.2019. [Online]. Available: https://sourceforge.net/p/frevo/wiki/Tutorials/

Adaptive Software Deployment

Ichiro Satoh

National Institute of Informatics
2-1-2 Hitotsubashi Chiyoda-ku Tokyo 101-8430 Japan
Email: ichiro@nii.ac.jp

Abstract—**Individual IoT devices may not be able to provide enriched services because they tend to have limited or imbalanced computational resources, e.g., lacking keyboards or displays. To solve this problem, we propose a dynamic federation of computational resources of smart objects as a virtual distributed system according to users' requirements and context. The approach presented in this paper has two key ideas. The first is to federate multiple smart objects or application-specific services as a virtual computer and the second is to separate between services for users from context-aware policies of such services. The approach was constructed as a general-purpose middleware system for executing and deploying application-specific software at smart objects.**

Keywords-Software deployment; Component coordination; Distributed system; Self-organization.

I. INTRODUCTION

Internet of Things (IoT) has been used in a variety of infrastructures, such as power plants, energy distribution networks, transportation systems, water supply networks, and also the systems supporting the concept of smart houses, smart buildings and smart factories. Nevertheless, the bandwidth of networks between IoT devices tends to be narrow because such networks are based on low-power connections and radio communications. Furthermore, computational resources of IoT devices are not or well-balanced, in comparison with personal computers and smart phones. For example, IoT devices may lack any keyboards or displays. Although individual IoT devices do not have enough resources, their federations may be able to provide enriched services, which need computational resources, e.g., processors, memory, input/output devices beyond the resources of individual IoT devices.

To solve the problems discussed above, we propose to federate computational resources of IoT devices as a virtual distributed system. Such federations also should be adapted to contextual information, e.g., the locations of users and computers in addition to the computational resources of IoT devices. Our approach provides the notion of adaptive federations between the devices for software components running on IoT devices. It is characterized in introducing metaphors inspired from nature: *gravitational* and *repulsive* forces between software for defining services and target entities, including people or spaces that the services are provided for in the real world (Figure 1). This is because, like large-scale distributed systems, the scale and complexity of such a context-aware system is beyond our ability to manage using conventional approaches, such as centralized or top-down approaches. The former force dynamically deploys software for defining services at computers nearby the targets and executing them there. It is introduced as relocations between users and services or between services. The latter force prevents software for defining services from being at computers nearby the locations of the targets. It is used as a relocation technique between similar services.

Some of the metaphors in the approach were discussed in our previous paper [10]. In this paper, we address an application of the metaphors to a context-aware system in the real world. The approach is constructed as a general-purpose middleware system for federating IoT devices with the metaphors. To ensure independence from the underlying location systems, the system introduces virtual counterparts for the target entities and spaces. This paper presents the design and implementation of the system and our evaluation of our approach through a case study of it.

The remainder of this paper is organized as follows. In Section 2 we outline our basic idea behind the approach. Section 3 presents the design and implementation of the proposed approach. In Section 4 we describe our experience with the approach through an example. Section 5 surveys related work and Section 6 provides a summary.

II. APPROACH

This section discusses our requirements and then outlines idea behind the proposed approach.

A. Requirements

IoT devices are connected with one another via wired or wireless networks. They also tend to be various because they are often designed to their given purposes rather than any general-purposes.

- Individual IoT devices may not be able to provide enriched services because they tend to have only limited resources, e.g., lacking keyboards or screens.

- Since IoT devices are used in the real world, services provided from such devices often depend on contextual information. Nevertheless, the services themselves should be defined independently of context so that they can be reused in various context.
- Our middleware system should be independent of any underlying sensing systems to capture contextual information in the real world in addition on any application-specific services running on the system.
- IoT devices are often managed in a non-centralized manner to support large-scale context-aware services, e.g., city-level ones.

B. *Adaptive federation of IoT devices*

To satisfy the above requirements, we introduce the following approaches into our system.

- The first is to dynamically federate multiple IoT devices or application-specific services as a virtual computer. To satisfy the first requirement, the system dynamically makes a virtual computer on IoT systems by federating of hardware and software components according to their capabilities.
- The second is to separate between services provided for users from context-aware policies of such services. When contextual information changes, a federation among IoT devices should adapt itself to changes rather than individual components running on the devices.
- The system supports software or hardware components. It enables application-specific services to defined within such components rather than the system.
- It is constructed as a distributed system consisting of IoT devices, where IoT devices are managed in a peer-to-peer manner.

Context-aware services themselves are common. To reuse such services in other context, the middleware systems provides contextual conditions that the services should be activated as policies defined outside the services. The policies can be classified into two types: *gravitational* and *repulsive* forces between services and the target entities and spaces.

1) Virtual counterparts: We abstract away the underlying systems, including location-sensing systems. Our middleware system has the following two kinds of software components, called agents, in addition to hardware components corresponding to IoT devices.

- Physical entities, people, and spaces can have their digital representations, called *virtual-counterpart* agents, in the system. Each virtual-counterpart is automatically deployed at computers close to its target entity or person or within the space. For example, a virtual-counterpart for users can store per-user preferences and record user behavior, e.g., exhibits that they have looked at.

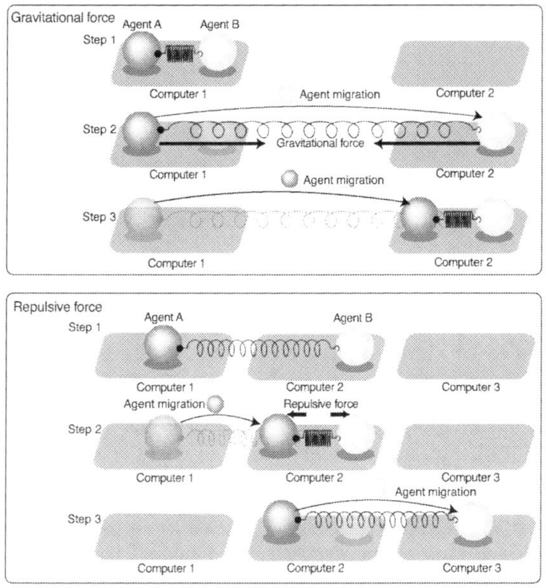

Figure 1. Component deployment based on *Gravitational* and *repulsive* policies

- The system assumes an application-specific service to be defined in a software component and executes the component as an autonomous entity, called a *service-provider* agent. In the current implementation, existing Java-based software components, e.g., JavaBeans, can define our services.

The first and second agent are executed in runtime systems and can be dynamically deployed at the runtime systems different computers. They are executed as mobile agents [12] that can travel from computer to computer under their own control. When a user approaches closer to an exhibit, our system detects that user migration by using location-sensing systems and then instructs that user's counterpart agent to migrate to a computer close to the exhibit.

2) Federation and deployment as forces between agents: As mentioned previously, we introduce nature-inspired agent deployment policies based on two metaphors: *gravitational* and *repulsive* forces. Virtual-counterpart and service-provider agents are loosely coupled so that they can be dynamically linked to others. The current implementation has two built-in *gravitational* policies:

- An agent has a *follow* policy for another agent. When the latter migrates to a computer or a location, the former migrates to the latter's destination computer or to a computer nearby.
- An agent has a *shift* policy for another agent. When the latter migrates to a computer or a location, the former migrates to the latter's source computer or to a computer nearby.

Each service-provider agent can have at most one *gravitational* policy. Although the *gravitational* policy itself does not distinguish between virtual-counterpart and service-provider agents, in the above policies, we often assume the former to be a service-provider agent and the latter to be a virtual-counterpart agent. For example, when a visitor stands in front of an exhibit, the underling location-sensing system detects the location of the visitor and then the visitor's virtual counterpart agent is deployed at a computer close to the current location. When service-provider agents declare follow policies for the counterpart agent, they are deployed at the computer or nearby computers.

The current implementation has two built-in *repulsive* policies. Each service-provider agent can have zero or more repulsive policies in addition to the *shift* policy.

- An agent has an *exclusive* policy for another agent. When the former and latter are running on the same computer or nearby computers, the former migrates to another computer.
- An agent has a *suspend* policy for another agent. When the former and the latter are running on the same computer or nearby computers, the former is suspended until the latter moves to another computer.

Each service-provider agent can have at the most one *repulsive* policy. To avoid the redundancy of agents whose services are similar at the same computers, we should use *repulsive* force between service-provider agents.

III. Design and Implementation

This section describes the design and implementation of our middleware system. As shown in Figure 2, it consists of two parts: (1) context information managers, (2) runtime systems for application-specific services. The first provides a layer of indirection between the underlying locating-sensing systems and agents. It manages one or more sensing systems to monitor contexts in the real world and provides neighboring runtime systems with up-to-date contextual information of its target entities, people, and places. The second is constructed as a distributed system consisting of multiple computers, including stationary terminals and users' mobile terminals, in addition to servers. Each runtime system runs on a computer in the real world and is responsible for executing and migrating virtual-counterpart and service-provider agents with nature-inspired deployment policies. It evaluates the deployment policies of agents and then deploys the agents at runtime systems. Application-specific services are defined as virtual-counterparts or service-provider agents, where the former offers application-specific content, which is attached to physical entities, people, and places, and the latter can be defined as conventional Java-based software components, e.g., JavaBeans.

A. Contextual Information Management

Each Context Information Manager (CIM) manages one or more sensing systems to monitor context in the real world,

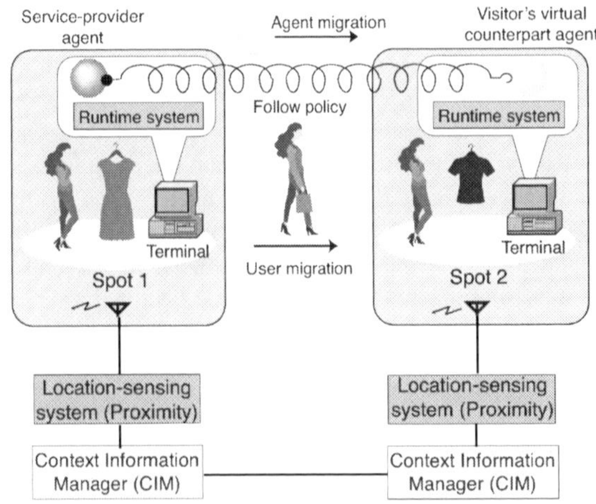

Figure 2. Architecture.

e.g., people and the locations of the target entities and people. Among many kinds of contextual information on the real world, location is one of the most important and useful in managing services in IoT networks. Therefore, this paper focuses on sensing location of IoT devices and users although the manager itself can support a variety of context. The current implementation of CIM supports active Radio Frequency IDentifier (RFID)-tag systems to locate computers and users. CIM monitors the RFID-tag systems, detects the presence of tags attached to people and entities, and maintains up-to-date information on the identities of RFID tags that are within the zones of coverage of its RFID tag readers. To abstract away the differences between the underlying locating systems, each CIM maps low-level positional information from each of the locating systems into information in a symbolic model of the location. The current implementation represents an entity's location, called a *spot*, e.g., spaces of a few feet, which distinguishes one or more portions of a room or building. A CIM either polls its sensing systems or receives the events issued by the sensing systems or other CIMs. Each CIM has a database for mapping the identifiers of RFID tags and virtual counterparts corresponding to physical entities, people, and spaces attached to the tags. These database may maintain information on several tags. When a CIM detects the existence of a tag in a spot, it multicasts a message containing the identifier of the tag, the identifiers of virtual counterparts attached to the tag, and its own network address to nearby runtime systems.

B. Runtime system

Since services are defined as software components, the middleware systems provides runtime systems that can execute and migrate components to other runtime systems running on different computers through TCP channels using mobile-agent technology [12].

1) Execution and deployment of services: Each runtime system is built on Java virtual machine (Java VM) version 8 or later, which conceals differences between the platform architectures of the source and destination computers as shown in Figure 3. It governs all the agents inside it and maintains the life-cycle state of each agent. When the life-cycle state of an agent changes, e.g., when it is created, terminates, or migrates to another runtime system, its current runtime system issues specific events to the agent.

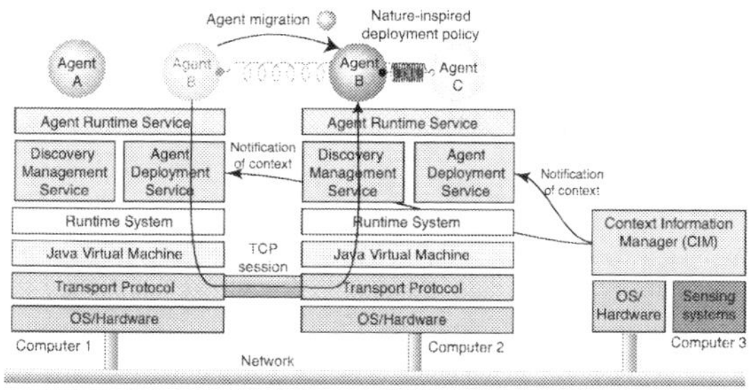

Figure 3. Runtime system

When an agent is transferred over the network, not only its code but also its state is transformed into a bitstream by using Java's object serialization package and then the bit stream is transferred to the destination. Since the package does not permit the stack frames of threads to be captured, when an agent is deployed at another computer, its runtime system propagates certain events to to instruct it to stop its active threads. Arriving agents may explicitly have to acquire various resources, e.g., video and sound, or release previously acquired resources.

The system only maintains per-user profile information within those agents that are bound to the user. It instructs the agents to move to appropriate runtime systems near the user in response to his/her movements. Thus, the agents do not leak profile information on their users to third parties and they can interact with mobile users in a personalized form that has been adapted to respective, individual users. The runtime system can encrypt agents to be encrypted before migrating them over a network and then decrypt them after they arrive at their destinations.

2) Policy-based federation and deployment: Our adaptive deployment policies are managed by runtime systems without a centralized management server. When a runtime system receives the identifiers of virtual counterparts corresponding to physical entities, people, and spaces attached to newly visiting tags, it discovers the locations of the virtual counterparts by exchanging query messages between nearby runtime systems. Each runtime system periodically advertises its address to the others through User Datagram Protocol (UDP) multicasting, and these runtime systems then return their addresses and capabilities to the runtime system through a TCP channel.

When an agent migrates to another agent's runtime system, each agent automatically registers its deployment policy with the destination. The destination sends a query message to the source of the visiting agent. There are two possible scenarios: the visiting agent has a policy for another agent or it is specified in another agent's policies. Since the source in the first scenario knows the runtime system running the target agent specified in the visiting agent's policy; it asks the runtime system to send the destination information about itself and about neighboring runtime systems that it knows, e.g., network addresses and capabilities. If the target runtime system has retained the proxy of a target agent that has migrated to another location, it forwards the message to the destination of the agent via the proxy. In the second scenario, the source multicasts a query message within current or neighboring sub-networks. If a runtime system has an agent whose policy specifies the visiting agent, it sends the destination information about itself and its neighboring runtime systems. The destination next instructs the visiting agent or its clone to migrate to one of the candidate destinations recommended by the target, because this platform treats every agent as an autonomous entity.

C. Service

Each mobile agent is attached to at most one visitor and maintains that visitors' preference information and programs to provide customized annotations. Each virtual counterpart agent keeps the identifier of the tag attached to its visitor. Each agent in the current implementation is a collection of Java objects in the standard JAR file format and can migrate from computer to computer and duplicate itself by using mobile agent technology. Each agent must be an instance of a subclass of the class pre-defined in the middleware system. Our system enables agents to define the computational resources they require. When an agent migrates to the destination according to its policy, if the destination cannot satisfy the requirements of the agent, the platform system recommends candidates that are runtime systems in the same network domain to the agent. If an agent declares repulsive policies in addition to a gravitational policy, the platform system detects the candidates using the latter's policy and then recommends final candidates to the agent using the former policy, assuming that the agent is in each of the detected candidates.

IV. Experience

To evaluate the performance overhead of the deployment policies presented in this paper, we implemented and evaluated a non-deployment policy version of the system. When this version detected the presence of a user at one of the spots, it directly deployed a service-provider agent instead of virtual counterpart agents. We measured the cost of migrating a null agent (a 5-KB agent, zip-compressed) and an annotation agent (1.2-MB agent, zip-compressed) from a source computer to a recommended destination computer that was recommended. The latency of discovering and instructing a virtual counterpart or service-provider agent attached to a tag after the CIM had detected the presence of the tag was 420 ms. Without any deployment policies, the respective cost of migrating the null and annotation agents between two runtime systems running on different computers over a TCP connection was 41 ms and 490 ms after instructing agents to migrate to the destination. When the null or annotation agent had a *follow* policy for the virtual counterpart agent, the respective cost of migrating the null and annotation agents between two runtime systems running on different computers over a TCP connection was 185 ms and 660 ms. These results demonstrate that the overhead of our deployment policy can be negligible in context-aware services.

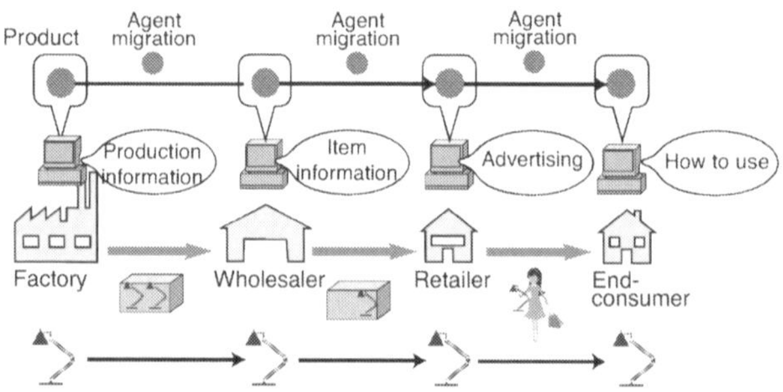

Figure 4. Forwarding agents to digital signage when user moves.

A. Advertisement media for appliances

We experimented and evaluated an advertisement system for appliances, e.g., electric lights, with the approach. It does not support advertising for its target appliance but also assist users to control and dispose the appliance. We attached an RFID tag to an electric light and provide a mobile agent as an ambient media for the light. As shown in Figure 4, it supports the lifecycle of the item from shipment, showcase, assembly, using, and disposal.

- **In warehouse:** While the light was in a warehouse, its counterpart object declared a *follow* policy to a services that should have been deployed and running at the computers of the warehouse's operators in the warehouse. The service displayed the item's specification, e.g., its product number, serial number, date of manufacture, size, and weight.
- **In a store's showcase:** While the light is being showcased in a store, its counterpart object declared two *follow* policies. The first policy was a relocation relation to an advertisement service fetched from the factory and the second policy was a relocation relation to price-tag service fetched from the store. The advertising service was deployed at a computer close its target item, which could display its advertising media to attract purchases by customers who visit the store. Two images, as shown in Figure 5 a) and b), are maintained in the agent that display the price, product number, and manufacturer's name on the current computer. The price-tag service communicated with a server provided by the store to know the selling price of its target, electric light and displayed the price on the display of its current computer.
- **In a store's checkout counter:**When a customer carried the item to the cashier of the store, the item's counterpart declared a *shift* policy to an order service. The service remained at a store to order another item for the factory as an additional order.
- **In house:** When a light was bought and transferred to the house of its buyer, its counterpart declared a *follow* policy to an instruction service at a computer in the house and provides instructions on how it should be assembled. The active media for advice on assembly are shown in Figure 5 c) and d). The service also advises how it was to be used as shown in When it was disposed of, the service presents its active media to give advice on disposal. As shown in Figure 5 e), the service provides an image to illustrate how the appliance is to be disposed of.

Our experiment at a store is a case study in our development of pervasive-computing services in large-scale public spaces. However, we could not evaluate the scalability of the system in the store, because it consisted of only four terminals. Even so, we have a positive impression on the availability of the system for large-scale public services. This is because the experimental system could be operated without any centralized management system. The number of agents running or waiting on a single computer was bound to the number of users in front of the computer.

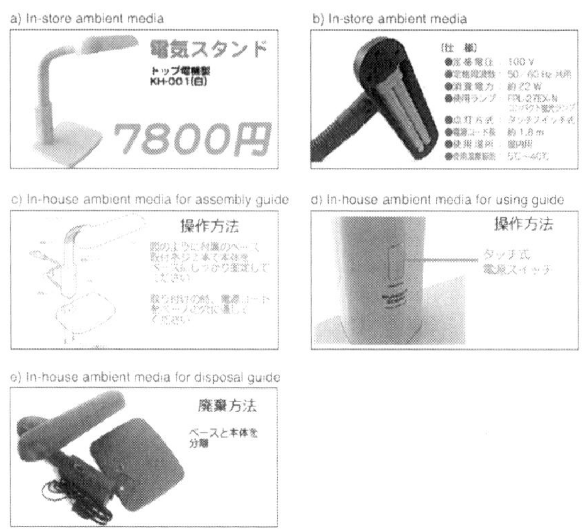

Figure 5. Agents for appliance

V. Related Work

There have been many attempts to manage IoT devices as a distributed system [3][6][7][5]. Govoni, et al. [5] proposed a middleware system, called SPF, to support IoT application and service development, deployment, and management. However, SPF did not support any dynamic deployment and coordination between services and devices. Fortino et al. [6] proposed an agent-based middleware system for discovering IoT devices in IoT through a REST interface, for registering, indexing, and searching IoT devices and their events, but their system did not support any deployment and federation of software. Smart-Its [2] was a platform specifically designed for augmentation of everyday objects to empower objects with processing, context-awareness and communication instead of the deployment of services. Several researchers proposed the notion of disaggregated computing as an approach to dynamically composing between devices, e.g., displays, keyboards, and mice that are not attached to the same computer, into a virtual computer in a distributed computing environment. Leppaanen et al. [9] proposed a mobile agent-based middleware for IoT devices. Although it enabled software to be dynamically deployed at IoT devices, it lacked any mechanisms for federating software and devices.

That system presented in this paper is an application of our previous bio-inspired system [10]. The system was a general-purpose test-bed platform for implementing and evaluating bio-inspired approaches over real distributed systems. It enabled each software agent to be dynamically organized with other agents and deployed at computers according to its own organization and deployment policies. In contrast, this paper addressed a practical system with nature-based approaches used in the real world with real users for real applications. We presented an outline of mobile agent-based services in public museums in our earlier versions of this paper [11], but did not describe any nature-inspired deployment policies in those works.

VI. Conclusion

This paper presented a context-aware service middleware system with an adaptive and self-organizing approach. The system enabled two individual agents to specify one of the deployment policies as relocations between the agent and another. It can not only move individual agents but also a federation of agents over a distributed system in a self-organized manner. We evaluated the system by applying it to visitor-assistant services. When visitors move from exhibit to exhibit, the visitors' virtual counterpart agents can be dynamically deployed at computers close to the current exhibits to accompany the visitors via their virtual counterpart agents and play annotations about the exhibits. Visitors and service-provider agents are loosely coupled because the agents are dynamically linked to the virtual counterpart agents corresponding to them by using our deployment policies.

In conclusion, we would like to identify further issues that need to be resolved. We plan to evaluate existing bio-inspired approaches to distributed systems with the platform. We also plan to apply the system into other applications.

References

[1] O. Babaoglu, H. Meling, and A. Montresor, "Anthill: A Framework for the Development of Agent-Based Peer-to-Peer Systems," Proceeding of 22th IEEE International Conference on Distributed Computing Systems, pp. 15-22, IEEE Computer Society, September 2002.

[2] M. Beigl and H. W. Gellersen, "Smart-Its: An Embedded Platform for Smart Objects," Proceedings of the smart object conference (SOC'2003), pp. 15–17, Springer, 2003.

[3] G. Bravos, "Enabling Smart Objects in Cities Towards Urban Sustainable Mobility-as-a-Service: A Capability – Driven Modeling Approach," Proceedings of International Conference on Smart Objects and Technologies for Social Good (GOODTECHS'2016), pp. 342-352, Springer, July 2016.

[4] B. L. Brumitt, B. Meyers, J. Krumm, A. Kern, and S. Shafer, "EasyLiving: Technologies for Intelligent Environments," Proceedings of International Symposium on Handheld and Ubiquitous Computing, pp. 12-27, January 2000.

[5] M. Govoni, J. Michaelis, A. Morellil, N. Suri, and M. Tortonesi, "Enabling Social- and Location-Aware IoT Applications in Smart Cities," Proceedings of International Conference on Smart Objects and Technologies for Social Good (GOODTECHS'2016), pp. 305-341, Springer, July 2016.

[6] G. Fortino, M. Lackovic, W. Russo, and P. Trunfio, "A Discovery Service for Smart Objects over an Agent-Based Middleware," International Conference on Internet and Distributed Computing Systems (IDCS'2013) pp. 281-293, LNCS, Vol.8223, Springer, October 2013.

[7] G. Fortino, A. Guerrieri, W. Russo, and C. Savaglio, "Middlewares for Smart Objects and Smart Environments: Overview and Comparison," in Internet of Things Based on Smart Objects pp. 1-27, Springer, 2014.

[8] B. Johanson, G. Hutchins, T. Winograd, and M. Stone, "PointRight: experience with flexible input redirection in interactive workspaces," in Proceedings of 15th ACM symposium on User interface software and technology, pp. 227-234, October 2002.

[9] T. Leppänen, J. Riekki, M. Liu, E. Harjula, and T. Ojala, "Mobile Agents-Based Smart Objects for the Internet of Things," In Internet of Things Based on Smart Objects: Technology, Middleware and Applications, (G. Fortino and P. Trunfio (ed.)), pp. 29-48, Springer 2014.

[10] I. Satoh, "Test-bed Platform for Bio-inspired Distributed Systems," in Proceesings of 3rd International Conference on Bio-Inspired Models of Network, Information, and Computing Systems (BIONETICS'2008), November 2008.

[11] I. Satoh, "A Context-aware Service Framework for Large-Scale Ambient Computing Environments," in Proceedings of ACM International Conference on Pervasive Services (ICPS'09), pp. 199-208, ACM Press, July 2009.

[12] I. Satoh, "Mobile Agents," Handbook of Ambient Intelligence and Smart Environments, pp. 771-791, Springer, 2010.

[13] P. Tandler, "The BEACH application model and software framework for synchronous collaboration in ubiquitous computing environments," Journal of Systems and Software, Vol.69, No.3, pp. 267-296, 2004.

Personalized Learning Coach:

An adaptive application for mindset and motivation

Rachel Van Campenhout
Dept. of Instruction and Leadership in Education
Duquesne University
Pittsburgh, United States
email: vancampenhoutr@duq.edu

Abstract—**This paper outlines an idea for an adaptive application which would integrate with other digital learning platforms to generate a profile for a learner on their mindset, goals, and motivation. This adaptive system would then provide personalized coaching through prompts based on the learner's profile and engagement within the learning platform, in order to shift mindsets and increasing learning outcomes.**

Keywords—learning; motivation; mindset; goals; outcomes; adaptive; prompts.

I. INTRODUCTION

Digital technology is revolutionizing every industry, creating pathways to new efficiencies and more effective use of resources. The education industry is changing as well with personalized learning, blended classrooms, virtual reality, and a variety of other technology advances [1]. There are decades of research on how and why we learn, but the internet as a learning tool allows for data to be gathered, analyzed, and acted upon. What if the body of research on learning mindset and motivation could be utilized as a personal adaptive learning coach for any online learning tool? A Personalized Learning Coach (PLC) could integrate with online learning system such as language learning apps, children's coding apps, massive open online courses (MOOCs), professional training, and more. The PLC would gather information on a learner's goals and mindset and then adaptively deliver advice, reinforcement, and encouragement based on the learner's unique profile and actual engagement with the learning content, all with an aim to improve the learner's outcomes.

This proposed application is an idea resulting from my learning and motivation research as a doctorate student, and experience working in educational technology. While the technical implementation is beyond the scope of this paper, I will outline the motivation and learning theory which would drive the functionality of the application (Section II), the proposed adaptive behavior of the application (Section III), and the outcomes and significance (Section IV).

II. LEARNING AND MOTIVATION THEORY

Motivation is a complex and multifaceted concept with significant research looking at types and approaches within an educational setting [2]. While there are many approaches to motivation, the PLC would target shifting mindsets and beliefs to better support motivation to learn, as learners with this type of motivation continue to engage in activities even if not immediately interested do so because they find the program valuable and desirable [8]. "Motivation to learn refers to a student's propensity to value learning activities: to find them meaningful and worthwhile, and to try to get the intended benefits from them. In contrast to intrinsic motivation, which is primarily an affective response to an activity, motivation to learn is primarily a cognitive response involving attempts to make sense of the activity, understand the knowledge that it develops, and master the skills that it promotes" [2]. The PLC would utilize many strategies to help students increase or maintain motivation to learn.

A critical theory behind the PLC is understanding the mindset and beliefs of the user. Learners who believe they can learn new things (incremental theory) often display better learning outcomes and self-esteem than those who believe their abilities to learn limited (entity theory) [3][4]. Intervention studies have shown that shifts can occur from entity to incremental thinking through stimulation [5]. One main strategy of the learning coach would be to attempt to replicate these findings that mindsets can be shifted from incremental to entity.

Understanding a learner's goals can illuminate why they are engaged with a particular learning activity and how to best support them. There are two distinct types of goals which are useful for this project: purpose goals which explain why something is being learned, and target goals which express how something will be learned [6]. Explicit goal setting can be especially helpful for learners struggling with motivation or self-efficacy. Guiding students through the process of setting goals and reflecting on their own learning can lead them to engage in activities with motivation to learn. With a model for setting goals and significant reinforcement, learners have shown development and growth of motivation to learn [7].

III. AN ADAPTIVE APPROACH

Computer tutoring systems focused on content are nearly as effective as human tutoring [9], so an adaptive program aimed at addressing non-domain specific content could be equally as effective. This PLC could integrate with any digital learning application for which a user creates an account, and could track a user from one learning tool to the next. A critical component of integration with other learning platforms would be the ability to receive and analyze data as learners answer practice questions and engage with the content in the native platform.

The purpose of the Personalized Learning Coach is to shift mindsets and improve learning outcomes by gathering information about the learner and adaptively delivering prompts and content based on the learner's profile and subsequent learning actions. The first step, then, is to create the learner's profile. The learning coach would begin by delivering a battery of validated surveys on growth mindset, self-efficacy, goals, and motivation. The learner would be asked to enter their purpose goal for why they want to learn the material, and decide on target goals for the content. Based on the learner's answers, the coach would provide an analysis of the learner's mindset and beliefs, and suggestions for learning strategies. This profile and the resulting suggestions (derived from learning theory) is the first personalized set of content delivered to the learner.

With the learner's profile established, the PLC would then engage with the learner periodically through notification pop-ups, or prompts. Adaptive prompts have shown promising results and could help shift mindsets and improve learning outcomes [10]. One type of notification would be based on performance on formative learning activities such as answering questions or completing tasks. For learners who indicated they had a fixed/entity mindset about learning and their abilities, the coach would periodically congratulate correct answers and remind the learner that learning is an achievable process. Incorrect responses would elicit prompts reminding the learner that mistakes are part of the learning process, and to keep going. The purpose of these PLC notifications is to shift to growth and incremental mindsets.

The PLC could also respond to the learner's progress by delivering prompts to help learners identify themselves as the active controller in the learning process. The causal attribution of success or failure can impact motivation for learners. Learners demonstrate more sustained effort and persistence when attributing success to internal forces, namely sufficient ability and reasonable effort [2]. If learners with fixed mindsets or low motivation can see their outcomes as a mix of their current knowledge and level of effort, then they can shift their mindset to understand that learning is controllable.

Using a learner's goals to reinforce motivation to learn is also a tool the PLC can act on. Every learner will have different goals for the content they are trying to learn, and the number and types of goals have shown to have an impact on how successful learners are [11]. The coach can use those goals to determine when and how to encourage continued engagement and reinforce goals. The coach can also use the learner's goals to cultivate motivation to learn by emphasizing authentic activities, phrasing goal statements in terms of learning accomplishments rather than tasks completed, revisiting goals post-activity, and creating summaries of the learner's accomplishments [2]. Each of these methods would be personalized to each learner depending on their profile and how the learner answers practice questions and works through the content.

The PLC would deliver the same validated surveys toward the end of the learning experience to determine if the adaptive prompts were able to successfully shift mindsets where applicable. Learners would be notified if their results changed. The PLC cycle is delivering surveys to generate a profile, tracking data from the native learning environment, adaptively delivering prompts, and re-evaluating learners. The PLC could do this process on many learning platforms for a single user.

IV. Further Research and Significance

Further research is needed to determine the technical requirements to develop an application such as this. The PLC would need integration tools for current learning technology, and a database to store user profiles and learning data. Machine learning tools would need to be tested to determine the best method of analyzing data and make decisions on the type of prompts to deliver. A review of artificial intelligence techniques could help the PLC determine when to deliver prompts to different types of learner profiles.

Any person of any age should know that learning is a process which is accessible and achievable. Children should grow up knowing that they can learn anything they set their minds to. Adults looking to grow or make a change in their lives should understand how best to engage with learning content. Research into learning mindsets and motivation have shown that certain beliefs and practices help people learn more efficiently, persist longer, and have better self-concepts [2]. Could an adaptive application incrementally improve global learning through surfacing mindsets, goals, and motivation to learners of all types?

References

[1] D. Newman, Top 6 digital transformation trends in education, Retrieved from Forbes.com, 2017.

[2] K. R. Wentzel, and R. E. Brophy, Motivating students to learn. New York, NY: Routledge, 2014

[3] L. Blackwell, K. Trzesniewski, and C. Dweck, "Implicit theories of intelligence predict achievement across an adolescent transition: A longitudinal study and an intervention" Child Development, 78, 2007, pp. 246–263.

[4] R. Robins, and P. Pals, "Implicit self-theories in the academic domain: Implications for goal orientation, attributions, affect, and self-esteem change" Self and Identity, 2002, pp. 313–336.

[5] C. Dweck, "Can personality be changed? The role of beliefs in personality and change" Current Directions in Psychological Science, 17, 2008, pp. 391–394.

[6] J. Harackiewicz, and A. Elliot, "The joint effects of target and purpose goals on intrinsic motivation: a mediational analysis" Personality and Social Psychology, 24, 1998, pp. 675–689.

[7] A. Assor, "Allowing choice and nurturing an inner-compass: Educational practices supporting students' need for autonomy." In S. L. Christenson, A. L. Reschly, and C. Wylie (Eds.), *Handbook on student engagement*, pp. 421–440. New York: Springer. 2012

[8] M. Nisan, "Beyond intrinsic motivation: Cultivating a "sense of the desirable." In F. Oser, A. Dick, & J. Patry (Eds.), Effective and responsible teaching: The new synthesis, pp. 126–138. San Francisco: Jossey-Bass. 1992

[9] K. VanLehn, "The relative effectiveness of human tutoring, intelligent tutoring systems, and other tutoring systems" Educational Psychologist, 46, 2011, pp. 197-221.

[10] R. Schwonke, S. Hauser, M. Nückles, and A. Renkl, "Enhancing computer-supported writing of learning protocols by adaptive prompts" Computers in Human Behavior, 22, 2006, pp. 77-92.

[11] A. Valle, R. Cabanach, J. Nunez, J. Gonzalez-Pienda, S. Rodriguez, and I. Pineiro, "Multiple goals, motivation and academic learning" British Journal of Educational Psychology, 73, 2003, pp. 71–87.

Adaptive Serious Gaming for the Online Assessment of 21st Century Skills in Talent Selection

Gabrielle Teyssier-Roberge
School of Psychology
Université Laval
Québec, Canada
gabrielle.teyssier-roberge.1@ulaval.ca

Sébastien Tremblay
School of Psychology
Université Laval
Québec, Canada
sebastien.tremblay@psy.ulaval.ca

***Abstract*— 21st century skills are key factors sought by organizations in the 4th Industrial Revolution. Our objectives are twofold: 1) To test the use of serious games for detecting the 21st century skills among highly qualified personnel (HQP); and 2) To develop an adaptive and gamified system for boosting skill acquisition and for talent selection of HQP candidates. The main findings represent a first encouraging step towards measuring skill proficiency through serious gaming which in turn could serve to trigger personalized content and interactivity.**

Keywords-serious gaming; cognition; non-technical skills; human resources; talent selection.

I. Introduction

The number of ways interactive games can be used is expanding beyond the traditional areas of entertainment and education. Serious games and gamified simulations are widely recognized for their potential to foster learning and the acquisition of non-technical skills. Serious games can be a very powerful tool for developing skills such as an analytical capacity for decision making. There is growing interest in making serious games adaptive – games that would adjust their content, storyline, difficulty level and feedbacks to the players' interactivity, preferences and fluctuating affective-cognitive state. We wish to present innovative ideas related to the use of such adaptive systems in talent selection. These ideas have emerged from an ongoing research endeavor concerned with the development of adaptive serious gaming and the capability to monitor human performance, behavior and functional state in near real-time. Adaptive games could boost the ability of serious games to contribute to the training and assessment of 21st century skills such as systemic thinking, creativity and cognitive flexibility. In the present project, one key objective is to establish whether adaptiveness could be based on the monitoring of indicators of skill acquisition and mastery. We seek to identify a set of gaming behaviors and measures of the functional state that can provide an assessment of the ability to think in a critical manner, to be creative and to be flexible in making decisions.

Personnel selection is based on the use of traditional tools (e.g. interviews and questionnaires) to assess the suitability of a candidate for one position. Among highly qualified personnel (HQP), the 21st century skills – systemic thinking, adaptability and creative problem solving – are key factors sought by organizations in the era of the 4th Industrial Revolution [12][8]. While the selection interview – including the semi-structured job-oriented interview – and psychometric testing represent the most common ways organizations use to determine the best candidate to fill out a position, the shortcomings raised by several authors (e.g. traditional tools are not adequate to assess whether the candidate holds one or more 21st century skills – see [13]) denote the importance of reviewing how to carry out the selection process by using new tools such as serious games [2]. Considering that a large number of organizations worldwide are using at least one serious game as a training tool, it is relevant that research now focus on serious games as a way to select candidates as opposed to conventional staffing methods [1]. In the present project, we wish to use serious games in order to detect the 21st century skills among HQP and develop an adaptive and gamified system for talent selection and assessment of HQP candidates.

II. Measurement

In order to provide an assessment capability, a game should be capable of capturing a variety of in-game user behaviors such as "information seeking", "making a decision", or "reviewing alternatives", as well as the context in which those behaviors occur within the game [5]. It should capture context at a high level, such as the level of difficulty, the level of stress that the user is under [6], or the number of decision constraints the user is facing [4]. The focus should also be on measuring changes in performance and skill indicators under different conditions (e.g., high/low time pressure) and over time (e.g., track progress). The choice of human performance measures depends in part on the importance of the underlying skill in the context of a specific scenario. For cognitive dimensions such as information seeking and the management of workload, systems that track head and eye movements can provide unobtrusive information about the current locus of visual fixation that enables inferences about the locus of attention [10]. Eye-tracking data can provide a large range of metrics that can be very informative about dynamic decision making. For instance, scanpath measures – which relate to saccade-fixation-saccade sequences of eye movements – can index the efficacy in information seeking, while fixation metrics, which measure how long the gaze is relatively stationary, can help estimate the processing (or encoding) time [11]. Combinations of behavioral measures can also provide information about time-sharing and multitask performance. A key dimension of the measurement – psychometrics at the basis of the skill assessment – is to operationalize each skill in measurable indicators imbedded within the game [5].

III. PRELIMINARY STUDY

As an initial step towards the development of the adaptive serious gaming approach to non-technical skill assessment, we designed a study looking at the convergent validity. In this section, the method and the preliminary results of the study are described.

A. Method

Ten participants were candidates going through the selection process of a small high-tech company. All had engineering, AI or computing backgrounds. Participants first played four times 12 rounds of the game Democracy 3. In this game, the player is a head of government, must manage state affairs and the end goal is to be re-elected. Democracy 3 portrays complex decision-making and requires systemic thinking, creative problem solving and cognitive flexibility (see [3]). Each game test was followed by a subjective assessment of skill acquisition (self-report and observer ratings on a scale of 1 to 10). Order of tasks was counter-balanced – across self and peer assessment, each skill to be assessed and playing Democracy 3.

B. Results

Performance scores were calculated as a product of re-election polls and financial budget. 60% of the participants managed to be re-elected with an average poll of 52%. Performance scores proved to be sensitive to individual differences. There was little relation between the results associated to the assessment of the skills and those associated with playing Democracy 3. Interestingly, overall, re-elected participants seem to show greater skill assessment – save for the self-reporting of adaptability (see Table I).

TABLE I.

	Re-elected	Not Re-elected
Nb	6	4
Average Poll	52%	6%
Adaptability Self	0.70	0.88
Adaptability Peers	0.73	0.69
Creative Self	0.76	0.60
Creative Peers	0.80	0.71
Systemic Self	0.86	0.70
Systemic Peers	0.75	0.72

The delta between the self-assessment questionnaires and the peer assessment varies considerably across participants (see Table II). Our findings represent a first encouraging step towards measuring skill proficiency through serious gaming which in turn could serve to trigger personalized content and interactivity.

TABLE II.

	Mean	Standard Deviation
Adaptability Self	0.76	0.19
Adaptability Peers	0.72	0.10
Creative Self	0.71	0.23
Creative Peers	0.77	0.09
Systemic thinking Self	0.87	0.10
Systemic Thinking Peers	0.74	0.11

IV. ARCHITECTURE OF THE ADAPTIVENESS

The components of the adaptive system would be comprised of modules for content delivery, online assessment of skills and for directing adaptation. The purpose of the content delivery module is to present the game and tests content to the candidate [7]. This is the component of the system with which the candidate (player) interacts. The presentation of the game content is controlled by the adaptation module. The delivery module must report outcomes and user interactions as required by the evaluation module. The purpose of the evaluation module is to update the model or assessment profile of the candidate based on measurements of the candidate. In the case of a first assessment through the system, the model of the candidate does not contain any data besides initial self-reports. The evaluation module should be capable of direct measurements using eye tracking, physiological and "face reading" devices, as well as indirect monitoring of performance from user interactions reported by the content delivery module, such as key presses, decision accuracy, timings, quiz results, and so on. The purpose of the adaptation module is to adapt the delivery of content based on the evolution of the candidate model (profile). The adaptation module must examine the difference between the candidate's performance and skill evaluation with the expectations and desired skill profile of potential employers. Mechanisms of adaptation may include: adapting the pace of information delivery; adapting the complexity of the game; altering the assessment content and objects that are presented.

V. CONCLUSION

Initial results are promising in validating the assumption according to which performance at playing Democracy 3 is related to other means of assessing non-technical skills. The recommended architecture would be the foundation of the adaptive serious game for the assessment of non-technical skills. Such a customizable system that takes into account inputs from potential employers and focuses its assessment on skill proficiency and attitude rather than expert knowledge will greatly contribute to improve the efficiency and user-friendliness of the talent selection process.

ACKNOWLEDGMENT

The authors would like to thank B. Bussière, S. Savage and E. Guillemette for their contribution to the empirical work and to G. Foin for proofreading. This work was funded by the Social Sciences and Humanities Research Council of Canada (SSHRC).

REFERENCES

[1] M. B. Armstrong, R. N. Landers and A. B. Collmus, "Gamifying Recruitment, Selection, Training, and Performance Management: Game-Thinking in Human Resource Management", in Handbook of Research Trends in Gamification, H. Gangadharbatla and D. Z. Davis Eds. Pennsylvanie, PE: IGI Global, pp.140-165, january 2016.

[2] M. Fetzer, "Serious Games for Talent Selection and Development", The Industrial-Organizational Psychologist, vol. 52, pp.117-125, january 2015.

[3] D. Lafond, J-F. Gagnon, S. Pronovost, M. Ducharme and S. Tremblay, "Behavioral test for prediction of individual differences in dynamic decision making ability," Proceedings of the 7th International Conference of AHFE, Orlando, CA, july 2016.

[4] D. Lafond, B. R. Vallières, F. Vachon and S. Tremblay, "Judgment analysis in a dynamic multitask environment: Capturing non-linear policies using decision trees," Journal of Cognitive Engineering and Decision Making, vol. 11, pp.122-135, 2017.

[5] C. S. Loh and Y. Sheng, Y. "Measuring expert-performance for Serious Games Analytics: From data to insights," in Serious Games Analytics: Methodologies for Performance Measurement, Assessment, and Improvement, C. S. Loh, Y. Sheng and D. Ifenthaler, Eds. New York, NY: Springer, pp.101-134, 2015.

[6] M. Parent, J.-F. Gagnon, T. H. Falk and S. Tremblay, "Modeling the operator functional state for emergency response management," Proceedings of the 13th International Conference on Information Systems for Crisis Response and Management (ISCRAM). Rio de Janeiro, Brazil, may 2016.

[7] M. Peeters, K. Van Den Bosch, J-J. C. Meyer and M. A. Neerincx, "Situated cognitive engineering: The requirements and design of directed scenario-based training," Proceedings of the 5th International Conference on ACHI, Valencia, Spain, pp.1-8, 2012.

[8] M. Romero, M. Usart and M. OTT, "Can Serious Games Contribute to Developing and Sustaining 21st Century Skills? ," Games and Culture, vol. 10, pp.148-177, 2015.

[9] H. A. Spires, "21st Century Skills and Serious Games: Preparing the N Generation," in Serious Educational Games: From Theory to Practice, L. A. Annetta, Eds. Rotterdam, The NetherlandsArticle in a journal, pp.13–23, january 2008.

[10] S. Tremblay, D. Lafond, C. Chamberland, H. M. Hodgetts and F. Vachon, "Gaze-aware cognitive assistant for multiscreen surveillance," in Advances in Intelligent Systems and Computing, vol. 722. Intelligent Human Systems Integration, W. Karwowski and T. Ahram, Eds. Basel, Suisse: Springer International Publishing AG, pp. 230-236, 2018.

[11] F. Vachon and S. Tremblay, "What eye tracking can reveal about dynamic decision-making," in Advances in Cognitive Engineering and Neuroergonomics, K. Stanney and K. S. Hale, Eds. Boca Raton, FL: CRC Press, pp. 157-165, 2014.

[12] E. van Laar, A. J. van Deursen, J. A. van Dijk, J. de Haan, "The relation between 21st-century skills and digital skills: A systematic literature review", in Computers in Human Behavior, vol.72, pp.577-588, march 2017.

[13] J. VOOGT and N. P. Roblin, "A comparative analysis of international frameworks for 21st century competences: Implications for national curriculum policies," Journal of Curriculum Studies, vol. 44, pp.299–321, 2011.

Architectural Concepts and Their Evolution Made Explicit by Examples

Mirco Schindler

Institute for Software and Systems Engineering
Technische Universität Clausthal, Germany
Email: mirco.schindler@tu-clausthal.de

Andreas Rausch

Institute for Software and Systems Engineering
Technische Universität Clausthal, Germany
Email: andreas.rausch@tu-clausthal.de

Abstract—**During the evolution of a software-intensive system, deviations may occur between the implementation and the architecture of the system. One of the main reasons for this is the incomplete knowledge of developers and architects, which is based in the fact that the complexity of today's systems cannot be understood by one person in detail. In addition, there is the language gap between source code representation and architecture description. Following the technique of Programming By Example, the presented approach built up an understanding of architectural concepts with the help of examples, i.e., Architecture By Example. A approach is established to extract architectural concepts from source code and its integration into an evolutionary and incremental development process.**

Keywords*–*Software Architecture; Architecture Erosion; Managed Architectureevolution; Agile Architecturedevelopment; Machine Learning; Architecture By Example;

I. INTRODUCTION

Typical activities within the scope of software development are development or maintenance of software systems, the implementation of new functionalities, the extension and the reuse of components or software artifacts. What all these activities have in common is a certain understanding of the source code and its underlying architecture required for its successful realization [1].

It is also typical that in smaller projects the architect and developer build a personal union and often an architectural description exists only implicitly, i.e., it is not really comprehensibly documented. If the roles in larger projects are distributed among different people, this usually improves the documentation, but this does not guarantee that the architecture description is conform to the implementation [1]. Furthermore, if the conformance is still given during the development time, knowledge is lost over time, e.g., by a personnel change, which can often lead to an architecture erosion for a long-term evolution, as described in [2] and [3].

Considering implementation and architecture, both are a subject to an evolution that is not always synchronized. New technologies influence the solutions more than in any other field in type, scope and speed. Therefore, the introduction of new technologies is often accompanied by a paradigm or a change of concepts.

On the other hand, the requirements for a system change over time, requirements are added, changed or even disappear. This leads necessarily to the fact that also the architecture is exposed to changes, because the architecture once developed does not need to fit any longer to the future requirements.

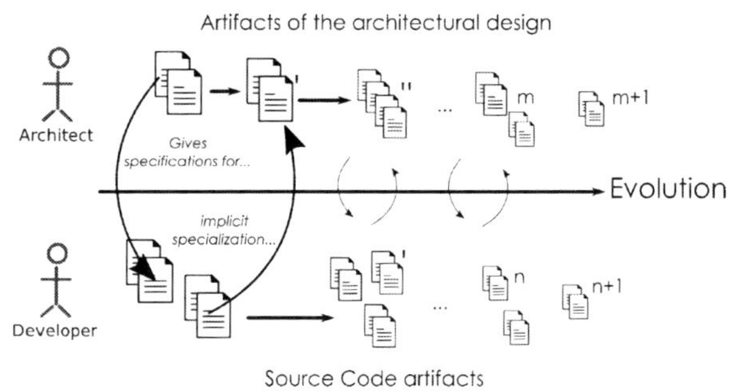

Figure 1. Evolution of Architecture- and Source Code artifacts

Whereas the verification of the specifications can be managed by the architecture, e.g., by rule-based approaches [4], the concepts of the developer are usually not directly played back to the architectural level. One reason is the different language of artifacts the architect and the developer are working with. In addition, it is not that easy to extract best practices directly from the source code artifacts, usually the architect has to exchange information directly with the developer.

The area of tension between abstract architecture description and concrete implementation is illustrated in Figure 1. If the artifacts of the architecture design define the scope for the developer, then the resulting source code artifacts should influence the architecture as well. The compromise that has to be achieved here is between full specification of the software architecture and the creative autonomy of the developer. But this compromise leads to a number of general problems in software engineering, architecture knowledge is incomplete and not up to date, architectural concepts are not well understood especially within different contexts, the same for best practices of implementation. The presented approach address the extraction of architectural concepts of source code artifacts. The occurring interaction between architect and developer will be explained in more detail in the following Section II using an example scenario and introduce to the specific problem space. In Section III, the solution approach is presented in detail and its application in different systems is explained. It ends with a conclusion and outlook.

II. Problem Description

In this section, the challenge of making architectural concepts explicit is introduced with the help of a clear application example and a dialog between architect and developer, which can reflect a typical situation in the daily work between architect and developer.

A. A manageable Example System

To illustrate the problem space a software system was chosen, which was designed within the project CoCoME [5]. Both architecture description as well as implementation is existing and can be found in [6].

The system implements the functionality required for a supermarket warehouse, from cash desk systems to report generation and ordering of new goods. The section that is considered here deals with the information system, whose structure is visualized in Figure 2. For clarity reasons, multiplicities and a complete labeling of the interfaces were avoided, for a complete illustration see [5]. The chosen architecture is a classic Three-Tier architecture with Service-Oriented interfaces [7] [8].

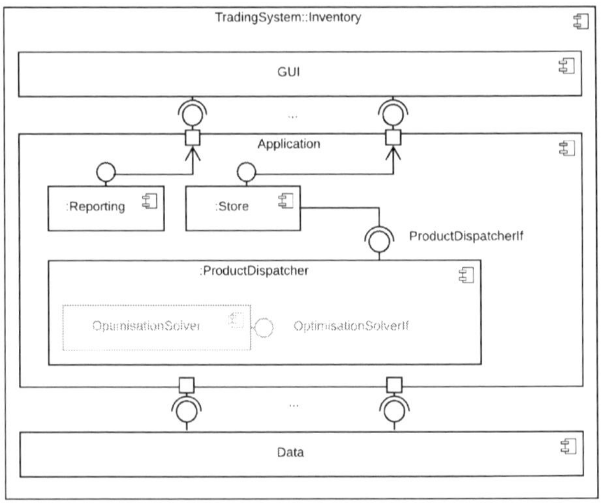

Figure 2. Structural View of the information system of the CoCoME system `TradingSystem::Inventory`

This system has also been studied in the work of Herold [4]. He describes an approach for automatically verifying compliance between a given architecture and implementation using architecture rules. Specifically, this means for the selected section of the application layer with its three internal components (see Figure 2) that the interfaces offered by these components have to be realized as Service-Oriented interfaces. The corresponding architectural rule can be simplified and not formally formulated as follows (a formal description as first-order logic statements see [4] page 139-145):

```
A Service-Oriented interface only
has service methods. A service
method is a method that only has
parameters that are primitive in
type, or the type is a Transfer
Object (TO). A TO also uses
only data types that are either
primitive or TOs.
```

Let us take a look at a typical situation and dialog that can occur during development:

B. Scenario

The SW developer Hannes gets the task to realize the component `OptimisationSolver` in the current iteration, which should be integrated into the component `ProductDispatcher`. He implements the functionality of an optimization algorithm for the distribution of goods to different supermarkets in a functionally correct way.

Afterwards the SW-Architect Bo checks the realization concerning the architecture rules presented in the previous Section II-A. However, the result is not positive, the rule is violated! But Hannes does not understand why, the functionality is implemented correctly, the system does what it is supposed to do!

For the developer Hannes, the architecture rules have no relation to the code. Bo shows Hannes code examples which represent the rule and thus correctly implement this architectural concept, as well as the lines where it deviates from it (see Figure 3). In this case, the examples belong to the same system, so the developer might know them or the context in which they are used. Also, for the violations, they are linked to concrete lines and contexts within the source files.

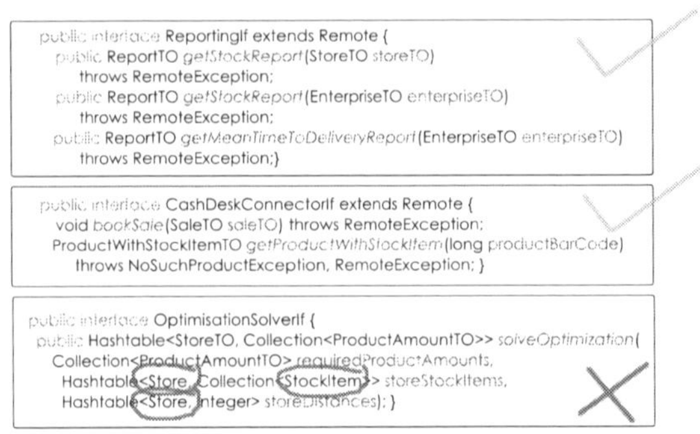

Figure 3. Examples of correct implementation and detected deviations

What does the deviation between the specified rule and the implementation mean? As specified for a Service-Oriented interface only primitive types or Transfer Objects are allowed as parameters. Our developer Hannes now understands his mistake after reviewing the examples and uses the Transfer Objects. Bo checks the result again and it fits, it is all good and a new code example that implements the architecture concept of a service-orientated interface also exists.

In the next iteration Hannes gets the task to implement a new database query. Following the realization the architect Bo checks the implemented code artifacts, but all rules fail. Form his perspective it seems, that Hannes did something completely wrong. He shows him code examples, which are correct realizations of the failed rules. But Hannes replies that he swapped the database framework and changed the access concept, as the new technology recommends a different concept that increases data security, but this requires a different way of handling the data. The architect is familiar with this and tells him: "All right, then we need to adjust the rules that will apply to data storage components from now on in this system".

BO select new rules representing the new concept, checks the code with the new rules and all is well!

As the scenario shows, an architectural violation can be solved in two ways, by adapting the architecture or by adapting the implementation. But how can we decide which way makes more sense in which case? The presented approach will support this decision making process by extracting the concepts from source code with the goal to get an understanding of what the developer did to get an indication of the type of violation. It can be summarized in a general research question as follows:"How can developers' best practice be identified and reflected to the architecture level?" This includes the representation and the extraction of concepts, as well as the way the acquired knowledge can be used to support the software engineering process.

III. SOLUTION AND ITS APPLICATION

In this section, the approach, which is making architectural concepts explicit, is explained and each step is illustrated with the help of an application example.

An architectural concept is defined in this work as:

```
"A characterization and
description of a common, abstract
and realized implementation-,
design-, or architecture solution
within a given context represented
by a set of examples and/or rules."
[9]
```

According to this definition, this covers a wide range of concept candidates, a few examples of which are given below:

- *Conventions:* Naming, package- and folder structure, vocabulary, domain model ...; *Desig-Pattern:* Observer, Factory, ...;
- *Architecture-Pattern:* client-server system, tiers, ...;
- *Communication Paradigms:* Service-orientated, message based, ...;
- *Structural Concepts:* Tiers, Pipes, Filter, ... or
- *Security Concepts:* encryption, SSO, ...

A. The Overall Approach

The holistic approach is visualized in Figure 4 and consists essentially of three activities (SELECTION, EXTRACTION and GENERALIZATION), which are explained in detail in the following Section III-B.

A **Concept** c is described as a set of **Properties** P. Furthermore, for a **Element** e there is a so-called **Detector** D is defined. A **detector** is a binary function $d_{p_j} \in D$, which maps a concrete property $p_j \in P$ and a concrete element $e_i \in E$ as follows:

$$d_{p_j}(e_i) = \begin{cases} 1 & \text{, iff the element } e_i \text{ fullfills the property } p_j \\ 0 & \text{, else} \end{cases} \tag{1}$$

An element can be a system artifact such as a class, a method, or a relationship between two elements in a realized system. The considered source code artefacts are transformed in the so-called **System Snapshot** $\mathfrak{S}$. This language independent model representation M, which is an extension of the models of [4] [10] [11], still contains the link to the specific lines within the source code files. This link ensures traceability between the extracted architectural concepts and the source code. The following applies, that the set of elements E is a true subset of the model M, $E \subset M$. A special kind of element are associations A, which are representing dependencies between elements.

The model instance of a given software systems, which is stored in the System Snapshot, is transformed into the **facts base** $\mathfrak{F}$, which describes the fulfillment of concepts for the concrete elements. In addition, it is the repository of the new learned or derived facts. The facts are stored within the fact base in two different ways, a data structures that are organized in a table structure $\mathfrak{F}_E^{|P|\times|E|}$, lists facts that refer to elements or associations, and a graph structure that describes facts about elements, their context and their dependencies between them. In the following the structure of the matrix $\mathfrak{F}_E^{|P|\times|E|}$ is given, combining the System Snapshot with the selected detectors:

P \ E	e_1	$e_2 \cdots e_i\, a_1\, a_2 \cdots$	a_n
p_1	$d_{p_1}(e_1)$	$\cdots \quad \cdots$	$d_{p_1}(a_n)$
p_2 $\vdots$	$\vdots$	$\ddots$	$\vdots$
p_j	$d_{p_j}(e_1)$	$\cdots \quad \cdots$	$d_{p_j}(a_n)$

$, with\ A \subset E$

The concrete graph structure is defined as a common weighted graph $G(V, E', w)$ with a given set of vertexes V and edges E'. Whereby in this approach the vertexes are referred to the set of elements $E \setminus A, wherby A \subset E \subset M$ and the edges are linked to the set of associations A, $\mathfrak{F}_{G(E\setminus A, A, w)}$:

$$e_i \xrightarrow{w_{ij}} e_j \quad , with\ w_{ij}\ number\ of\ assoziations\ of\ the\ same\ type$$

The last of the three data pools is the **Concept Space** Ω. All known concepts are stored in it, whereby a concept is represented as a named element and linked with its detectors and examples, i.e., with concrete source code examples that fulfill this concept.

$$c_i \in \Omega := \{\text{identifier}_i, D_i, R_i\} \tag{2}$$

In this definition D_i is the set of detectors, which are able to check a given element if this fulfills the concept c_i or not. The set R_i includes all known elements, which are fulfill the concept c_i.

The central artifact is the **Configuration** Σ. In each iteration, i.e., with each new execution of the selection step, a new instance $\sigma_i \in \Sigma$ is created. The configuration is used for the information exchange between the three activities and contains all decisions which are made during the execution, both by humans and by the algorithms. The result of the approach is the so-called **Concept Performance Record**. This record informs about the concepts that are in the analyzed system realization.

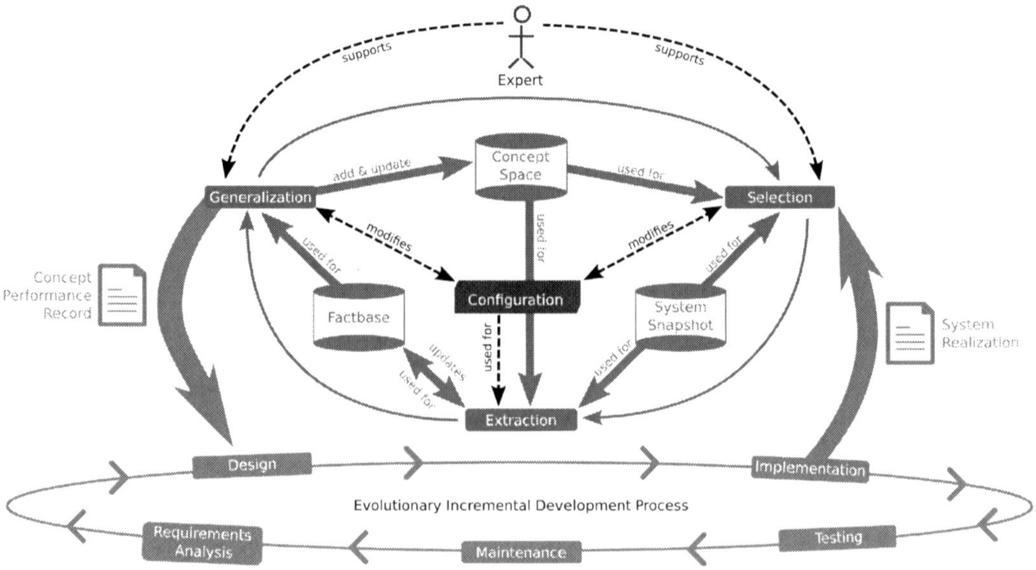

Figure 4. Overview of the solution approach and integration into a development process

In the following, this extraction process is described in detail, as well as how it can be integrated into an evolutionary and incremental development process and can support both architect and developer in their work.

B. The Extraction Phase

Altogether the defined process for the extraction of architectural concepts consists of three activities Selection, Extraction and Generalization (blue boxes in Figure 4), which are carried out iteratively and together are called the extraction phase.

Selection: In this step, an expert decides which parts of the system to analyses and what is the initial set of concepts to use. So it may be possible to reduce the number of initial concepts, since some basic knowledge of the system is usually available, like e.g., whether the system was developed object-oriented or not.

The selected subset of the system or the total system if no selection has been made and the initial selected concept set represented by its detectors are stored in the configuration and serve as input for the next step. In addition, as already described, the source code artifacts are transformed into a language-independent representation and stored as a system snapshot.

Extraction: This step is fully automated. First the fact base is created for all selected elements by executing each selected detector for each element. Each element is therefore assigned to a set of positive and negative properties according to the detector definition.

Subsequently, different algorithms from the field of machine learning are used to extract possible new facts or combinations from them. These so-called **Concept Candidates** $\hat{C}$ are added to the fact base as non-validated concepts. This also includes references to the **representatives** R of these concept candidates, i.e., elements that fulfill this newly extracted concept.

Generalization: After enriching the fact base with new facts respectively potential new concepts, an expert will validate these facts in the generalization step. The expert decides on the basis of the representatives of concept candidates whether it is a relevant concept or not. These decisions are stored in the configuration. Thus, the configuration contains the information about selected detectors and system artifacts as well as the newly extracted and validated concepts on this basis, whereby concept candidates, which were classified as not valid, are stored as so-called anti-pattern for this system snapshot.

Based on this decision process, new detectors are generated. This can be done manually or automatically, manually by storing e. .g. rules, which can be checked and automatically by training a so-called neural network detector with the examples. Finally, this new knowledge has to be integrated into the Concept Space, where it is checked whether the newly extracted concepts are already contained and simply not selected in this iteration. If a concept with this identifier is already contained, the expert has to decide whether it is the same or a different concept or variant, i.e., whether it should be added as a new one or whether the existing detector should be trained with the new representatives.

Implementation of the approach The algorithms listed below describe only one possible selection for the implementation of the individual activities, i.e., the algorithms mentioned fulfill the required characteristics. At this point, however, it cannot be guaranteed that there will be methods that perform better.

During selection, the expert can be supported by static code analysis procedures or clustering techniques, for example, to obtain different views of the system in order to select the source code artifacts and detectors relevant to the given task. Tools like SPAA [12] [13] [14] can be used. Also the visualizations of the software as Software City [15] would be conceivable to assist the expert.

In order to derive new concept candidates from the fact

base, various clustering methods and statistical methods were evaluated. Statistical analysis based on frequency and distribution analyses provide a first clue for concept candidates, but are not suitable for the automation of the extraction step like the clustering methods.

Different clustering methods were chosen to group elements that are similar in terms of their properties in order to derive potential candidates from them. The following were examined: Neural Gas [16], Growing Neural Gas [17], as well as Self-Organizing-Maps (SOM) [18], whereby in particular the work of Matthias Reuter [19], [20] was taken into account.

These algorithms were used to find concepts at element level, such as special data objects like the transfer objects described in the example [5]. In addition, they were used to extract similar properties of dependencies between elements, to extract different types of dependencies such as special communication channels or different types of relationships such as an inheritance relationship typical for an object-oriented realization.

The following algorithms were used to extract new facts from the facts represented by the graph structure: Graph Kernels [21], graph clustering approaches such as SPAA [13] [12] [14] and t-SNE [22] to find similarities and anomalies within the graph. An example in which the coordinator pattern as a candidate results from such an extraction is described in [2].

A SOM is also used for the creation of new detectors within the framework of generalization by training with the representatives. The selection and parameterization of adequate methods in all activities, is the focus of the current, further and ongoing work.

C. The Evolution Phase

As shown in Figure 4, the approach described in the previous section can be embedded into any evolutionary and incremental development process. This means that after each implementation step the source code can be analyzed and these results are available for the next evolution step in the design activity.

This results in a holistic approach that considers the evolution of architectural concepts on two levels. On the one hand an identified concept itself is subject to changes, e.g., it can be refined or degenerated by further examples and on the other hand the application of architectural concepts to a concrete system can change during development by switching to another technology for example.

The generated Concept Performance Record can support the system architect in understanding the realized concepts. This information can be combined with the results of a conformity check, i.e., with a list of architecture violations referring to concrete source code artifacts.

If, for example, the developer was not familiar with the architecture and this is the reason for the violation, it can be fixed by the developer in the next implementation step so that no erosion occurs. On the other hand, it can be decided that the reason for the violation is an unsuitable architecture. In this case, the Concept Performance Record can support the planning of architectural changes by making the aspects the developer has in mind explicit at the architectural abstraction level through examples.

Another aspect is the improvement of the development and maintenance process through monitoring. We can assume that the configuration and all data pools (fact bases and concept spaces) are stored and versioned in a common repository. As already introduced, a concept stored in a concept space consists of a triple, its identifier, at least one detector, and a set of examples that fulfill this concept. As a result of the use of new technologies, frameworks or programming paradigms, it can lead to new concepts that may replace old concepts, so that once extracted concepts disappear over time and are no longer identified. The comparison of two Concept Performance Records from different versions of a product can lead to indications of mutations of concepts. This can also help to detect the erosion of the product or even a product line architecture at an early stage and to react in a managed way.

D. Scenario Mapping

If we have a look to the scenario defined in Section II-B, than the described activities can support it.

We assume that in the first conflict, where no transfer objects were used as parameters, the concept Transfer Object is known, stored in the Concept Space and was also selected. This means that at least one detector and corresponding examples of Transfer Objects are existing. In this case, the execution of the detector will result for the parameters of the `solveOptimization` method (see Figure 3) not positive. With the knowledge that these elements concept a indication for a deviation is given. Furthermore the architect has a direct linkage to the examples for the following discussion with the developer.

In the second case, where the database framework and with it a concept change is implemented, the following can be observed. A concept that has been detected or extracted before is no longer recognized - it has disappeared. On the other hand, previously unknown concepts have been extracted. The fact that an element no longer satisfies a concept fulfilled in the previous iteration and is now referenced in a newly extracted concept is a strong indication of a concept change.

IV. CONCLUSION AND OUTLOOK

The central element of the approach are the directly referenced source code examples through which machine-learned models become explainable, architectural concepts explicit and the adaption of a software architecture takes place in a managed way driven by the extracted knowledge from source files.

The approach presented here contributes to making software architectures explicit. The developer's understanding of architectural concepts is increased by code examples, i.e., a representation he is familiar with. The architect is supported during the decision making process, as he gets additional information about the architecture deviations with whose help he can decide whether the resolution of the violation is brought about by an adaptation in the source code or by a change in the architecture and thus the ideas of the developer are transferred to the architecture level. In this case, it is the examples that provide the architect with the information, with the focus on the properties and concepts that are fulfilled by the source code artifacts concerned.

With regard to the scenario described in Section II-B another question arises here: *Must be the interface* `OptimisationSolverIf` *realized as a service-oriented interface at all?* As visualized in Figure 2, it is only used within the application layer and not provided for external access, i.e., a possible solution for the conflict would also be to allow different types of implementation related to the context of the interface. In this case, the approach supports describing the context by the kind of the connection which exist between interface and its environment, and the differences between the different realization kinds which become understandable by the description of their characteristics.

Also described in the scenario is a technology change. Referring to the prototypical development or testing in the context of a product line as described in [9], the change becomes explicit. For example, it becomes clear which concepts are lost and which are added and which elements are affected. With regard to the rolling out of a concept change to variants of the product line, the detectors can simply determine which elements are affected by the no longer permissible concept.

As an outlook we would like to mention the evaluation with different OpenSource systems (e.g., Java Path Finder[23]. (approx. 178,000 LOC), jEdit[24] (ca. 58,400 LOC), PMD[25] (ca. 110.350 LOC), log4j[26] (approx. 158,600 LOC) and the enrichment of the fact base with semantic information, such as functional information or data describing the runtime behavior.

The statement: *"Satisfying rules can be a hard job for software developer!"* is not surprising considering that software development is a highly creative process [27] and therefore not every architectural violation is basically bad; rather it is necessary to explain the deviation in its context. To achieve this, it is necessary to make the architecture implicitly implemented by the developer explicit. If we also take into account that agile development methods are increasingly used, which are carried out with sprint cycles of e.g., two weeks, that architecture, too, is progressing at this rate of evolution, or it can at least be ensured that it does not erode. A managed architecture evolution in short cycles is only possible if both architect and developer have a basis that both understand.

As well as a common understanding, evolution also takes place on both levels, driven on the one hand by new requirements, which may no longer be met by the current architecture, and on the other hand driven by new technologies or programming paradigm and best practices.

Just like the Programming By Example [28] approach an understanding is here created through examples, too - but at the architectural level, with the goal to bring the architectural and the coding perspective together.

References

[1] M. Gharbi, A. Koschel, A. Rausch, and G. Starke, Software Architecture Fundamentals: A Study Guide for the Certified Professional for Software Architecture – Foundation Level – iSAQB compliant. Heidelberg: dpunkt, 2018.

[2] A. e. a. Grewe, "Automotive Software Product Line Architecture Evolution: Extracting, Designing and Managing Architectural Concepts," in International Journal on Advances in Intelligent Systems. IARIA, 2017, pp. 203–222.

[3] C. e. a. Knieke, "A Holistic Approach for Managed Evolution of Automotive Software Product Line Architectures," in ADAPTIVE 2017. Wilmington, DE, USA: IARIA, 2017, pp. 43–52.

[4] S. Herold, Architectural compliance in component-based systems: Foundations, specification, and checking of architectural rules, 1st ed., ser. SSE-Dissertation. München: Verl. Dr. Hut, 2011, vol. 5.

[5] A. Rausch, R. Reussner, R. Mirandola, and F. Plasil, Eds., The Common Component Modeling Example: Comparing Software Component Models (Lecture Notes in Computer Science / Programming and Software Engineering), 1st ed. Springer, 2008.

[6] http://www.cocome.org/, accessed: 2018-12-12.

[7] C. Szyperski, Component Software: Beyond Object-Oriented Programming (2nd Edition), 2nd ed. Addison-Wesley Professional, 2002.

[8] R. Reussner, Ed., Handbuch der Software-Architektur, 1st ed. Heidelberg: Dpunkt-Verl., 2006.

[9] A. e. a. Grewe, "Automotive Software Systems Evolution: Planning and Evolving Product Line Architectures," in ADAPTIVE 2017. Wilmington, DE, USA: IARIA, 2017, pp. 53–62.

[10] C. Deiters, Beschreibung und konsistente Komposition von Bausteinen für den Architekturentwurf von Softwaresystemen, 1st ed., ser. SSE-Dissertation. München: Dr. Hut, 2015, vol. 11.

[11] Malte Mues, "Taint Analysis: Language Independent Security Analysis for Injection Attacks," Master's Thesis, Technische Universität Clausthal, Clausthal, 2016.

[12] M. Schindler, C. Deiters, and A. Rausch, "Using Spectral Clustering to Automate Identification and Optimization of Component Structures," in Proceedings of 2nd International Workshop on Realizing Artificial Intelligence Synergies in Software Engineering (RAISE), 2013, pp. 14–20.

[13] M. Schindler, "Automatische Identifikation und Optimierung von Komponentenstrukturen in Softwaresystemen," Diploma Thesis, Technische Universität Clausthal, 2010.

[14] M. Schindler, A. Rausch, and O. Fox, "Clustering Source Code Elements by Semantic Similarity Using Wikipedia," in Proceedings of 4th International Workshop on Realizing Artificial Intelligence Synergies in Software Engineering (RAISE), 2015, pp. 13–18.

[15] R. Wettel, "Software Systems as cities," PhD Thesis, Università della Svizzera Italiana, Switzerland, Lugano, 2010.

[16] M. Cottrell, B. Hammer, A. Hasenfuss, and T. Villmann, "Batch and median neural gas," Neural Networks, vol. 19, no. 6-7, 2006, pp. 762–771.

[17] B. Fritzke, "A growing neural gas network learns topologies," in Advances in neural information processing systems, 1995, pp. 625–632.

[18] T. Kohonen, "The self-organizing map," Neurocomputing, vol. 21, no. 1, 1998, pp. 1–6.

[19] M. Reuter and H. H. Tadijne, "Computing with Activities III: Chunking and Aspect Integration of Complex Situations by a New Kind of Kohonen Map with WHU-Structures (WHU-SOMs)," in Proceedings of IFSA2005, Y. e. Liu, Ed. Springer, 2005, pp. 1410–1413.

[20] M. Reuter, "Computing with Activities V. Experimental Proof of the Stability of Closed Self Organizing Maps (gSOMs) and the Potential Formulation of Neural Nets," in Proceedings World Automation Congress (ISSCI 2008). TSI, 2008.

[21] A. Gisbrecht, W. Lueks, B. Mokbel, and B. Hammer, "Out-of-sample kernel extensions for nonparametric dimensionality reduction," in ESANN, vol. 2012, 2012, pp. 531–536.

[22] L. van der Maaten and G. Hinton, "Visualizing data using t-SNE," Journal of Machine Learning Research, vol. 9, no. Nov, 2008, pp. 2579–2605.

[23] http://babelfish.arc.nasa.gov/hg/jpf/jpf-core, accessed: 2018-12-12.

[24] http://www.jedit.org/, accessed: 2018-12-12.

[25] https://pmd.github.io/, accessed: 2018-12-12.

[26] https://logging.apache.org/log4j/2.x/, accessed: 2018-12-12.

[27] M. Gu and X. Tong, "Towards Hypotheses on Creativity in Software Development," in Product focused software process improvement, ser. Lecture Notes in Computer Science, F. Bomarius, Ed. Berlin [u.a.]: Springer, 2004, vol. 3009, pp. 47–61.

[28] H. Lieberman, Your wish is my command: Programming by example, ser. Morgan Kaufmann series in interactive technologies. San Francisco: Morgan Kaufmann Publishers, 2010.

Data-driven Component Configuration in Production Systems

Daning Wang, Christoph Knieke, Andreas Rausch
Technische Universität Clausthal, Institute for Software and Systems Engineering
Arnold-Sommerfeld-Straße 1, 38678 Clausthal-Zellerfeld, Germany
Email: {daning.wang|christoph.knieke|andreas.rausch}@tu-clausthal.de

Abstract—**In many factories, trying to model and develop a complex production system is considered a hard task, requiring efforts and time to the process engineers and system engineers. The production system is treated as a closed data driven system where the system development is motivated by the production time and the quality of products. The corresponding technical solutions for the evaluated result (e.g., for production time) are considered as the driving data of the production system, which can be developed to improve the productivity of the production system. On the other side, the production system is a cyber-physical system, which presents a unified view of computing systems that interact strongly with their physical environment. In order to raise the productivity, the production time and the quality of products must be evaluated regularly. The components in production systems must follow these results of evaluation and be configured with a new architecture to achieve the new requirements. Thus, the challenge is how to follow the driving data to get the new component configuration in production system, particularly cyber-physical system. This paper will give an approach for modeling of the production system and generating of a candidate of component configuration in consideration of the driving data.**

Keywords–Architecture Evolution; Semantical Matching; Configuration of Components; Cyber-physical System.

I. Introduction

Cyber-Physical Systems (CPS) play important roles in many areas, e.g., smart factory, digital manufacturing, smart logistics, and energy efficiency. The modern mechanical engineering products are increasingly being supplemented by programmable controllers. Production system is a classical Cyber-Physical System. It is in constant evolution and should permanently be operated in order to raise the productivity or meet the continuously and fast changing requirements [1]. However, in general a production system is not defined perfectly at the beginning. And sometimes, it has to monitor itself for its productivity. Besides, driven by availability of new technology the production systems are repeatedly enhanced and extended in their prolonged life time.

An existing production system (see Figure 1) can be modeled with a component oriented modeling language. By using of an equivalent representation, the component oriented model for the existing production system is transformed to a graph structure, which keeps the system structure and properties from the original component oriented model [2]. This graph structure evolves into more different graphs by using of graph-based algorithms. Each new graph represents a new components configuration. By using combination rules, which are defined by system engineers, a part of the new component configurations, which meet the requirements of the driving data, can be found out. One of these configurations will be simulated and as a new production system implemented. This new one is named target 1 and will be continually evaluated into the second iteration.

In this paper, an approach is introduced to model and generate a candidate of component configurations for a plan of new production system according to the driving data. Firstly, the related work about the solutions of this problem will be introduced in Section II. Then, an example is presented in Section III reflecting the data driven evolution of production system. The necessary basics and fundamentals of this approach will be introduced closely related to the example system in Section IV. The approach is described in two parts in Sectionn V : the system architecture and algorithms. Finally, Section VI concludes and gives an outlook on further work.

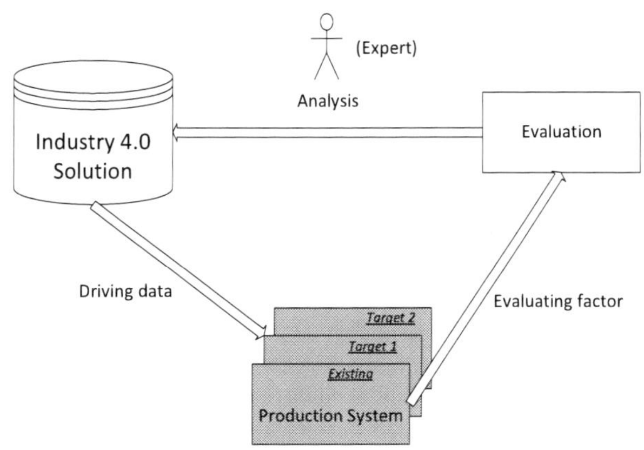

Figure 1. Data driven development of a production system

II. Related Work

The "Industry 4.0" (I4.0) – also called "smart manufacturing" or "industrial internet of things" – in production is synonymous with highly flexible production, which enables companies to offer highly individualized products by linking the internet to conventional processes and services, and to actively involve their customers very early in the development process [3]. Currently, there are very less opportunities for the small and medium-size enterprises (SMEs) to gather the information which they need to adopt I4.0 solutions. In [4], an information portal is presented providing access to the results of a study commissioned by Stechert and Franke [5]. It reveals basic approaches to digitization and helps to identify business areas, such as product development that can be influenced by specific I4.0 functional areas. But the link to concrete I4.0 technologies does not take place here.

As part of the project "Intro 4.0" [6], the implementation strategies of I4.0 solutions are developed based on four applications for participating industrial partners. Here, the specific I4.0 solutions are developed and introduced to industrial partners. The findings on the development and implementation of I4.0 solutions will then be used to derive recommendations for action on risk and potential estimation when implementing the I4.0 solutions [6]. However, the development of a simulation environment or the evaluation methodology for the comparison of alternative solutions is not planned.

The modeling of processes and information flows offers the sufficient resource for networking of the production planning systems, the control systems of machines, building systems and logistics systems [7]. The projects ENOPA [8] and EnHiPro [9] mainly committed to modeling between production planning systems and control systems of machines and logistics systems. The project PROFILE mainly devoted to description models for companies and the innovation and knowledge management in production networks. That is also the main work in the projects SynProd [10] and GINA [11].

The Functional Mock-up Interface (FMI) defines a standardized interface and is developed by Daimler within the framework of the MODELISAR project for the coupling of various simulation modules [12]. This approach is used to integrate simulation modules into other simulation modules with a common interface. A master simulation is defined, in that the appropriate different modules can be coupled. The data exchange between the modules must also be modeled in the master.

All these previous solutions have in common that although they allow a technical integration of different models they do not give a set of suitable concepts for structuring and integration of the concrete I4.0 solutions in the existing production system. So, the I4.0 solutions must be integrated in the existing production system before the evaluation of the I4.0 solutions.

III. EXAMPLE SYSTEM

Figure 2 shows a battery manufacturing system as an example. It consists of a 3D-print station, a quality assurance station, a battery module assembly, an electronics assembly, a final assembly, a storage for assembly (such as caps, batteries and electronics), a logistic system, a central controller and two robot grippers as transportations. The manufactured batteries will be transported into a warehouse and stored there.

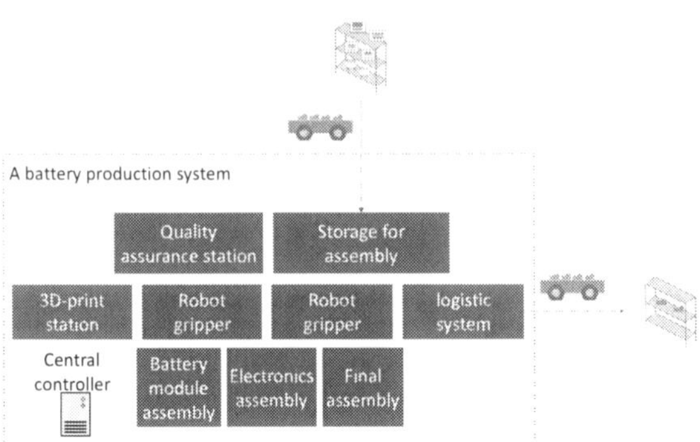

Figure 2. Battery production system as example

This battery manufacturing system is a classical CPS. The manufacturing parameters and the description of production processes are provided from another system as the input data to the central controller. The central controller networks the work stations, assemblies and other subsystems together to execute the production plan. The material and resources are transported into the storage for assembly and after the production the batteries are transported out from this system.

In this case, the production time is an important evaluating to reflect the productivity. Therefore, an evaluation system is monitoring this evaluating factor and in this way makes the evaluation of productivity. The evaluation results are analyzed to obtain one industry 4.0 solution. In this case, "Track and Tracing with RFID" technology is selected using to optimize the production time (see Figure 3): One or more new RFID-reader sensors will be integrated into the existing production system and the RFID-chips must be integrated into the transport trays.

But there are many possible implementations to integrate the RFID-reader sensors into the existing production system. Thus, before the implementation or simulation of one integration concept, a decision support is necessary.

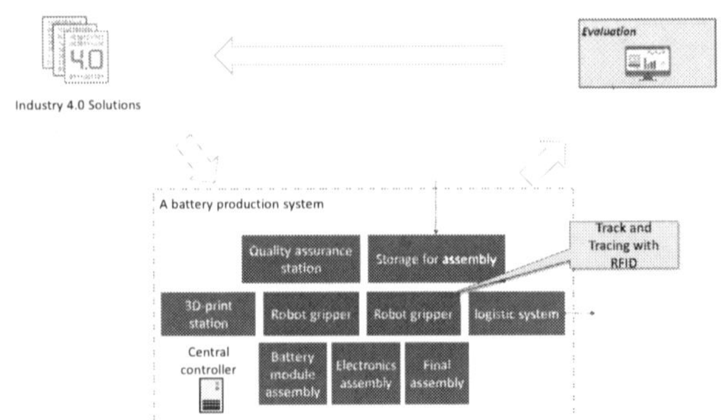

Figure 3. The technical solutions of the evaluated result for this battery production system as example

IV. BASICS AND FUNDAMENTALS

A. Component-based modeling

Internal Block Diagram (IBD) is a UML 2 based standard component oriented modeling language and used in Systems Modeling Language (SysML) for systems engineering [13]. The IBD consists of system components, interfaces in the form of ports and connections. Their symbols and interpretations are described in Figure 4.

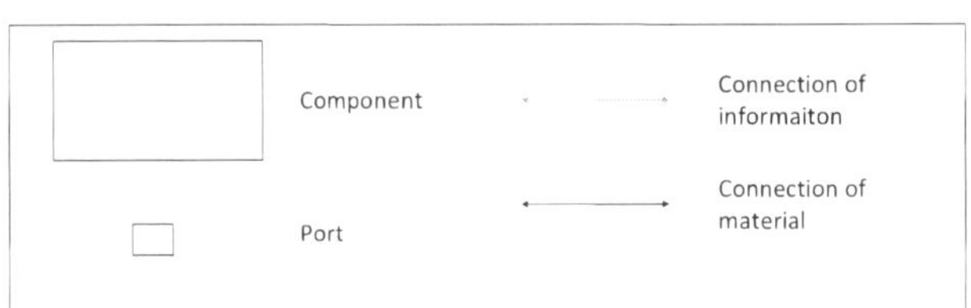

Figure 4. The interpretations of the symbols in IBD

The above mentioned existing state of the battery manufacturing system is modeled model with IBD in Figure 5.

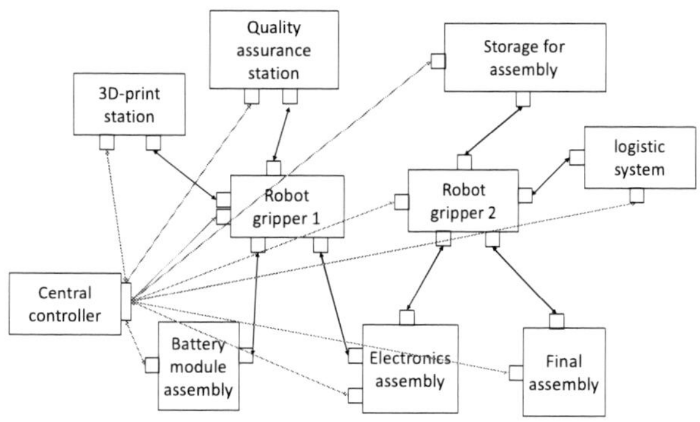

Figure 5. The existing production system modeled with IBD

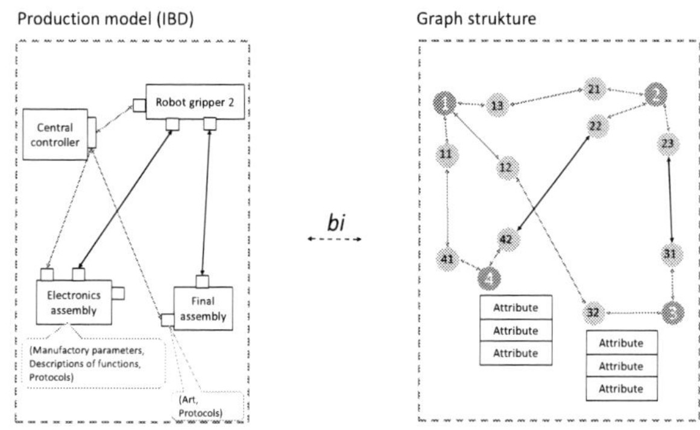

Figure 6. The graph representation of the existing production system

B. Graph structure

In order to describe the system evolution from exsiting state to a target state, a directed graph structure is introduced in definition (1). The elements in the set V represent the nodes of the graph structure G. Any element in the set E represents a directed edge (arrow) in G. The edges can be also described with $E := V \times V$. The functions src and tgt are two connection relationship functions for every edge, which connects to its source node with function src, as well as its target node with tgt. Every node and edge has attributes to store the semantic information (description information). Every attribute has a key-value structure, where P represents the power set of key-value pairs. The keys are identification keys and help identify the various kinds of description information, which are stored in values.

$$\begin{aligned} \mathcal{G} &:= (V, E, src, tgt) \\ src &:= src|_{E \to V} \\ tgt &:= tgt|_{E \to V} \end{aligned} \tag{1}$$

$$\begin{aligned} attributes &:= V \cup E \to P(Key \times Value) \\ Key &:= a\ set\ of\ values \\ Value &:= a\ set\ of\ values \end{aligned} \tag{2}$$

C. Transformation between models and graph structure

A transform function bi represents the transformation between IBD models and graphs. This transformation is defined as an equivalent and reversible transformation.

$$bi(m_{IBD}) \leftrightarrow g_{IBD} \tag{3}$$

Following the example of battery manufactoring system, a representative part in the full system is selected to clearly and detailedly introduce the transformation for every elements. In that, the system components and ports are transformed into nodes, and all connections to edges. (see Figure 6)

The system components like central controller, robot gripper 2, electronics assembly and final assembly are transformed to nodes 1, 2, 3, and 4 (see Figure 7). The belonging descriptions, like the manufactory parameters, descriptions of functions and protocol, are transformed into the attributes of the corresponding node. All of the interfaces are transformed to nodes in the graph. In this example, the digital (second) interface of the final assembly system component is transformed to node 32 in the graph, and its descriptions, like art and protocols, are saved in the attributes of node 32. All of the material flows and information flows are transformed to edges in the graph, at the same time the connection relationships are kept through this transformation.

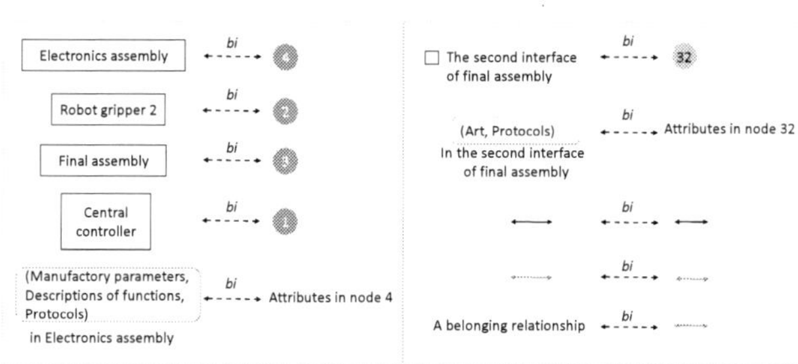

Figure 7. The interpretations of transformation between the IBD elements and graph elements for the existing production system

V. Approach

A. System architecture

Our approach is based on a subsystem named candidates generator. Figure 8 shows a new system architecture of data driven development of production system with this approach.

The inputs of candidates generator consist of one production model, which describes the existing state of the production system with IBD (1) and one Industry 4.0 solution (2). The outputs of candidates generator is a set of models for a target production system (3), which is integrated with the given industry 4.0 solution. At the same time, this set of models must be implementable. In the case of battery manufacturing system, the candidates for a new production system should consider with the integration of RFID-reader sensors into the existing production system. In the circumstances, any model in the candidates who cannot satisfy this condition will be removed from the candidates.

The filtered models will be continually evaluated with evaluating factors (4), such as production time and so on. After the evaluation, one production model is selected as a target model (5) and analyzed by experts (6) again. These processes

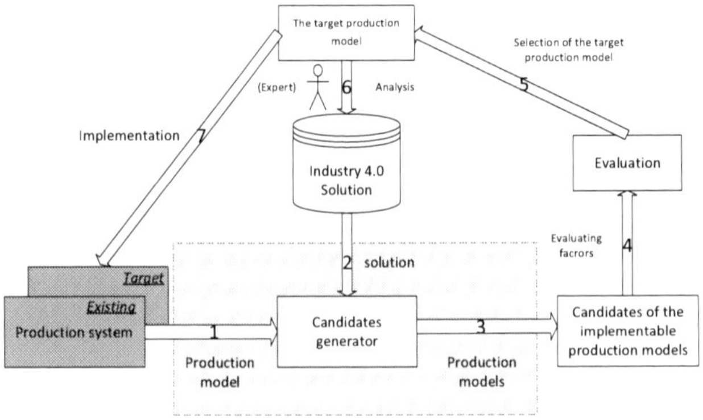

Figure 8. A new system architecture of data driven development of production system with our approach

make the generating an iterative loop possible, in order to apply more than one Industry 4.0 solution on a production system. After the integrations for all of Industry 4.0 solutions, the finally selected target production model will be implemented (7) to a new (target) production system. The new production system can be continually developed in the second iterative process into candidate generator.

B. Algorithms

The production model for the existing state is transformed into graph structure without information loss and structural changes by using the transformation function bi (see definition 3). On the graph structure, the algorithms in graph theory, e.g. depth-first search, breadth-first search, path/walk morphism and shortest path problem, can easily be used to generate new graphs. The transformation function bi makes the reversible from graph structure to production model possible and without information loss and structural changes.

VI. Conclusion and Further Work

We proposed an approach which supports the further development of complex cyber-physical systems. In the application example, the algorithm used in our approach had to give recommendations for integrating RFID-reader sensors in the existing production system. The existing models were first abstracted to a common graph-based description. The candidates generator was then used to determine candidates with a possible integration of the new components. Based on this set of candidates, an optimal integration of the new components can be identified.

The underlying concept is currently being continuously further developed and applied in the research project "Synus" to optimally integrate Industry 4.0 solutions into existing systems. This is intended to provide SMEs in particular with a decision-making aid for the introduction of new technologies.

Acknowledgment

This paper evolved of the research project "Synus" (Methods and tools for the synergetic conception and evaluation of Industry 4.0 solutions) which is funded by the European Regional Development Fund (EFRE — ZW 6-85012454) and managed by the Project Management Agency NBank.

References

[1] H. Giese, B. Rumpe, B. Schätz, and J. Sztipanovits, "Science and engineering of cyber-physical systems (dagstuhl seminar 11441)," Dagstuhl Reports, vol. 1, no. 11, 2012.

[2] H. Grönniger, J. O. Ringert, and B. Rumpe, "System Model-Based Definition of Modeling Language Semantics," Formal techniques for distributed systems, 2009, pp. 152–166.

[3] MCKINSEY DIGITAL, "Industry 4.0: How to navigate digitization of the manufacturing sector." [Online]. Available: https://www.mckinsey.de/files/mck_industry_40_report.pdf

[4] VDMA - FORUM INDUSTRIE 4.0, "Industrie 4.0 konkret - Lösungen für die industrielle Praxis." [Online]. Available: http://industrie40.vdma.org/documents/

[5] C. Stechert and H.-J. Franke, "Requirements models for modular products," ICORD 09: Proceedings of the 2nd International Conference on Research into Design, Bangalore, India, 07.-09.01.2009.

[6] J. Schmitt, D. Inkermann, C. Stechert, A. Raatz, and T. Vietor, "Requirement oriented reconfiguration of parallel robotic systems," Robotic Systems-Applications, Control and Programming, 2012.

[7] S. Thiede, Energy efficiency in manufacturing systems. Springer Science & Business Media, 2012, ISBN: 978-3-642-25914-2.

[8] M. Schönemann, C. Schmidt, C. Herrmann, and S. Thiede, "Multi-level modeling and simulation of manufacturing systems for lightweight automotive components," Procedia CIRP, vol. 41, 2016, pp. 1049–1054.

[9] M. Schönemann, C. Herrmann, P. Greschke, and S. Thiede, "Simulation of matrix-structured manufacturing systems," Journal of Manufacturing Systems, vol. 37, 2015, pp. 104–112.

[10] C. Müller, M. Grunewald, and T. S. Spengler, "Redundant configuration of automated flow lines based on "industry 4.0"-technologies," Journal of Business Economics, vol. 87, no. 7, 2017, pp. 877–898.

[11] T. Vietor, C. Herrmann, and T. S. Spengler, Synergetische Produktentwicklung: unternehmensübergreifend erfolgreich zusammenarbeiten; Ergebnisse des Verbundprojekts SynProd. Shaker, 2015, ISBN-10: 3844034374.

[12] T. Blochwitz, M. Otter, J. Akesson, M. Arnold, C. Clauss, H. Elmqvist, M. Friedrich, A. Junghanns, J. Mauss, D. Neumerkel et al., "Functional mockup interface 2.0: The standard for tool independent exchange of simulation models," in Proceedings of the 9th International MODELICA Conference; September 3-5; 2012; Munich; Germany, no. 076. Linköping University Electronic Press, 2012, pp. 173–184.

[13] E. Huang, R. Ramamurthy, and L. Mcginnis, "System and simulation modeling using SysML," Proceedings - Winter Simulation Conference, Jan 2008, pp. 796–803.

Modeling of Automotive HVAC Systems Using Long Short-Term Memory Networks

Peter Engel
TU Clausthal
Institute for Software and Systems Engineering,
Clausthal, Germany
e-mail: peter.engel@tu-clausthal.de

Sebastian Meise
TLK-Thermo GmbH,
Braunschweig, Germany
e-mail: s.meise@tlk-thermo.de

Andreas Rausch
TU Clausthal
Institute for Software and Systems Engineering,
Clausthal, Germany
e-mail: arau@tu-clausthal.de

Wilhelm Tegethoff
TLK-Thermo GmbH,
Braunschweig, Germany
e-mail: w.tegethoff@tlk-thermo.de

Abstract— **Adaptive and fast-calculating HVAC and climate models are gaining increasing importance in the automotive development process. Physically motivated thermal models achieve high quality results, but have a disadvantage in terms of their computing speed due to their complexity. One possible approach for the fast and precise simulation of thermal systems is deep learning with artificial neural networks. This paper aims to determine the extent to which neural LSTM are suitable for modeling the complex dynamic behavior of vehicle air conditioning. For this purpose, a physical reference model of a passenger car air conditioning system including a vehicle cabin is set up in the simulation environment Dymola with the component library TIL Suite. Furthermore, a model structure of a LSTM -based deep neural network to map the dynamic thermal behavior correctly is proposed. For the purpose of training the ANN, the overall system has been broken down into subsystems. The subsystems are individually trained open-loop and then linked to form a closed-loop overall model. For evaluation purposes, models with the same model structure but based on feed forward network (FFN) architectures are implemented, trained and tested.**

Keywords - BEV; Applied Machine Learning; HVAC; LSTM; ANN;

I. Introduction

In the automotive development process, simulations of the vehicle climate are required in order to test components, assemblies, system concepts and control variants in a cost-effective and time-efficient manner. Furthermore, simulations of the vehicle's climatization systems are currently gaining more and more of a focus on research, as they are used within Model-Predictive Controllers (MPC) to optimize HVAC control.

Previous work has shown that physical modeling shows good results and provides a good picture of real thermodynamic processes. A number of studies have focused on a detailed physical modeling of the cabin climatization for simulation purposes [1]-[14]. In addition to the vehicle interior temperature, energy consumption, air humidity and, in some cases, air quality and thermal comfort are also calculated in the form of a Predicted Mean Vote (PMV). With the modeling methods described here, it was possible to achieve high prediction accuracy in the sense of the accordance of measurement and simulation results. However, these models have a significant disadvantage of the modeling effort and the high runtime and are therefore not suitable for use in a model predictive controller. A compromise between run-time and prediction accuracy with relatively low modeling effort is provided by adaptive learning methods with modeling of the controlled system by Artificial Neural Networks (ANN). Previous work on simulating the cabin climate with ANN showed promising results for short forecast horizons. However, for longer forecasting horizons and at large operating range, the known works are only limitedly suitable for simulation in the vehicle development process or in use within an MPC. One reason for this is the error accumulation due to the multiple consecutive one-step-ahead predictions. The output of each prediction step along the prediction time window is used as the input for the following one. As a result, the error also propagates and resonates, resulting in high inaccuracies.

An alternative architecture of recurrent neural networks, which is particularly suitable for the prediction of time series, has been introduced with Long Short-Term Memory (LSTM) networks [15]. With the use of LSTM in their products, the major technology companies Apple, Alphabet and Microsoft have achieved great success in recent years. Based on this network structure, a deep neural network for the simulation of the cabin climate will be presented in this paper.

The modeling of physical systems using machine learning methods is subject to two major challenges. On the one hand, the right architecture, which is suitable for mapping the system dynamics well, must be found. The other problem consists in the quality of the learning data as the essential basis of all learning methods. The values of physical quantities obtained by measurements of physical processes are subject to deviations due to measurement uncertainties and measurement deviations. Since the quality of learning systems is limited by the quality of the learning data, preprocessing of the signals, e.g., by smoothing and filtering, is required. Since this work examines the suitability of the architecture for mapping the system dynamics, the training is based on learning data generated by a conventional system model. For this purpose, a complex detailed reference system model was created in a first step. Based on this reference system model, the quality of the examined learning methods was evaluated.

The following Section II describes the state of the art in terms of physical thermal modeling and modeling with ANN. In Section III the reference system model is presented. Subsequently in Section IV, the structure of the LSTM-based deep neural network is explained in more detail. Finally in Section V, simulation results of the comparison of NARX-based networks and LSTM-based networks are presented and discussed.

II. Modeling of Thermal Systems

A. Physical Thermal Modelling

The simulation of thermal models is an established element of the vehicle development chain. One reason is that development times are greatly reduced, since component tests can take place virtually without having to set up or modify a new test bench. The requirements on the models are not only a realistic representation of the real component but also the speed at which the model can be simulated. This requirement is particularly important for models that are used on real-time systems. Furthermore, the simulation time has a great influence on the duration of the development cycles and thus has a direct effect on the costs, which underlines the importance of this requirement once again. The demands posed to the model are matched by the challenges of modelling. These are among others:

- Realistic mapping of system and component complexity
- Transfer of the characteristics of individual components by means of parameterization
- Implementation of the physical behavior of individual components
- Checking the thermal behavior of circulation systems

One way to generate fast and realistic thermal models of components and systems is to use physical models. These use thermodynamic relationships to realistically model the interaction of a component with its environment. The advantage of the physical approach lies in the inherent quality of the representation of reality, provided that the laws can be fully captured and implemented. However, since even a seemingly simple component, e.g., the refrigerant pipe of an air conditioning system already spans a complex network of thermal dependencies. This makes physical modelling of thermal systems very demanding and therefore time-consuming. It can take several weeks until the modelling of a car air conditioning system has been modeled and validated. The more complex a model becomes, the more time it can take to simulate it. Here, the quality of the simulation result competes with the simulation speed.

1) Model exchange using FMU

A further argument for the model-based component development is the possibility of parallel work of different departments on a component by means of model exchange. This can be done, for example, by transferring a Functional Mock-up Unit (FMU) [16]. The creator of the model exports the model from his modeling software into the standardized FMU format. This creates a container file which contains all equation systems of the original model in the form of a DLL and thus makes them generally usable. Beside the DLL there is also an XML, which contains the interface description. With the FMU export, it is also possible to integrate the required licenses and thus make the simulation of the integrated model possible in the first place. In order to restrict the use of the license, it is limited to the simulation of the FMU. The user of the FMU can now integrate the original model (e.g. Modelica code) in the format of an FMU into his own software environment (e.g. Matlab or MS Excel) and simulate it.

B. Modeling of Themal Systems with ANN

In various previous works, the modeling of thermal systems with neural networks was investigated. The majority of the work is focused on the simulation of building HVAC systems. Thus, e.g. in [17] and [18], nonlinear autoregressive networks with exogenous inputs (NARX) are used to predict the indoor temperature and humidity in rooms. The networks are essentially Feed Forward networks, usually multilayer perceptrons (MLP), with the outputs being fed back. In addition to the current independent (exogenous) inputs and the previous outputs, time-delayed values of these variables are also used as input. Figure 1 shows the common used NARX architecture.

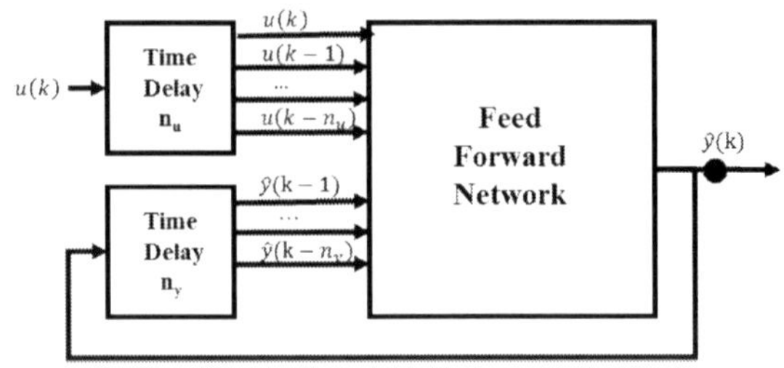

Figure 1 NARX Architecture

The training of the network is accomplished, without feedback, in a serial structure. Here, the true outputs $y(k-1, k-2, \dots, k-n_y)$ are used instead of the predicted output $\hat{y}(k-1, k-2, \dots, k-n_y)$. This has the advantage on the one hand that the exact inputs of the network are used. And on the other hand, a static backpropagation method such as the Levenberg Marquardt algorithm can be used as a learning method.

Based on this principle, several papers dealing with the modeling of building HVAC systems have been published. For example, in [19], multiple autoregressive RBF-ANNs are used to predict the PMV. The forecast result is used here within an MPC to reduce energy consumption while achieving maximizing thermal comfort. In [20], a series of recurrent models is used to predict humidity and indoor temperature in buildings. [21] also describes the use of a neural network to model a building HVAC system. This model is used as part of an intelligent energy management system in combination with a genetic algorithm to optimize the cooling energy requirement. The model consists of several submodels for the different components of the HVAC system, which are constructed as multi-layer perceptron (MLP) in feed forward structure with a hidden layer of 20 neurons, one bias and one hyperbolic activation function. The models predict the resulting exhaust temperature, fan pressure and compressor output. The model has a resolution of 1 minute. The mean average error MAE tested was 0.52K for the temperature model and 0.58 KW for the energy consumption.

The modeling of vehicle HVAC systems by neural networks was discussed in detail in [21]-[23]. In [22] and [23], the modeling of an experimental automotive air conditioning system with a recurrent, time-delayed neural network is described. The model is again used within a model predictive control to optimize the refrigeration cycle, in particular a variable speed compressor. The network has a hidden layer with 5 neurons and a time delay of 5 samples for the input and 3 samples for the feedback output. The data sampling rate was 8 seconds. The training was done on- and offline with a Levenberg-Marquardt algorithm. Tests using one-step-ahead and 10-steps-ahead prediction were performed. Here, it was determined that the feedback caused a fault accumulation, which is why an error resetting was performed after the 10 steps.

An artificial neural network architecture alternative to NARX exists with LSTM networks. In this case, as with all recurrent structures, not individual data points but entire sequences of the data are processed further. The feedback takes place here on the level of individual cells. Unlike traditional RNNs, the problems of exploding or vanishing gradients in training LSTMs have a much smaller impact. While the base element in feed forward networks is a single neuron with associated weights and an activation function, individual LSTM-units respectively LSTM-blocks are the base elements in LSTM networks. The common architecture of an LSTM-unit consists of one cell and three gates. The cell represents the memory of the unit. During each calculation step, the output of the LSTM-unit h_t (hidden state) and the state of the cell c_t are calculated.

The output of the LSTM-unit is calculated from the state of the cell and the output of the output gates. The cell state is calculated from the previous value of the cell state and the outputs of the input gates and the forget gate. In each of the three gates, as in a neuron in a feed forward network, each output is calculated from a weighted sum and an activation function. Through the training, the weights of the gates are adjusted and thus learned to what extent information from previous steps are stored or removed. The detailed description of the method can be found in [15].

Based on this basic architecture, Section IV proposes a deep neural network for mapping the thermal behavior of vehicle interior climate control. This model is trained on the data of a reference model, which is explained in more detail in the following chapter.

III. Physical Reference Modell

A. Model Design

In the simulation environment Dymola, the model of a mobile refrigeration system and a car cabin was created using the modeling language Modelica, the ModelicaStandardLibrary and the model library TIL Suite [24]. The air conditioning system used as a reference system comes from a Volkswagen e-Golf, which was available as a measuring vehicle for several months. The data collected was used to create a model of the vapor compression cycle, the climate control system and the cabin. The coarse structure of the refrigeration system model is shown in Figure 2.

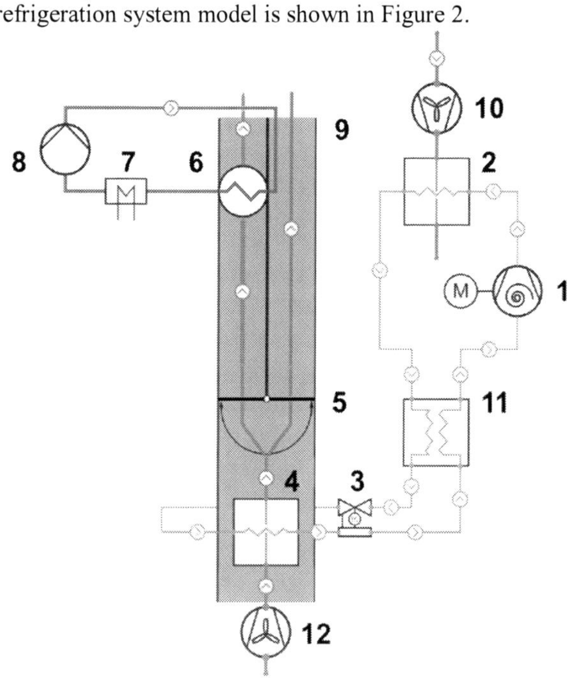

Figure 2 Refrigeration cycle with a scroll compressor (1), a high-pressure-side external air-refrigerant heat exchanger as condenser (2) with a fan (10), an internal heat exchanger (11), an expansion element (3) and the inner heat exchanger as evaporator (4). In the air duct (9) there is a temperature flap (5) which divides the air flow coming from the fan (12) and, depending on the operating point, directs it via the heat exchanger in the water-glycol cycle (6) of the heating circuit. The medium is heated by a high-voltage PTC (7) and circulated by a pump (8).

B. Refrigeration System Model

Compressor: The refrigeration cycle is operated with the refrigerant R-1234yf and consists of a scroll compressor taken from the TIL standard library. By adjusting its displacement volume and efficiencies, it was adapted to the compressor from the real refrigeration cycle. Internal pressure and friction losses as well as heat dissipation to the environment are also mapped by the model.

Heat exchangers: The refrigerant-side heat exchangers used are from the TIL AddOn Automotive [25] and have been adapted to the dimensions of the e-Golf heat exchangers. The heat exchangers can be adapted to the real component via several parameters for geometry (see Figure 3), as well as heat transfer and pressure loss relationships.

Following the recommendation of Rohsenow et al. [26], the correlation of Gnielinski [27] for Reynolds numbers less than 2300 and the correlation of Dittus/Boelter [28] for Reynolds numbers greater than 104 was used for the calculation of the refrigerant-side heat transfer coefficient for the case of turbulent flow. For the phase change in the condenser, the correlation of Shah [29] was used. The air-side forced heat transfer was determined with the correlation established by Haaf [30]. For the refrigerant-side pressure loss during the phase change, the McAdams approach [31] in combination with the Swamee/Jain formulation [32] was used for Reynolds numbers greater than 2300 on the basis of the homogeneous calculation model. The implementation of the airside pressure loss was neglected.

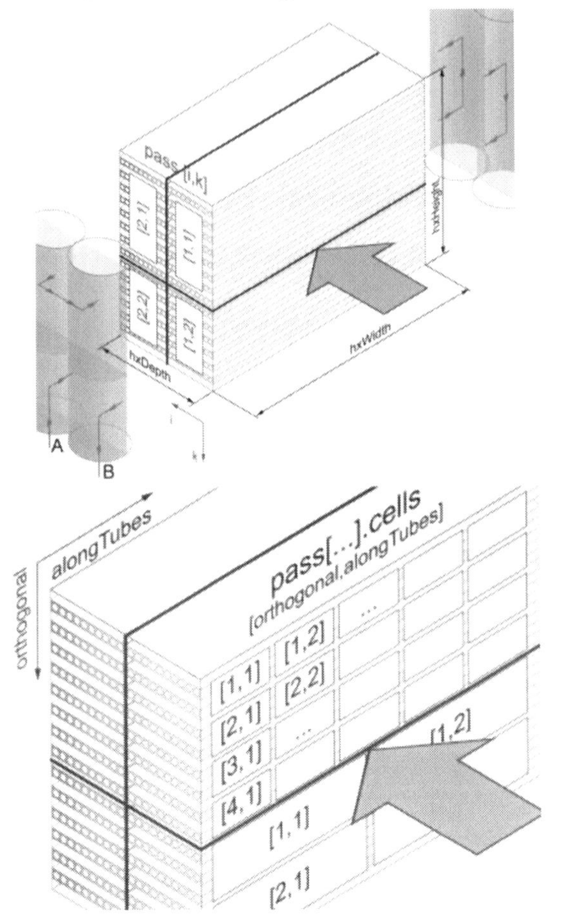

Figure 3 Modelling of heat exchangers with the TIL AddOn Automotive. The geometry of the heat exchangers can be completely adapted to that of the original component (upper illustration). Furthermore, the heat exchanger can be divided into cells (lower illustration). This allows a three-dimensional analysis of the heat exchanger [25].

High-voltage PTC: The high-voltage PTC was implemented via a heat source that transfers a loss-free heat flow to a tube model. The coolant, which absorbs the heat flow of the PTC with a defined heat transfer coefficient, is conducted through this tube model.

Expansion Valve: The expansion element is a thermostatic expansion valve. The opening behavior of the valve was implemented in the model based on manufacturer data. The nominal high- and low-pressure values are 9.7 bar at 235 cm³/h and 3.7 bar at 160 cm³/h. The maximum operating point is 7 bar at 35°C.

Fans: The fans are implemented as simple models which convey a defined air volume flow. Since no reliable air-side measurement data was available, no air-side pressure losses were integrated.

C. Vehicle Cabin System Model

The interior model comes from the TIL AddOn Cabin [33] and is based on an ideally mixed zero-dimensional air volume (moist air), which is thermally coupled to the passengers and surrounding surfaces (walls, windows, floor, ceiling, dashboard, seats) and these in turn to the environment (see Figure 4). The surface elements were implemented using parameters for geometry, material properties and heat transfer relationships.

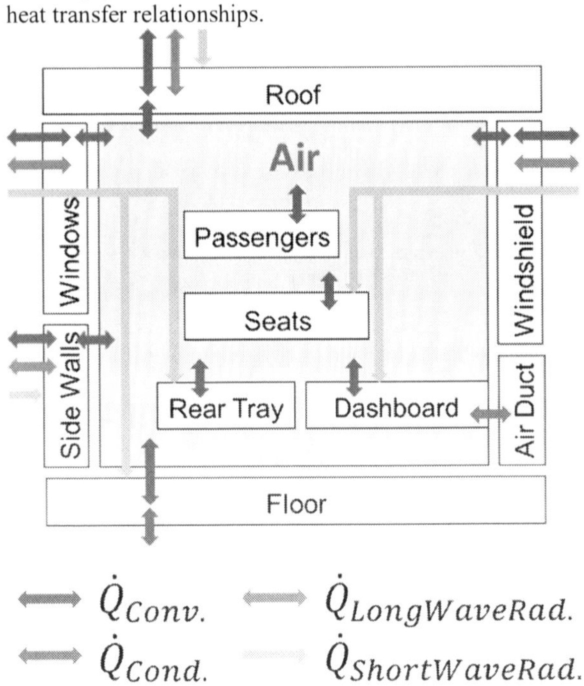

Figure 4 Structure of the cabin model with thermal connections of the individual components. In order to maintain the clarity, the representation of the long-wave radiation exchange of all components among each other, which is determined by view factors, was omitted

The air duct was modelled with a tube model available in TIL and thermally coupled to the underside of the dashboard. The passenger was integrated into the cabin model as heat and moisture source.

D. Comparison of Simulation and Measurement

The model was calibrated with several measurement runs and adapted via a fitting process. Since the climate control system uses the interior temperature as the central reference value, this quantity in particular is an important quality criterion for the model. Figure 5 shows a comparison of an exemplary simulation of a heating case. It can be seen that the interior model is not able to reproduce small temperature changes of the sensor. This is due to the ideal mixing of the air volume based on the zero-dimensional approach. However, the average heating behavior of the interior is very well represented. This results in a deviation of the interior temperature determined by the model of a maximum of 4.8K during the heat-up phase and a maximum of 0.9K in control mode over all evaluated test runs.

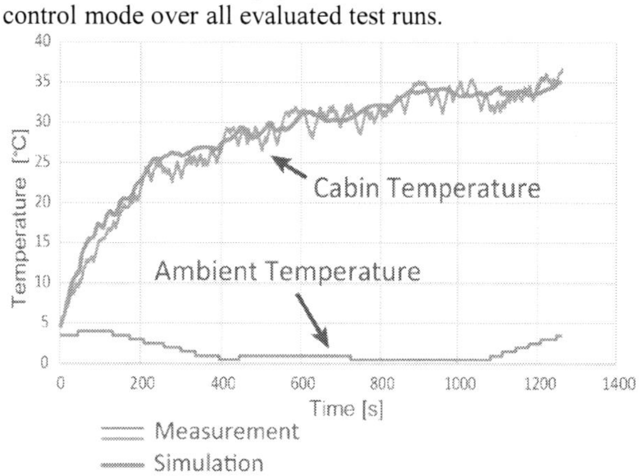

Figure 5 Comparison of measurement and simulation data of a test drive at an outside temperature between 0°C and 5°C.

The climate control system of the model was based on a typical control unit for electric vehicles. The model can dynamically map the following operating states:

- Heating
- Cooling
- Dehumidification
- Re-heating
- Ventilation

For the work presented here, the focus was on the operating states of heating and dehumidification. The resulting model of HVAC system and cabin consists of 9947 dependent parameters, 468 continuous time states, 199 linear equation systems with at most 2nd order, 32 non-linear equation systems with at most 1st order. The average CPU time is 240 seconds for 1000 simulated seconds. It was exported as FMU to perform the further process of ANN learning in Matlab and Python.

IV. Modeling of the Climate System with ANN

A. Model structure

The overall model consists of 6 linked submodels. Each submodel consists of an individually trained network. The submodels were each selected according to the sensors present in the vehicle, so that the signal trajectories of the inputs and outputs can be used as training data. The inputs of each subnet consist of feedback outputs of its own and other subnets, the direct outputs of other subnets and external inputs. Figure 6 shows simplified the overall model structure.

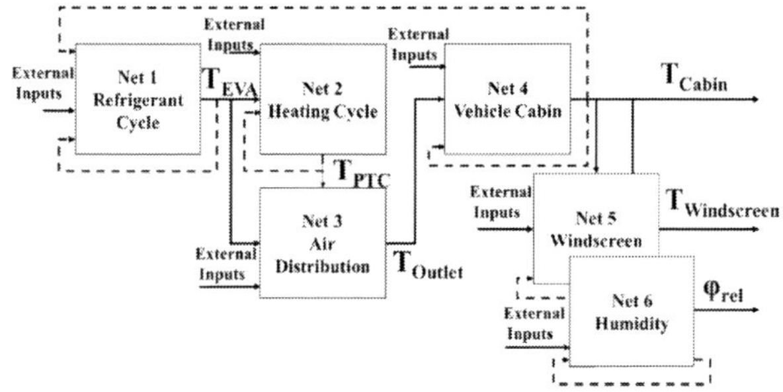

Figure 6 Model structure of the ANN-model

In the first subnet named the refrigerant cycle, the air temperature after the evaporator is predicted. For this purpose, the trajectories of the inside temperature, the outside temperature, the relative humidity inside and outside, the recirculation flap position, the fan power and the compressor power are used as inputs, each in the form of a sequence.

The second network represents the heating circuit. The trajectories of the electrical power of the PTC element, the air temperature after evaporator, the past air temperature after the heat exchanger, the temperature flap position and the fan power serve as input to predict the current air temperature behind the heat exchanger of the heating circuit. The predicted output values of the first two nets are used together with the position of the temperature flap and the blower output as input for the third network, the air distribution, to predict the outlet temperature at the vents to the cabin interior.

In the fourth network, the new internal temperature is calculated from a number of external inputs, such as outside temperature, direct and diffuse solar radiation power, vehicle speed, fan power, passenger number and past internal temperature and outlet temperature. From this, the new windscreen temperature and the resulting new relative humidity are predicted in the last two networks.

B. Network Architecture / Parameterization

1) NARX

The NARX networks were designed as in the work described in Section II.B, each with a hidden layer with different numbers of neurons (5, 10 and 20). The input signals of the networks were prepared according to the different tested delays of 3 and 6 delay steps. For preprocessing of the signals, the training data of the inputs and outputs was normalized by their mean value and their standard deviation. To generate the training data, 11 simulation runs were carried out with simulated journey duration of approx. 1 hour each. Here, a total of 40810 data samples were generated with a sampling rate of one second. The training data was subdivided as usual into learning, test and validation sets. As a learning function, the Levenberg-Marquardt algorithm was chosen with mean square error (MSE) as performance indicator. The training was carried out for each submodel with the different architectures and tested on 3 further unseen simulation runs with 10586 data samples. A maximum number of 200 learning epochs was defined as abort criterion for the learning processes. However, this never occurred because of the rapid convergence of the learning function. The RMSE was selected as benchmark for the evaluation of the test result.

2) LSTM

The LSTM networks were designed with a sequence input layer, a LSTM layer with different number of LSTM-units (5, 10 and 20), a fully connected layer and an output regression layer. Sequence lengths of 3 and 6 samples were examined. The input data was prepared as described above. For network training the adaptive moment estimation optimizer (ADAM), stochastic gradient descent optimizer (SGD) und the root mean square propagation optimizer (RMSProp) were tested. Here, too, a maximum number of 200 learning epochs was defined as the abort criterion of the learning processes. All learning methods showed a significantly weaker convergence compared to the NARX training procedures, so that the learning processes were always aborted due to the reached maximum number of learning periods. The SGD method proved to be the most efficient learning method. A mini batch size of 50 data samples per iteration was chosen. The test procedure was carried out as described above.

3) Combined Overall Model

To simulate the holistic system model, the individual subnetworks were linked according to the model structure shown in Section III.4. Here, the inputs were replaced by the direct and feedback outputs of the coupled individual subnets. The overall system was then tested by the three additional generated unseen test drive simulations.

V. Test of the Submodels and the Combined Overall Model

In accordance with the test methodology described in Chapter IV, the individual subnets were first tested using unseen described test data. In the first test series, the individual subnets were tested open loop with perfect input. This corresponds to the quality of a one-step-ahead prediction. Tables I and II show the results with the RMSE over all 3 test drives. It should be noted that the subnets 1-5 each have a temperature in K as a prediction variable and the subnet 6 a relative humidity in %.

The predictions of the NARX networks have significantly lower error rates compared to the predictions with LSTM networks. The error rates of the LSTM networks decrease with increasing network architecture complexity.

TABLE I. *Results of the NARX openloop subnet test*

Number of Hidden Layer Neurons	Number of Delays	RMSE Net 1	RMSE Net 2	RMSE Net 3	RMSE Net 4	RMSE Net 5	RMSE Net 6
5	3	0,0031	0,0035	0,0096	0,0004	0,0001	0,0111
5	6	0,0037	0,0031	0,0024	0,0013	0,0005	0,0052
10	3	0,0036	0,0045	0,0046	0,0017	0,0008	0,0167
10	6	0,0136	0,0031	0,0076	0,0004	0,0001	0,0059
20	3	0,004	0,0029	0,0019	0,0003	0,0003	0,0061
20	6	0,0059	0,018	0,0066	0,0002	0,0005	0,0067

TABLE II. *Results of the LSTM openloop subnet test*

Number of LSTM Units	Number of Delays	RMSE Net 1	RMSE Net 2	RMSE Net 3	RMSE Net 4	RMSE Net 5	RMSE Net 6
5	3	0,1493	0,3373	0,4015	0,1285	0,0918	0,5018
5	6	0,1223	0,3766	0,2651	0,0986	0,0729	0,4065
10	3	0,1087	0,2451	0,2132	0,0806	0,0779	0,3441
10	6	0,1332	0,3416	0,2305	0,0787	0,0723	0,327
20	3	0,1106	0,2442	0,2095	0,0592	0,0692	0,3236
20	6	0,134	0,2909	0,2175	0,0725	0,06	0,3039

In a second test series, the input values of the true past outputs were replaced by the feedback outputs of each subnetwork. This highlighted the error accumulation generated by each subnetwork. Tables III and IV show the results with the averaged RMSE over all 3 test drives. As can be seen from the test results, the error rates for both network types increase in the partially closed loop. The NARX subnet error rate in this test series increases so dramatically that only 4 NARX subnets (Network 1, 2, 4, and 5) perform better than the LSTM subnets.

TABLE III. *Results of the NARX partial closed loop subnet tests*

Number of LSTM Units	Number of Delays	RMSE Net 1	RMSE Net 2	RMSE Net 3	RMSE Net 4	RMSE Net 5	RMSE Net 6
5	3	0,1493	0,3373	0,4015	0,1285	0,0918	0,5018
5	6	0,1223	0,3766	0,2651	0,0986	0,0729	0,4065
10	3	0,1087	0,2451	0,2132	0,0806	0,0779	0,3441
10	6	0,1332	0,3416	0,2305	0,0787	0,0723	0,327
20	3	0,1106	0,2442	0,2095	0,0592	0,0692	0,3236
20	6	0,134	0,2909	0,2175	0,0725	0,06	0,3039

TABLE IV. *Results of the LSTM partial closed loop subnet tests*

Number of LSTM Units	Number of Delays	RMSE Net 1	RMSE Net 2	RMSE Net 3	RMSE Net 4	RMSE Net 5	RMSE Net 6
5	3	1,1777	4,9163	2,3134	0,5887	0,9752	8,8424
5	6	0,5883	5,1189	2,1451	0,586	0,987	13,897
10	3	0,6478	4,2755	2,2007	0,5778	0,969	5,1603
10	6	0,6148	4,9479	2,1204	0,4728	0,9435	4,5458
20	3	0,6237	4,4588	2,1995	0,6136	0,9106	5,547
20	6	0,5667	4,747	2,1876	0,4748	0,8591	3,9582

In the final test series all coupled inputs were replaced by the linked direct and feedback outputs of the coupled individual subnets. For the combined overall model, the sub network structure, which performed best in the second test series, was selected for the respective network types. Table V shows the results with the RMSE for both network types for all 3 test drives. As can be seen from the results, the error rates of the NARX networks increase significantly, while the error rate in the LSTM subnets is almost unchanged compared to the second test series. The error rates of the NARX networks have a greater spread compared to the error rates of the LSTM networks. This is an indication for a better generalization capability of the LSTM networks.

TABLE V. RESULTS OF THE LSTM *OVERALL* CLOSED LOOP TESTS

NARX	RMSE Net 1	RMSE Net 2	RMSE Net 3	RMSE Net 4	RMSE Net 5	RMSE Net 6
Test Drive Simulation 1	7,7141	5,7805	2,6185	9,8997	4,7859	37,936
Test Drive Simulation 2	1,5486	1,2762	0,9869	0,3264	0,1003	43,264
Test Drive Simulation 3	6,3908	1,6349	2,6705	8,4168	4,0662	37,749
LSTM	RMSE Net 1	RMSE Net 2	RMSE Net 3	RMSE Net 4	RMSE Net 5	RMSE Net 6
Test Drive Simulation 1	0,8787	4,8565	2,243	0,7314	0,8758	5,4002
Test Drive Simulation 2	0,5962	2,7291	1,73	0,3627	0,8197	3,7709
Test Drive Simulation 3	0,8667	7,2622	3,3382	0,6307	1,0455	6,5789

In summary, the test results of the overall models for the cabin air and windscreen temperature (Output Network 4 and Network 5) and the relative humidity (Output Network 6) show on average smaller error rates for the LSTM-based overall model.

VI. CONCLUSION

In the experiments, the overall LSTM-based model outperformed the overall NARX-based model for the simulation data tested. This leads to the conclusion that LSTM-based neural networks offer a promising alternative to traditional neural network modeling approaches. However, no conclusion can be drawn regarding the general suitability of the procedures. On the one hand, only a small subset of possible external climatic conditions was mapped with the generated reference data, so that no valid statement can be made about the generalizability for a broad spectrum of climatic boundary conditions. In addition, the networks were trained with "perfect" training data. Therefore, no statement can be made about the ability of the networks to what extent noisy signals or measurement inaccuracies can be compensated. For further evaluation, a wider range of test and training data must be used. To reduce the quality gap to physical reference models, more complex LSTM networks with longer input sequences, a higher number of LSTM units, and a larger number of training epochs may be required. These questions will be the subject of subsequent research based on this paper.

ACKNOWLEDGMENT

The authors acknowledge the financial support by the Federal Ministry of Education and Research of Germany in the framework of "KMU-innovativ: Informations- und Kommunikationstechnologien" within the project "Kataloggestützte interdisziplinäre Entwurfsplattform für Elektrofahrzeuge (KISEL)".

REFERENCES

[1] R. Baumgart, Reduzierung des Kraftstoffverbrauches durch Optimierung von Pkw-Klimaanlagen, Chemnitz, Germany: Dissertation TU Chemnitz, 2010.

[2] C. Haupt, Ein multiphysikalisches Simulationsmodell zur Bewertung von Antriebs- und Wärmemanagementkonzepten im Kraftfahrzeug, München, Germany: Dissertation, TU München, 2012.

[3] D. Ghebru, Modellierung und Analyse des instationären thermischen Verhaltens von Verbrennungsmotor und Gesamtfahrzeug, Frankfurt am Main: Dissertation, Karlsruher Institut für Technologie, 2013.

[4] F. Schueppel, Optimierung des Heiz- und Klimakonzepts zur Reduktion der Wärme- und Kälteleistung im Fahrzeug, Berlin, Germany: Dissertation TU Berlin, 2015.

[5] K. Schröder, S. Wagner, M. Ellinger, „Gekoppelte Simulation der Klimaanlage und Fahrgastzelle unter Berücksichtigung variierender Randbedingungen," in *PKW_Klimatisierung II- Klimakonzepte, Regelungsstrategien und Entwicklungsmethoden heute und in Zukunft*, Essen, expert verlag, 2002, pp. 210-223.

[6] H. Tummescheit, J. Eborn, K. Proessl, S. Foersterling und W. Tegethoff, „AirConditioning: Eine Modelica-Bibliothek zur dynamischen Simulation von Kältekreisläufen," in *PKW-Klimatisierung IV- Klimakonzepte, Zuheizkonzepte, Regelungsstrategien und Entwicklungsmethoden*, Essen, expert verlag, 2007, p. 196214.

[7] R. Domschke und M. Matthes, „In-the-Loop Simulation of Electronic Automatic Temperature Control Systems: HVAC Modeling," in *PKW-Klimatisierung IV- Klimakonzepte, Zuheizkonzepte, Regelungsstrategien und Entwicklungsmethoden*, Essen, expert verlag, 2006, pp. 215-231.

[8] K. Martin, R. Rieberer, S. Alber, J.-J. Robin und T. Schaefer, „Einsatz von numerischer Simulation bei der Entwicklung von Kältekreisläufen," in *PKW-Klimatisierung V-Effiziente Kältekreisläufe, Klimakonzepte für Hybridfahrzeuge und Strategien zur Komfortverbesserung*, Essen, expert verlag, 2007, pp. 77-91.

[9] S. Park, A Comprehensive Thermal Management System Model for Hybrid Electric Vehicles, Michigan, USA: Dissertation, The University of Michigan, 2011.

[10] B. Flieger, Innenraummodellierung einer Fahrzeugkabine in der Programmiersprache Modelica, RWTH Aachen: Dissertation, 2013.

[11] D. Marcos, F. J. Pino, B. Carlos und J. J. Guerra, „The development and validation of a thermal model for the cabin of a vehicle," *Applied Thermal Engineering 66*, pp. 646-656, 2014.

[12] M. Fritz, Entwicklungswerkzeuge für die Fahrzeugklimatisierung von Nutzfahrzeugen, Karlsruhe, Germany: Dissertation, Karlsruher Institut für Technologie (KIT), 2015.

[13] F. Netter, Komplexitätsadaption integrierter Gesamtfahrzeugsimulationen, Karlruhe, Germany: Dissertation, Karlsruher Institut für Technologie (KIT), 2015.

[14] D. Moller, J. Aurich, R. Tröger und C. Grünig,

„Gesamtheitliche Betrachtung des Thermomanagements in Elektrofahrzeugen - Interaktion der Klima- und Kühlsystemkomponenten im Gesamtverbund," in *19. MTZ-Fachtagung Simulation und Test 2017*, Darmstadt, Germany, 2017.

[15] S. Hochreiter und S. Jürgen, „Long Short-Term Memory," in *Neural Computation 9(8): 1735-1780*, München, Germany, 1997.

[16] T. M. Association, „FMI - Functional Mock-Up Interface," [Online]. Available: https://fmi-standard.org/. [Zugriff am 01 03 2019].

[17] G. Mustafarraj, J. Chen und G. Lowry, „Thermal behavior prediction utilizing artificial neural networks for an open office," in *Applied Mathematical Modelling 34 (2010) 3216-3230*, Uxbridge, Middlesex, United Kingdom, 2010.

[18] T. Lu und M. Viljanen, „Prediction of indoor temperature and relative humidity using neural network models: model comparison," in *Neural Comput & Applic 18: 345–357*, Espoo, Finland, 2009.

[19] P. M. Ferreira, A. E. Ruano, S. Silva und C. E.Z.E, „Neural networks based predictive control for thermal comfort and energy savings in public buildings," in *Energy and Buildings 55 238–251*, Portugal, 2012.

[20] A. E. Ruano und P. M. Ferreira, „Neural Network based HVAC Predictive Control," in *Proceedings of the 19th World Congress IFAC*, Cape Town, South Africa, 2014.

[21] T.-Y. Lee, Prediction of Car Cabin Temperature Using Artificial Neural Network, München: Master-Thesis Technische Universität München, 2007.

[22] B. C. Ng, D. I. Z. Mat, H. Jamaluddin und H. M. Kamar, „Application of adaptive neural predictive control for an automotive air conditioning system," in *Applied Thermal Engineering 73 (2014) 1242-1252*, Johor, Malaysia, 2014.

[23] B. C. Ng, D. I. Z. Mat, H. Jamaluddin und H. M. Kamar, „Dynamic modelling of an automotive variable speed air conditioning system using nonlinear autoregressive exogenous neural networks," in *Applied Thermal Engineering 73 (2014) 1253-1267*, Johor, Malaysia, 2014.

[24] TIL Suite: Software package to simulate thermal systems, TLK-Thermo GmbH, Braunschweig, March 2019.

[25] TIL AddOn Automotive: Software package to simulate thermal systems with focus on automolie applications, TLK-Thermo GmbH, Version 3.6.0 [Computer Software], Braunschweig, März 2019.

[26] Rohsenow, M. W.: Boiling, in: Rohsenow, M. W.; Hartnett, P. J; Ganic, E. N. (Editor): Handbook of Heat Transfer Fundamentals,
2. Edition, McGraw-Hill, 1985.

[27] Gnielinski, V.: Neue Gleichungen für den Wärme- und den Stoffübergang in turbulent durchströmten Rohren und Kanälen, in: Forschung im Ingenieurwesen - Engineering Research Vol. 41, Pt. 1, Springer-Verlag, 1975, pp. 8 – 16.

[28] Dittus, F. W.; Boelter, L. M. K.: Heat Transfer in Automobile Radiators of the Tubular Type, in: Publications on Engineering Vol. 2, University of California at Berkeley, 1930, pp. 443 – 461.

[29] Shah, M. M.: A New Correlation for Heat Transfer during Boiling Flow Through Pipes, in: ASHRAE Transac-tions Vol. 82, Pt. 2, American Society of Heating, Refrigerating and Air-Conditioning Engineers - ASHRAE Inc., 1976.

[30] Haaf, S.: Wärmeübertragung in Luftkühlern, in: Steimle, F. (Editor); Stephan, K. (Editor): Handbuch der Kälte-technik Vol. 6, Pt. B, Springer-Verlag, 1988.

[31] McAdams, W. H.; Woods, W. K.; Heroman, L. C.: Vaporization inside horizontal tubes-II-benzene-oil mix-tures, in: Trans. ASME Vol. 64, Pt. 3, The American Society of Mechanical Engineers, 1942, pp. 193 – 200.

[32] Swamee, P. K.; Jain, A. K.: Explicit Equations for Pipe-Flow Problems, in: Journal of the Hydraulics Division, Vol. 102, Pt. 5, ASCE - American Society of Civil Engineers, 1976, pp. 657 – 664.

[33] TIL AddOn Cabin: Software package to simulate thermal systems with focus on automobile interiors, TLK-Thermo GmbH, Version 3.6.0 [Computer Software], Braunschweig, März 2019.

Flood Prediction through Artificial Neural Networks

A case study in Goslar, Lower Saxony

Pascal Goymann, Dirk Herrling, and Andreas Rausch
Institute for Software and Systems Engineering
Clausthal University of Technology
Clausthal-Zellerfeld, Germany
e-mail: {firstname.lastname}@tu-clausthal.de

***Abstract*—In this project, a system was developed, which allows a flood prediction based on given data sets for a level measuring station in the Goslar area for a period of four hours. First, existing neural networks, which were developed during a seminar at the TU Clausthal, were extended with the help of the framework Tensorflow and investigated whether larger water level values and further flood scenarios allow good qualitative prognoses. Furthermore, the influencing factors of possible floods were identified based on past scenarios. In addition to gauge and precipitation measuring stations in the immediate vicinity of Goslar, weather data from the Institute of Electrical Information Technology (IEI), which have been available every 15 minutes since 2003, were also taken into consideration. These data sets were processed and evaluated accordingly, so that a qualitative prediction can be made for exact water gauge heights. In addition, in order to reduce the training time, a dimension extraction was performed using a Principal Component Analysis (PCA), in which main components were identified and the data set examined for patterns in order to determine the possibility of a dimension reduction. In order to transfer the neural network to further scenarios, a prediction was made for the area of Bad Harzburg, where two measuring stations with additional weather data were used as inputs.**

Keywords-Machine learning; Neural networks; PCA; Feedforward neural networks; Flood prediction.

I. INTRODUCTION

Floods are events, which, depending on the region and their characteristics, can have devastating consequences for people and their homes. At first, it is not always quite clear which exact interrelationships have been involved in the development of these events and have led to the subsequent catastrophe. Even if several flood events have occurred in the same region over the years, different reasons may have led to the individual incidents. This also applies to the area around Goslar, a town in the northwestern part of the Harz in the federal state of Lower Saxony. In July 2017, probably the most devastating natural disaster of the last century occurred here. Within only two days, 306 l/m^2 (according to the records of Harzwasserwerke GmbH at the Eckertalsperre) of rainfall fell in the immediate vicinity. This rainfall could be recorded at the gauging stations installed there in the period from 24.07. 9:00 am to 26.07. 12:00 pm [1]. The reason for this high precipitation could be found quickly and can be traced back to the low-pressure area "Alfred", which led to many floods in other areas in the northern Harz.

Another example concerned 10 May 2018 (Ascension Day). Here, precipitation of up to 100 l/m^2 fell within a few hours, with the Abzucht, a tributary river of the Oker, which was still largely responsible for the flood in the previous year, remaining far below the critical limit. Both situations show that although precipitation can play an important role, it is limited to a certain catchment area and can lead to flooding due to the direction of water flow in the local environment. Experience has also shown that other variables, such as soil moisture or snow melting must also be considered in order to be able to make accurate statements about whether there is a risk of flooding.

An evaluation of all theoretically possible parameters and measuring stations would take a lot of time and is currently already being implemented by an external warning system from the "Harzwasserwerke". Different predictions e.g., for precipitation and temperatures are compiled and evaluated manually. The problem that arises at this point is the resulting warning time of approx. 20 minutes. This period is not sufficient for a complete preparation of the local fire brigade. In order to increase this early warning time and to be able to make a qualitative statement about a future flood, a self-learning neural network will be created which automatically predicts a future (possible) exceeding of a threshold value at a water gauge measuring station. For this purpose, historical weather data as well as water level and rainfall data from the immediate vicinity of Goslar are used, which are fed into the neuronal network and used for training. The network optimizes the data based on the previously processed data and then provides information on whether there is a risk of flooding for another independent set of test data.

In the beginning existing work was taken up to check whether a flood can be predicted. These were evaluated and improved in order to be able to predict exact water levels with a maximum deviation of 5cm. Finally, a transfer to another scenario in Bad Harzburg takes place, where a flood prediction for another environment is made using another measuring station.

Section 2 starts with two related works, which have already dealt with similar topics. In section 3 a short explanation of the preliminary work is given, which has already investigated this topic in the context of a seminar at the TU Clausthal. Based of this works, a forecast of floods in Goslar is finally made. This serves to investigate whether an improvement of their algorithms can be made. Then a prediction of exact water levels is made. This forecast is then examined for dimensional reduction using a Principal Component Analysis (PCA) and evaluated for another scenario in Bad Harzburg. Section 4 briefly lists and compares two further alternative learning methods. In the end section 5 concludes with an explanation of the further outlook.

II. Related Work

In this section, two related works are taken up, which deal with similar topics. The first work deals with a service provided by Google, which is part of the Google Public Alerts Program and can use Artificial Intelligence (AI) to predict floods in the Indian region and then send warnings to the inhabitants [2]. The second work deals with an AI technology for reliably predicting earthquakes in different parts of the world [3].

A. Google Public Alerts

In 2017, Google provided special warning services within Google Maps, Google Now and in the normal Google search to warn affected people of imminent disasters. These include storm warnings, hurricane evacuation alerts, forest fires and earthquakes. The data is made available by the cooperation partners from the USA, Australia, Canada, Colombia, Japan, Taiwan, Indonesia, Mexico, the Philippines, India, New Zealand and Brazil, collected by Google and displayed for all users worldwide. Only early flood warnings were not made available to users on this platform. Since these were not offered by the cooperating partners, Google has developed its own service, which uses Artificial Intelligence to predict flood catastrophes. Using historical weather and flood events, as well as river level measurement stations and terrain conditions, these data are processed and fed into a neural network and then simulated on maps [4]. The subsequent prediction results are stored in Google Public Alerts with the severity of the event.

For a first test with real data, Google Public Alerts was released in September 2018 in the Patna region in India and first floods were successfully predicted. India's central water authority is working closely with Google to achieve better results in the future, which can be better achieved by Google than by the authorities themselves due to its technical expertise and the computing power it provides. In the future, cooperation's with Europe will also be realized in order to make similar predictions and make them available to users. In this case, interfaces would have to be created to enable Google to have permanent access to data.

B. Artificial Intelligence based techniques for earthquake prediction

A second elaboration [3] also deals with an early warning system, which was built based on Artificial Intelligence. Here, the prediction was not of floods but of earthquakes, whereby different approaches for the realization of such systems were compared with each other. Basically, earthquakes can be characterized by two properties. This is on the one hand the magnitude and on the other hand the depth. Those that are classified as fundamentally dangerous are those that are at a shallow depth and have a high magnitude. These are weighted correspondingly higher in the neuronal network. Based on input data from southern California, archived in the Southern California Earthquake Data Center (SCEC), earthquakes were tested in a Probabilistic Neural Network (PNN) of various strengths, of which 102 out of 127 earthquakes were successfully detected in the test data sets of classes 1 to 3.
Stronger earthquakes were also used in the test data sets. These were not successfully detected according to the paper, so instead of PNNs RNNs (Recurrent Neural Networks) for magnitudes from 6.0 were investigated [5]. In data preprocessing, the area is divided into smaller regions and the time in which the earthquake occurred into several time slots. Subsequently, these sections were processed including their relation to larger earthquakes in the investigated region.
Another scenario presented here concerns Chile. For this purpose, a Novel Neural Network, which predicts whether an earthquake will occur or not over the next five days [6]. The earthquakes used for this purpose were taken from two earthquake catalogues [7] and [8], which record all seismological activities in South America. Earthquakes from a magnitude of 4.5 in the period from 1957 to 2007 were used for this purpose.

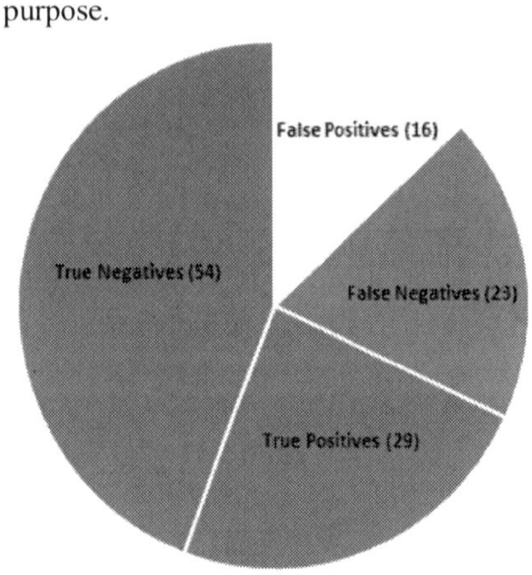

Figure 1. Pie chart for the earthquake forecast of the Chile Peninsula [6]

The training and test procedure took place in various regions in Chile, whereby different warning times and earthquake magnitudes were used. On average, results were close to 71%. From the 122 earthquakes defined in the test data, a pie chart was created, which is shown in Figure 1. Here, not only the occurrence of an earthquake was predicted, but also its strength, whereby a deviation of 1% flowed into the result.

III. Implementation and Results

A. Preliminary work

In the context of a seminar at the Clausthal University of Technology, three seminar papers on this topic were written, which dealt with the help of different AI frameworks (CNTK from Microsoft, Tensorflow from Google and Caffe from the University of California, Berkeley) and the previously defined

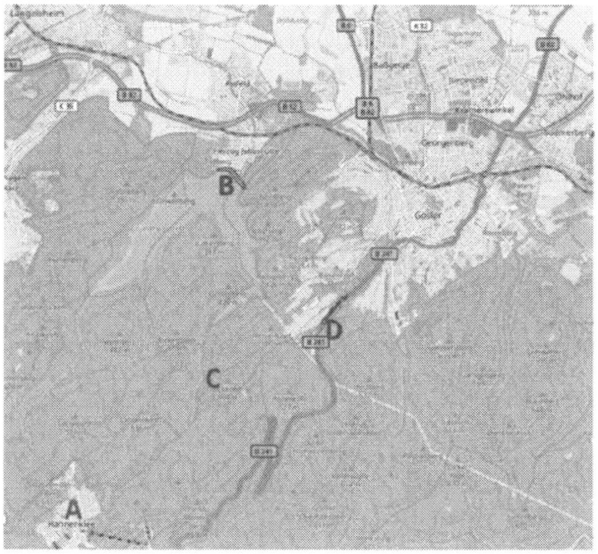

Figure 2. Used measuring stations: source (modified): openstreetmap.org

problem [9] [10] [11]. It was their task to create a neural network based on given data and to determine the data and result quality on this basis. It should be identified if that framework is suitable for this problem and how the result can still be improved. Two data sets were provided:

- A training data set from 01.11.2003 to 03.12.2012 consisting of approx. 80000 data points in 1-hour intervals
- A test data set from 14.06.2015 to 01.01.2018 consisting of approx. 22000 data points in 1-hour intervals

Both data sets contained the water levels (cm) and flow rates (m^3/s) at the water level measuring stations Sennhütte and the Margarethenklippe, rainfall data (mm) in Hahnenklee and the Granetalsperre. In addition, weather data were provided by the Institute for Electrical Information Technology at Clausthal University of Technology. These contained the temperature, the humidity, the air pressure, the solar radiation, the wind speed and the wind direction, whereby an average over the period of one hour took place. In addition, each data point was assigned a label $\in [0,1]$ indicating if flooding had occurred. Decisive for this was the water level at the water level measuring point Sennhütte, whereby it was defined that the water level of 40cm marked a flood. The measuring stations are shown in Figure 2 on a map (A: Hahnenklee, B: Granetalsperre, C: Margarethenklippe, D: Sennhütte).

The task was to make a flood prediction for the location Sennhütte with an early warning period of one or 48 hours. In order to achieve this, the provided data was processed. The average values of the last 2, 4, 8, 16 and 32 hours of rainfall were used for the input vector by a supposed connection between the water quantities in the rivers and the past precipitation values. The same procedure was used for the temperature values. Similarly, the seminar participants formed the averages of the individual water levels and air pressures over 1, 2, 3 and 4 hours. After processing, the data was fed into the neuronal network.

For all three seminar papers, the results for the prediction of one hour are presented in the Figures 3-5. For this purpose, a confusion matrix was created, which compares the results of the prediction and the results in the test data set. The correctly predicted results were highlighted in green, while the false alarms (false positives) were highlighted in yellow and the false negatives in red. This has the background that the false-negative results should be avoided altogether, as they would have devastating consequences by an incoming flood. The false positives should also converge towards 0, as this would result in unnecessary deployment of the emergency services. The consequences, however, would be manageable and have a lower damage potential.

Confusion matrix		Label	
		Flood	No Flood
Prediction	Flood	54	2
	No Flood	9	11008

Figure 3. Result with Framework Caffe [9]

Confusion matrix		Label	
		Flood	No Flood
Prediction	Flood	62	57
	No Flood	1	11053

Figure 4. Result with Framework CNTK [10]

Confusion matrix		Label	
		Flood	No Flood
Prediction	Flood	80	47
	No Flood	3	11031

Figure 5. Result with Framework Tensorflow [11]

In all three elaborations, a two-hour and four-hour forecast was discussed in more detail following the 1-hour forecast. Similar results could be achieved, which only worsened significantly with an increase to eight hours. For this reason, the further investigation of this work will concentrate on a 4-hour forecast, which would represent a considerable improvement in view of the warning time currently in use.

B. Prediction for higher water levels

Based on the preliminary work of the seminar participants, their algorithms should first be examined for major flood hazards. For this purpose, the water levels, which characterize floods, were increased to 50, 60, 70 and 80 cm. For better results, the data from the measuring stations were processed at 15-minute intervals instead of one hour. Like the preliminary work, the precipitation data at the measuring stations of the Granetalsperre and Hahnenklee were averaged over 1, 2, 4, 8, 16 and 32 hours and fed into the net as additional parameters. The values of the last 1, 2, 3, 4 and 5 hours were calculated for the outflow and water level measurements at the Margarethenklippe and the Sennhütte and fed into the neuronal network as additional dimensions.

In order to guarantee an even better quality, the same weather data set was used that was already used in the seminar papers. From these the average temperatures of the last 1, 2, 4, 8, 16, 32 hours were calculated and transferred together with the air humidity, the air pressure at the considered time, as well as before 1, 2, 3 and 4 hours into the input vector. The considered solar irradiation value and the wind speed were taken over in addition.

For the prediction of higher water levels, moving averages were formed which, in contrast to the arithmetic mean, are not formed over all data records, but only over a selected period. In this case, for example, this applies to temperatures of up to 32 hours and 128 data records. For the classification of the network, a label was created, which can be used for different Scenarios indicated if there was a flood (0=no flood, 1=flood). In order to consider data sets that indicate a flood hazard during the training process of the neural network more, an additional field is added to the input vector called "weight". This tells the network how often this data set should be trained in comparison to the data that do not represent a flood hazard. It is calculated from the ratio between the data sets with the label 1 and the label 0 used in the training data set. In addition to the data preparation, the scenarios to be tested were also determined. These were a total of 12, whereof the water levels of 50, 60, 70 and 80cm with a warning time of 1, 2 and 4 hours were considered. Good forecasts were achieved for all forecasts. This also affected the events with a four-hour warning time.

Two hidden layers with a neuron count of 128 and 64 neurons were used for the network architecture. The sigmoid function was used as activation function, which carried out the training with a learning rate of 0.001 and 10000 training steps. The optimization function for this case was the Proximal Adagrad-Optimizer. Figure 6 shows the confusion matrix at a water level of 50cm and an hour warning time.

Confusion matrix		Label	
		Flood	No Flood
Prediction	Flood	195	413
	No Flood	0	156024

Figure 6. Confusion matrix at 50cm water level and one hour warning time

The number of false negatives could be completely reduced to zero. This applies to all scenarios listed above in the same way. In addition, 413 results were issued as false alarms, which, like the preliminary work, was largely due to a better early warning period, in which the occurrence of a flood event was predicted too early. Since the confusion matrices for the other eleven scenarios contained similar values, these are not listed here.

C. *Prediction for concrete water levels*

After the prediction of flood events for different scenarios, the prediction of exact water levels will be dealt in the following. The same data basis was used as for the previous prediction. The forecast was made for the gauging station in Sennhütte. Since only a few floods were available in the database from 2003 to 2018 and their level levels varied, two different training and test data sets were distinguished for this prediction:

- A test data set from 2014 to 2018 and a training data set from 2003 to 2013
- A test data set from 2003 to 2008 and a training data set from 2009 to 2018

Since a neural network can only learn the water levels that were made available to it in the training set, it was not possible in the first case to correctly predict the water levels of the 2017 flood because these were outside the value range. For this reason, the order was reversed and this flood was integrated into the training data set.

In order to enable the neural network to correctly learn less frequently occurring water levels in the training set, all data points have been assigned a weight indicating how often the corresponding water level should be trained in the data set. The rarer the water level appears in the entire training data set, the higher the number of training runs in the neural network for this one data set.

In contrast to the prediction for higher water levels more neurons were used in this scenario. For the first hidden layer these were 512 and for the second hidden layer 256 neurons. Furthermore, the sigmoid function was used again as activation function and the Proximal Adagrad-Optimizer as optimization function, again with a learning rate of 0.001. Only the number of training steps was adjusted in the parameters. So, this has increased from 10000 training steps to 100000 steps, because the best prediction results could be achieved.

For the test cases, 170 (largest measured water level) different classes were created, which were used as classification basis for the data sets. In the prediction, the neural network finally assigned each data point to a class, whereby the actual and target states could be compared with each other. Tables 1 and 2 show the results of both predictions.

TABLE 1 PREDICTION FOR 2014-2018 (157611 RECORDS)

Difference greater than [cm]	**Number of data sets**	**Accuracy [%]**
0	7429	95.29
1	356	99.77
2	184	99.88
3	147	99.91
4	127	99.92
5	113	99.93

TABLE 2 PREDICTION FOR 2003-2008 (181026 RECORDS)

Difference greater than [cm]	**Number of data sets**	**Accuracy [%]**
0	12571	93.056
1	1741	99.04
2	740	99.59
3	367	99.8
4	207	99.89
5	131	99.93

On the one hand, the tables contain the number of data sets whose values in the prediction differ from those in reality by a certain amount and on the other hand the ratio of these to the total number of data sets. Both tables show good results, which show an accuracy of 99% at a water level difference of 1cm

D. Principal Component Analysis (PCA)

From the amount of data used so far, it is not possible to deduce which attributes have the greatest impact on the training and results of the neural network. An identification of the most important influencing factors allows a reduction of the input data and computing time, as well as a de-noising of the data set. An overfitting of the network is also limited by the dimension reduction, since a larger number of dimensions leads to a larger adjustment of the neural network. to get better results.

In the following, a Principal Component Analysis (PCA) is presented, which calculates possible main components based on linear combinations and enables a dimension reduction on of these. For this purpose, the original dimensions p are reduced to a smaller number of dimensions q, which summarize the essential information of the p dimensions.

First, the data set is standardized in order to ensure a correct distribution of the individual characteristics and to realize independence from the value ranges. From this standardized data set, a covariance matrix is created, which contains the covariance of each attribute with every other attribute. The eigenvalues and eigenvectors are calculated from this covariance matrix. The eigenvectors form the main components, while the corresponding eigenvalues signal how much information is contained in them [12]. The p eigenvectors with the largest eigenvalues are then filtered out. This serves to form a transformation matrix T consisting of m rows (number of dimensions) and p columns (number of eigenvectors). The following 12 attributes were selected for the realization of the PCA in this paper: rainfall from Hahnenklee and the Granetalsperre, outflow and water levels of the Margarethenklippe and the Sennhütte, as well as weather data consisting of temperature, air humidity, air pressure, radiation, wind speed and wind direction, in each case in the interval of one hour, resulting in 102040 data records. The first main component is obtained by minimizing the sum of the squared deviations of all variables. In other words, to extract the first component, the portion of variance that the component can explain across all variables is maximized. The remaining variance is then explained step by step. This means that the second component should clarify as much residual variance as possible. This procedure continues until the total variance of all data is theoretically explained by the main components.

The first seven main components of the Principal Component Analysis would be sufficient to maintain 90 percent variance. These account for 93.27 percent of the total variance, so a reduction from twelve to seven dimensions would only result in a 6.73 percent loss of information. Using these results, it can be concluded that all data from the measuring stations would be sufficient to have a large part of the information. The weather data only have an influence of 6.73 percent on the total information content and could therefore be discarded.

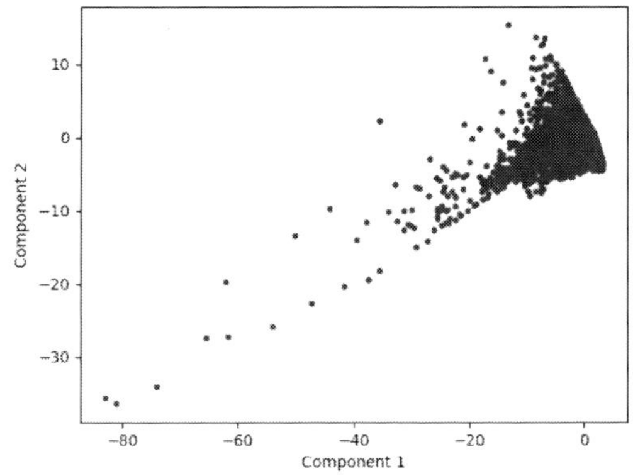

Figure 7. Reduction to 2 dimensions

The Reduction means that the computation time and memory problems can be decreased, as fewer dimensions are included in the calculation without a significant loss of the prediction quality. Figure 7 shows a reduction to two dimensions, with clustering of the data points around the coordinate origin.

E. Bad Harzburg area

The following is a review of the neural network for a further Scenario outside the previously considered catchment area. For this purpose, the region around Bad Harzburg with one precipitation and one outflow/level measuring station each installed at the Baste was examined more closely.

Since in contrast to Goslar only two measuring points were available, the values for soil moisture (only derived), air temperature and precipitation, provided by the "Deutschen Wetterdienst" at 10-minute intervals, were also used. In total, this resulted in 520128 data records.

The task was to predict water levels of 50, 60, 70 and 80cm for one, two and four hours and to evaluate them by the flood from 24.07.2017 to 27.07.2017. After the data preparation, the data set was labelled. All data points which exceeded the flood threshold value were assigned the code number 1. All other data points were given the value 0. Another field contained a weight that trained data sets that signaled flood hazard more frequently in the network than data that did not.

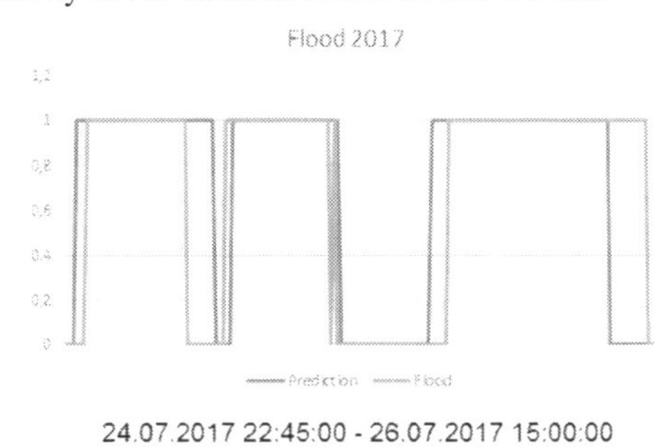

Figure 8. Prediction for Bad Harzburg at a water level of 80cm and two hours

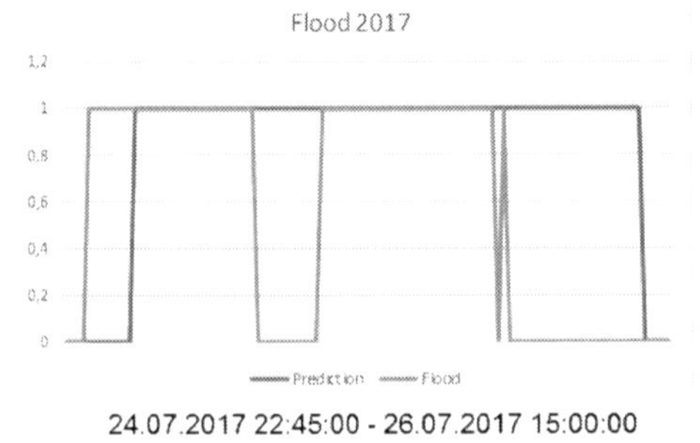

Figure 9. Prediction for Bad Harzburg at a water level of 80cm and four hours

The results of the prediction presented at Figure 8 and 9 are exemplary for a two- and four-hour prediction for a threshold value of 80cm. At first glance, it is clear that good results were obtained for an advance warning time of two hours, but that these results clearly deteriorated with an increase to four hours.

In order to enable a comparability with the results of the level measuring station Sennhütte, the same parameters were used for the creation, the training and the testing of the neuronal network. These parameters included the learning rate (0.001), the number of training sessions (10000) and the number of hidden layers (2 with a neuron count of 128 and 64 neurons). The activation function was the sigmoid function and the optimization function the Proximal Adagrad-Optimizer. For this reason, it can be concluded that the number and location of the gauge, outflow and precipitation measuring stations have a major impact on the quality of the results and that it might be advisable to add more for better results.

IV. Alternative Methods

This paper deals with Artificial Neural Networks (ANN), which in this case were excellently suited for supervised learning. There are also alternative methods such as Regression Trees or Ensemble Learning that can also be used. Regression Trees belong to the group of decision trees and deal with the mapping of decision rules to a branched tree, which is then traversed from the root to the individual leaves based on various decisions.

With regression trees a continuous value is mapped on the individual leaves (e.g., a time series analysis), so the aim of this method is the prediction of continuous values. This has the advantage that for small amounts of data it is easy to understand which decision is made at which moment. However, this clarity decreases considerably with an increasing number of decisions. A further problem here is the overfitting, in which the error increases continuously with new test data records at a certain point [13].

In contrast to other methods, Ensemble Learning uses several different learning algorithms at the same time. A set of predictors (ensemble) is formed, which together form an average (ensemble average). In this way, certain outliers can be corrected by other learning methods. If there is a method that is best suited to the problem, it will outperform most other learning methods in ensemble learning. Furthermore, the more methods used, the more difficult it will be to interpret the results. The biggest restriction, however is the learning time. The more methods are used, the longer the algorithm needs to calculate the prediction result, which is the reason why this work is limited to only one learning procedure [14].

V. Conclusions

The aim of this work was to establish, train and evaluate a neural network for the detection of flood hazards and concrete water levels in the area around Goslar. In addition, existing works were examined, trained and tested for the recognition of flood inlets starting from a higher water level. Increasing the warning time to four hours produced very good results. All floods in the period from 2003 to 2018 were successfully detected and predicted accordingly. A reduction of false alarms was successfully achieved, but some were left over time, which in some cases resulted in false positive predictions. This, however, was usually related to a danger that had already occurred shortly before. Further water level, precipitation and outflow measuring stations could be used to identify further floods outside the area (here: Sennhütte). For example, the flood of 10 May 2018 did not appear in the data, but was defined as a flood hazard.

In addition to the identification of floods, the prediction of exact water levels was also a task of this work. The same data sets as for the flood prediction were used to divide the data into two scenarios. For each scenario, it was necessary to predict the water levels at the Sennhütte with a maximum deviation of 5cm. The results showed an accuracy of close to 99% from a difference of 1cm, only higher water levels, which were either outside the value range of or only with a very small number in the training datasets were not detected and were above the 5 cm deviation limit. In order to obtain better results for the higher water levels, further floods in the training data would be necessary.

The consideration of a dimension reduction for the selected data set with 12 dimensions has shown that seven dimensions would be enough for over 90 percent variance conservation. As an alternative classification method an LDA [15] can be used. When using a discriminant function two or more groups can be examined simultaneously for a plurality of characteristic variables. Furthermore, new objects whose class affiliation is not known can be rearranged. Later collected data can be easily assigned.

The evaluation for the area of Bad Harzburg was also able to precisely detect and predict floods up to a warning time of two hours. When this time was increased to four hours, the accuracy was no longer sufficient. An addition of further measuring stations to determine the water levels, outflow quantities and precipitation could produce a similar result quality as for the area around Goslar.

Until now, the measurement of the prediction quality has only been calculated using confusion matrices, which did not provide a meaningful evaluation of false alarms. For a better determination of the quality of the neuronal network, another method can be used, called cross-validation method [16]. The most frequently used method is k-fold cross-validation. At the beginning there is a division of the data into k equal parts, also called folds. Subsequently, the network is run through k times, where k-1 folds are used as training data set and the remaining fold as test data set. With each further run a different fold is used as test data set, so at the end of the validation procedure k accuracies are available from which the arithmetic mean will be formed. The multiple runs of the net with different folds provide information about the sensitivity of the net, since each data point in the data set was available exactly once in the test data set.

The preprocessing of the time series of the different measuring stations and weather data can also be replaced by a recurrent neural network. Here, the data of the past time points are stored in the input layer. A recurrent neural network can use this information, which are stored internally.

ACKNOWLEDGEMENT

At this point I would like to thank all the people who supported me in the preparation of this paper. My special thanks go to the Harzwasserwerke (HWW) for providing the data from the measuring stations in Goslar and Bad Harzburg, as well as to the Institute of Electrical Information Technology for providing the data at the weather station located there.

REFERENCES

[1] NLWKN, The July flood 2017 in southern Lower Saxony, 2017

[2] J. Vincent, *Google is using AI to predict floods in India and warn users. [Online].* Available from: https://www.theverge.com/2018/9/25/17900018/google-ai-predictions-flooding-india-public-alerts. [retrieved: 04, 2019].

[3] F. Azam, M. Sharif, M. Yasmin, and S. Mohsin, "Artificial Intelligence Based Techniques For Earthquake Prediction: A Review", Science International, vol. 26, pp. 1495 – 1502, 2014.

[4] Y. Matias, *Keeping people safe with AI-enabled flood forecasting. [Online]. Available from:* https://www.blog.google/products/search/helping-keep-people-safe-ai-enabled-flood-forecasting/. [retrieved: 04, 2019].

[5] H. Adeli, and A. Panakkat, "A probabilistic neural network for earthquake magnitude prediction", Neural networks : the official journal of the International Neural Network Society, vol. 22, pp. 1018-24, doi: 10.1016/j.neunet.2009.05.003.

[6] J. Reyes, and V. H. Cárdenas, "A Chilean seismic regionalization through a Kohonen neural network", Neural Computing and Applications, vol. 19, pp. 1081-1087, doi: 10.1007/s00521-010-0373-9.

[7] Ceresis catalog. *Earthquake catalogue for South America.* [Online]. Available from: http//www.ceresis.org./. [retrieved: 04, 2019].

[8] Usgsr, *Earthquake Hazards Program.* [Online]. Available from: https://earthquake.usgs.gov/. [retrieved: 04, 2019].

[9] S. Rupsch, Prediction of floods through neuronal networks using the framework Caffe, unpublished.

[10] R. Kern, Flood prediction with the Machine Learning Framework Microsoft Cognitive Toolkit, unpublished.

[11] H. Rosenberg, Flood prediction with Tensorflow, unpublished.

[12] H. Lohninger, *Principal Component Analysis (PCA).* [Online]. Available from: http://www.statistics4u.info/fundstat_germ/cc_pca.html. [retrieved: 04, 2019].

[13] Popular Decision Tree: Classification and Regression Trees (C&RT). [Online]. Available from: http://www.statsoft.com/Textbook/Classification-and-Regression-Trees. [retrieved: 04, 2019].

[14] R. Polikar, Rowan University, *Ensemble learning.* [Online]. Available from: http://www.scholarpedia.org/article/Ensemble_learning. [retrieved: 04, 2019].

[15] V. Zeissler, Robust recognition of prosodic phenomena and emotional user states in a multimodal dialogue system, Studien zur Mustererkennung, Logos Verlag Berlin, pp. 165-166, 2012.

[16] A. C. Müller, and S. Guido, Introduction to Machine Learning with Python: Practical Data Science Knowledge, O'Reilly, pp. 236ff, , 2017.

A Data Driven Approach for Efficient Re-utilization of Traction Batteries

Christian Kreutzmann, Priyanka Sharma, Sebastian Lawrenz
Clausthal University of Technology, Institute for Software and Systems Engineering
Arnold-Sommerfeldstraße 1
Clausthal-Zellerfeld, Germany
email: { christian.kreutzmann|priyanka.sharma|sebastian.lawrenz}@tu-clausthal.de

***Abstract*— As electric cars become more and more affordable to broader parts of our society the number of new registrations start to increase. Inevitably, an increased number of resources consuming cars bring new challenges to raw material supply and electrical power networks based renewable sources. Traction batteries are used in electric cars for power. An approach to solve both issues is second -life applications for used traction batteries. Second-life applications are a way of reusing traction batteries, which cannot be used in electric cars anymore due to challenging requirements. One way of using the traction batteries in their second-life is to use them for maintaining a fixed frequency on electrical networks even if peaking demand cannot be matched by a sufficient supply. As high availability in these power networks requires suitable storage. It lowers material consumption for otherwise newly produced battery systems and reduces costs for the second-life applications users. Nevertheless, the current state of recycling and identification of potential second-life batteries are highly cost intensive but can be improved by usage and combination of data. In this paper, we explore an approach for using data to increase efficiency and reduce the cost of second-life applications of traction batteries in electric cars. But in order to move to a data driven approach for re-utilization of traction batteries, there are various challenges in the existing system. We identify these challenges and propose solutions.**

Keywords-recycling; electric-vehicles; traction batteries; data driven; blockchain

I. INTRODUCTION

The current change of mobility concepts from conventional to electric-cars leads to several upcoming challenges. First of all, the composition of the entire vehicle itself differs vastly from current vehicles as electric powertrains depend on rare and expensive raw materials. Just to name tantalum, nickel and lithium [1]. Furthermore, societies endeavor to alter their power supplies away from centralized and ecologically damaging power plants to smaller, decentralized and emission friendly technologies [2]. In order to maintain safe and reliable power supply, vast amounts of storage capacity have to be available. This is due to the nature of most renewable energy sources as they highly depend on wind or sun exposure. An approach to solve the lack of high available storage power is to use batteries in special facilities or even on a consumer level. The high cost for the batteries itself plays a big role in the economic feasibility and slower the spread of this approach.

One way to reduce costs and improve ecological impact is to reuse traction batteries after the vehicle or the battery exceeded an end of life criteria. Traction batteries are responsible to supply the electric powertrain with energy. They operate in high voltage spectrum. Since material consumption for producing new batteries can be avoided. This so called second-life approach which lowers the initial investment costs for battery-based power storage solutions and improves a net present value up to 33% after 20 years following for business orientated use [2]. Core process for a sufficient implementation of a second-life concept is the identification of traction batteries and their current state of health in order to be able to determine their potential for another use case or a safe recycling route. The current state of battery health can be determined by the battery impedance and the battery capacity [3]. Both information is saved in the battery management system of each battery but can so far only be accessed by the original equipment manufacturer. Third parties must rely on own measurements which involves a big workload and therefore costs for a save and reliable categorization. Just to name the process of capacity determination, it involves tempering each battery on a set temperature and load the battery till no more loading is possible. In a next step, the battery must be discharged, and the current has to be measured which results in a value for the available capacity. While present amounts of returning electric vehicles remain relatively low, compared to conventional vehicles, current dismantling processes and categorizing of each traction battery strongly relies on OEMs [4]. But with, further increasing flows third parties can be expected to play a big role in the whole dismantling industry.

During the life of an electric vehicle, a lot of data is generated by several participants, which, after being used for its initial purpose, is not being collected and put into relation to each other. An approach to increase the efficiency of the recycling industry is to improve the information exchange between all the stakeholders, which are part of the circular economy [5]. Especially second-life applications are using the data of the traction batteries throughout its lifecycle in order to define their further areas of application. If the battery could be tracked in its entire lifecycle the relevant data from it can be used to optimize the dismantling process and to determine the second-life applications of traction batteries. However, there are some challenges in the existing systems. We identify these challenges, such as access to the battery data, difficulties in estimating the batteries health easily and providing a secure and trusted platform for storing and accessing data.

The rest of the paper is structured as following. Section II. gives a brief overview of related work. The lifecycle of traction battery and the stakeholders are shown in Section III. Section IV. presents the identified challenges. An approach to solve the identified problems is described in Section V. In Section VI. an example of application scenario is presented. Section VII. shows the evaluation plan. Finally, Section VIII. concludes and gives insights of the future work.

II. STATE OF THE ART

As mentioned in the motivation of this paper the current number of new electric car registrations is strongly increasing in countries such as Germany. Nevertheless, remains relatively low compared to the number of conventional car registration [6]. Nevertheless, the prospects are seemingly good for battery-based mobility concepts and therefore a sufficient process for occurring waste streams should be conducted. An approach for a possible solution can be seen in China. Due to high amounts of emissions in local cities, policies were focusing and emphasizing electric vehicles over the last years. In order to obtain an efficient recycling route for upcoming amounts of waste streams, China introduced a first traceability management platform for traction batteries [7]. It aims to trace the whole lifecycle of a battery and use the data for a better recycling track. Not only original equipment manufacturers but also battery producers and recycling companies need to register themselves on the platform and each battery is tracked using a unique identification number.

Another corresponding approach in keeping track of used materials in the car industry is the International Material Data System [8] (IMDS). Currently 35 OEMs and around 120.000 suppliers provide data of used materials in their products. The IMDS is than for example the basis for an EU type approval.

Furthermore, there are already existing solutions for circular economy concepts. For end-of-life vehicles are existing already strategic planning and optimization approaches to find optimal network configurations [9]-[10].

In other industries, an increase in efficiency through the targeted use of data has long been established. A good example for this is logistic. Since the introduction of Enterprise Resource Management System, the efficiency was increased highly [11].

III. TRACTION BATTERY LIFECYCLE

Defining a relevant lifecycle for traction batteries used in electric cars is challenging. In order to keep a simple overview of the lifecycle, in this paper we present only the core relevant stakeholders. Figure 1 illustrates the adopted lifecycle of a traction batteries with previously mentioned stakeholders in focus.

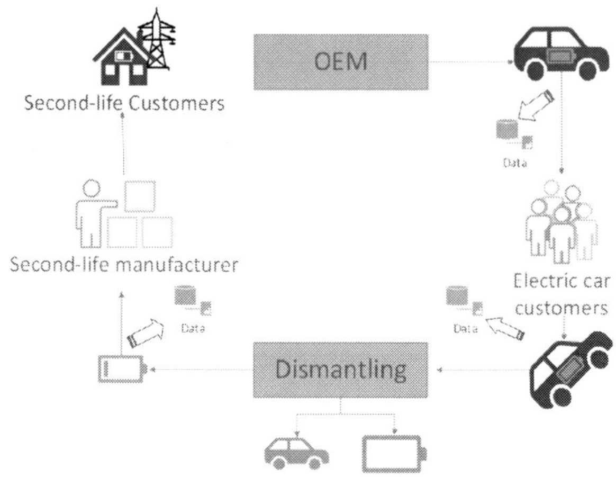

Figure 1: Lifecycle of traction battery.

The **Original Equipment Manufactur**er (OEM) can be seen as the starting point of the life of a traction battery and electric vehicle. First market design, production and sales are executed by the OEM. In this process a set of data such as installed battery technology, set up of battery management system and unique vehicle identification number is being generated but not accessible without the OEM's interfaces.

The next step of the examined lifecycle are the vehicle **customers**. Depending on the individual use case a vehicle can be transferred to numerous owners. Currently the only safe way to keep track of ownership are the corresponding vehicle registration documents. This data is sometimes not digital and therefore lost for other use cases. Furthermore, while being used the vehicle generates vast amounts of data. This includes data concerning the current state of health of a battery or general usage profiles. This data can if only be accessed by the OEM or associated partners and not by other participants.

After being used to a certain degree an electric vehicle will be brought back to a suitable dismantling process. Currently only the OEM's are qualified to dismantle high voltage systems from their own electric cars in a greater scale. It is to be assumed that with greater amounts of returning vehicles this process will be executed by third parties such as qualified **dismantlers**. Comparable solutions are already in place for conventional vehicles since many years. The dismantler needs to identify certain groups of batteries in order to decide for a different track. Either the batteries qualify for a second-life application or merely a recycling process. As explained in the motivation the data for a fast and reliable decision is only to be accessed by solutions provided by an OEM or must be conducted through a time and cost consuming process of measuring and evaluation each battery manually.

Following the end of first lifecycle, after being dismantled and potentially grouped in a qualified track, the batteries are being used by **second-life manufacturers** to build new products. In this process data of the state of health and potential use scenarios of each battery is needed and is, in an ideal case, provided by the dismantling shareholder.

The final second life product is than being used by a second life customer in a suitable use case. Vastly in a fixed location and till a second end of life criteria will be matched.

IV. IDENTIFIED CHALLENGES

Second-life applications of traction batteries have many advantages. Once the battery is no longer usable in the vehicle, they can be implemented in other systems such as maintaining electric networks. We identify that using the data of the battery lifecycles can help all the stakeholders in the chain. Mainly the second life manufacturer as they can easily determine the battery's health by seeing the data of its lifecycle. This on one hand reduces the cost of manufacturing second life applications and on other hand increases the efficiency of second life application as the health of the battery is well recognized. But there are various problems in the existing systems for the required data flow. We identify the following challenges as the main challenges for this paper.

1. Tracing of the batteries - In order to determine a precise battery health, it is very important to collect data about it through its entire lifecycle. The batteries cannot be easily traced currently throughout its lifecycle, thus it's very expensive to retrieve the battery health data when required.
2. Access to the data- Currently, it's not easy to access the battery data. The data is produced or collected by all the stakeholders but it's difficult for the other stakeholders to access it. Also, in most cases the batteries must be manually checked in order to access the health data from the battery management systems.
3. Secure platform to store and access data- The system should be able to store and give access to the data securely. The system should guarantee data security, i.e., the data is always secure from unwanted authorized users.
4. Trusted Platform- In the lifecycle of a traction battery, data is generated by various sources and stakeholders. In order to use data for efficient re-utilization of traction batteries the accuracy of the data is very important. If the data is not accurate or is tampered at any point the results of actual battery health state changes. Thus, the platform should be able to guarantee data integrity and trust, i.e., the data is consistent, accurate and not changed at any point in time.

Current technologies, such as RFID, do not fulfill all aspects in order to match the identified challenges. First of all, the maximum storage capacity of an RFID-Chip is limited and depending on the amount of data stored not sufficient enough. Furthermore, RFID does not offer a complete solution for sharing data while maintaining security and data integrity. Lastly in case of a damaged RFID-Chip all data would be gone and can't be retrieved.

V. PROPOSED SOLUTION

In order to reduce the costs and make the second-life applications of traction batteries more efficiently, we realized the health of the battery should be tracked through its entire lifecycle. The data about the battery's health can be used to optimize the dismantling process and to determine the second-life application of the battery based on its health. Thus, tracking the batteries through its lifecycle reduces the cost and error rather than checking it manually.

The first requirement for tracking a traction battery is that it should be unique. As a result, we propose that during the production, batteries should get a "unique address". Once the battery has a physical unique address this address must be stored somewhere as digital copy so that more data about it can be added as the batteries moves through various steps in its lifecycle. One way for keeping this digital data of the batteries is adding this to a database. Nevertheless, in order to provide more security and trust to the digital data we propose tracking the batteries lifecycle using blockchain technology (see Figure 2). This enables the creation of a decentralized environment, where the cryptographically validated transactions and data are not under the control of any third-party. Any transaction ever completed is recorded in an immutable ledger in a verifiable, secure, transparent and permanent way, with a timestamp and other details [12].

A blockchain is a decentralized, distributed database that is used to maintain a continuously growing list of records, called blocks. Each block contains a timestamp and a link to a previous block. By design and by purpose blockchains are inherently resistant to modification of the data. Functionally, a blockchain can serve as an open, distributed ledger that can record transactions [13]-[14].

In summary the blockchain is a distributed database existing on multiple computers at the same time. It is constantly growing as new sets of recordings, or 'blocks', are added to it. Each block contains a timestamp and a link to the previous block, so they form a chain. The database is not managed by anybody; instead, everyone in the network gets a copy of the whole database. Old blocks are preserved forever, and new blocks are added to the ledger irreversibly, making it impossible to manipulate by faking documents, transactions and other information. Blockchain is a transforming technology and can help the stakeholders on in the chain to securely trace the battery's data and access data. Further some blockchain technologies (for example Ethereum [15]) are providing smart contracts. A smart contract is a self-executing script that reside on the blockchain. This contract could be used to manage the data exchange between the different parties in a blockchain to involve them in a contractual agreement [14] [16] . Figure 2 illustrates an outline of the overall approach to enable the data exchange.

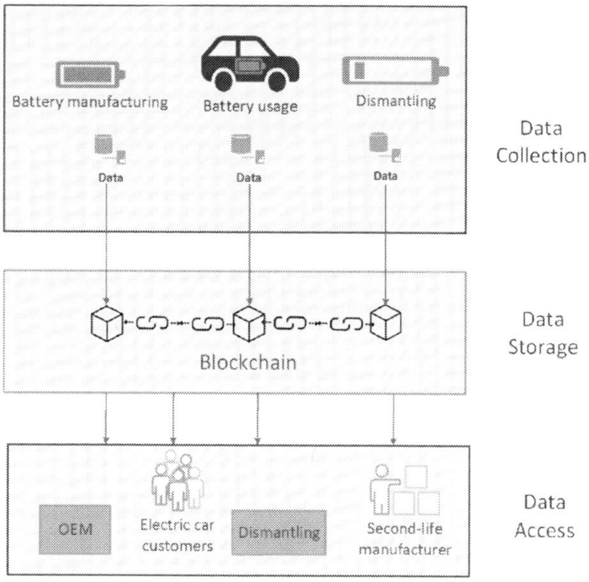

Figure 2: Overall approach.

As shown in Section IV. The proposed platform to store and access data should be secure and trustful. Data Integrity, i.e., guarantee that the data is consistent and accurate at every point is very important for using data driven approach for efficient re-utilization of traction batteries. The data could be changed by the stakeholders for benefits or can be accessed by unauthorized users and altered. Thus, the features of blockchain providing higher security, data integrity and immutability motivates us to use it as a database for tracking the lifecycle of traction batteries. Once the data is stored on blockchain it cannot be altered hence always providing accurate battery health.

In the moment the data is stored on blockchain it can be accessed from there whenever required. And as the data is stored on blockchain it becomes almost impossible to manipulate the data providing higher data integrity, i.e., it can be ensured that the data is accurate and consistent over its entire lifecycle.

Blockchains are mainly associated with cryptocurrencies but the its scope is far beyond just cryptocurrencies. There are various types of blockchains and a wide array of implementation approaches. It can be categorized in three types: Public, consortium and private.

A public blockchain is where anyone in the world can become a node in the transaction process. It is a completely open public ledger system. It is also be called permission less ledgers [17].

In private blockchains, the write permissions are with one organization or with a certain group of individuals. Read permissions are public or restricted to a large set of users [17].

Consortium blockchains let a group of people establish a distributed ledger. It can also be known as a permission private blockchain [17]. Thus, we propose using consortium blockchains for the tracking and data access of traction batteries as a distributed ledger between all the stakeholders is required.

Blockchain allows multiple competing parties to securely interact with the each other. It has shared immutable ledgers for recording transaction history and thus it can be used for tracking the batteries securely and lets the stakeholders access the data easily [18]. Thus, blockchain can be used as a standard interface to store and access data securely.

A uniform format should be sought for the data structure. An example of this would be the eCl@ss standard, which is the only worldwide ISO/IEC-compliant data standard for goods and services [19]. The advantage of one standard is that every stakeholder than finally has the same understand of the data and can use it easily.

VI. SCENARIO BASED ON PROPOSED SOLUTION

In this Section, we show a scenario of how data can be tracked with our proposed solution and be used for the re-utilization of traction batteries. Figure 3 shows the three layers- data collection, data storage and data access.

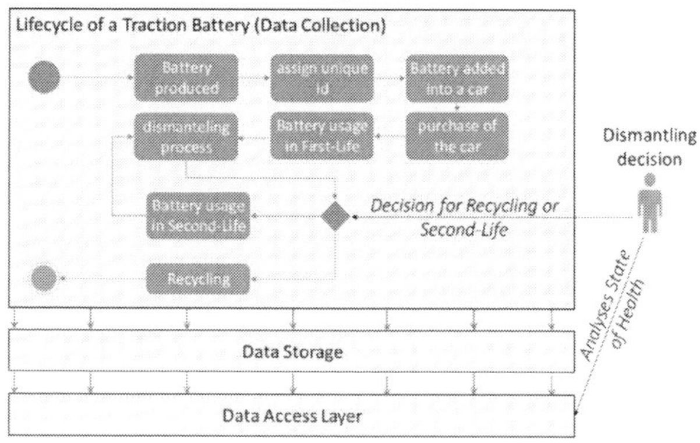

Figure 3: Example of an Application Scenario.

The data collection starts once the battery is produced. A timestamp of its production date is stored in the blockchain. The blockchain here is the data storage mechanism. While the battery is produced, we propose that the battery is given a unique id which can be used to track the battery. Thus, while production the battery's unique id and production timestamp is stored. After the production, the battery is added to the vehicle. The timestamp when the vehicle is sold can be added. During the battery's first life in the car, the health of the battery can be tracked through its charging cycles from various sources. One source to track the charging cycles is using the charging stations for it. This approach is benefiting from growing charging infrastructure provided by the OEMs themselves. All the data about the battery's health through charging cycles can be stored. After the battery is used in its first life it goes to the dismantling process where the decision whether it can be used for second life application or should be recycled is to be made. This decision can be easily made by analyzing the data of the battery's lifecycle, with our proposed solution as all the data is already stored and available rather than manually checking it. This reduces the cost of the process and helps in taking a precise dismantling decision. When the battery is still usable for a Second-Life application, data about its health can also be used to determine for which application, it can be used in. After the battery serves its second-life usage it returns to the dismantling process where a further use or recycling decision can be easily made by looking at the health data.

VII. Evaluation Plan

In order to implement the proposed solution suitable technologies and type of blockchain has to be selected. Public blockchains such as bitcoin and Ethereum are not suitable for this scenario. Thus, firstly we will evaluate the blockchains and related technologies. However, despite all the advantages of the Blockchain it does not make sense to store all the data in the Blockchain. Thus, depending on the size of data more advanced data storage mechanisms has to be selected. Possibilities are on-chain and off-chain data storage. In such as a mechanism only critical data such as timestamps and charging cycles data is only stored for access to everyone. Other data is stored in an off-chain system.

But further research in this is required. Also, a uniform format should be made for the data structure. An example of this would be the eCl@ss standard, which is the only worldwide ISO/IEC-compliant data standard for goods and services [19]. Currently, we are evaluating suitable blockchains, technologies and data structure for the proposed solution. The standard should be oriented on eCl@ss, which is the only worldwide ISO/IEC-compliant data standard for goods and services [19].

VIII. Conclusion and Outlook

In this paper we present a data driven approach for increasing efficiency of traction battery re-utilization by reducing related costs. In order to use data for this purpose we identified two major problems in the existing system. Primarily, there is no existing mechanism to track the battery's lifecycle and secondly the stakeholders who are a part of the chain do not have access to the data of the batteries. For this we propose a mechanism, using blockchain, through which the data throughout the battery's lifecycle can be tracked and accessed. Blockchain provides higher security, data integrity, transparency, immutability and trust. Once the record is saved on a blockchain it cannot be changed thus it can be ensured that the data is real and was not manipulated at any point. There are various ways to implement it, but in this scenario a public blockchain is not feasible. A shared database with authorized access is required. Consortium blockchains let a group of people establish a distributed ledger. Thus, we propose using a consortium blockchain for the stakeholders or partners who are a part of the battery's lifecycle. Currently we are evaluating the technologies and platforms to establish a permissioned blockchain for the scenario shown in this paper. Our next steps will be the implementation of the proposed solution for traction batteries.

Acknowledgment

This paper evolved from the research project “Recycling 4.0” (digitalization as the key to the Advanced Circular Economy using the example of innovative vehicle systems) which is funded by the European Regional Development Fund (EFRE | ZW 6-85017297) and managed by the Project Management Agency NBank.

References

[1] G. Zhao, *Reuse and Recycling of Lithium-Ion Power Batteries*. Singapore: John Wiley & Sons Singapore Pte. Ltd, 2017.

[2] S. Fischhaber, A. Regett, S. Schuster, and H. Hesse, “Studie: Second-Life-Konzepte für Lithium-Ionen-Batterien aus Elektrofahrzeugen. Analyse von Nachnutzungsanwendungen, ökonomischen und ökologischen Potenzialen.,” *Begleit. und Wirkungsforsch. Schaufenster Elektromobilität*, 2016.

[3] K.-B. Holve, “Auslegungsaspekte von Batteriepacks und Batteriemanagement-Systemen,” Universität Duisburg-Essen, 2018.

[4] J. Neubauer, K. Smith, E. Wood, and A. Pesaran “Identifying and Overcoming Critical Barriers to Widespread Second Use of PEV Batteries,” *Nrel*, no. February, pp. 23–62, 2015.

[5] C. Knieke, S. Lawrenz, M. Fröhling, D. Goldmann, and A. Rausch, “Predictive and flexible Circular Economy approaches for highly integrated products and their materials as given in E-Mobility and ICT,” *Circ. Econ. Mater. Components E-mobility – CEM²*, 2018.

[6] “Neuzulassungen von Pkw in den Jahren 2008 bis 2017 nach ausgewählten Kraftstoffarten.” [Online]. Available: https://www.kba.de/DE/Statistik/Fahrzeuge/Neuzulassungen/Umwelt/n_umwelt_z.html?nn=652326. [Accessed: 12-Apr-2019].

[7] “National NEV Monitoring And Mangement-Traction Battery Recycling And Traceability Platform.” [Online]. Available: https://www.tbrat.org/. [Accessed: 12-Apr-2019].

[8] “IMDS | Internationales Material Daten System.” [Online]. Available: https://www.mdsystem.com/imdsnt/startpage/index.jsp. [Accessed: 12-Apr-2019].

[9] O. Püchert, H.; Spengler, T. S.; Rentz, “Strategische

Planung von Kreislaufwirtschafts- und Redistributionssystemen - Am Fallbeispiel des Altautorecyclings," *Zeitschrift für Planung, 7 (1), pp. 27–44.*, 1996.

[10] F. Schultmann, B. Engels, and O. Rentz, "Closed-Loop Supply Chains for Spent Batteries," *Interfaces*, vol. 33. INFORMS, pp. 57–71.

[11] A. Rizzi and R. Zamboni, "Efficiency improvement in manual warehouses through ERP systems implementation and redesign of the logistics processes," *Logist. Inf. Manag.*, vol. 12, no. 5, pp. 367–377, 1999.

[12] M. C. Bacescu, "The 13 th International Scientific Conference eLearning and Software for Education Bucharest , April 27-28 , 2017," *13th Int. Sci. Conf. eLearning Softw. Educ.*, no. April, pp. 369–376, 2017.

[13] A. S. Bruyn, "Blockchain an introduction Research paper," 2017. *University Amsterdam* [Online]. Avaible: https://beta.vu.nl/nl/Images/werkstuk-bruyn_tcm235-862258.pdf [Accessed: 12-Apr-2019]

[14] M. Finck, "Blockchain Technology," in *Blockchain Regulation and Governance in Europe*, 2018, pp. 1–33.

[15] "Ethereum Project." [Online]. Available: https://www.ethereum.org/. [Accessed: 12-Apr-2019].

[16] A. Kosba, A. Miller, E. Shi, Z. Wen, and C. Papamanthou, "Hawk: The Blockchain Model of Cryptography and Privacy-Preserving Smart Contracts," in *Proceedings - 2016 IEEE Symposium on Security and Privacy, SP 2016*, 2016, pp. 839–858.

[17] "Paul Valencourt & Samanyu Chopra & Brenn Hill [Paul Valencourt] - Blockchain Quick Reference (2018, Packt Publishing)." .

[18] M. Santos and E. Moura, *Hands-On IoT Solutions with Blockchain*. 2019.

[19] "home: ecl@ss." [Online]. Available: https://www.eclass.eu/en.html. [Accessed: 12-Apr-2019].

Automated Generation of Requirements-Based Test Cases for an Automotive Function using the SCADE Toolchain

Adina Aniculaesei*, Andreas Vorwald* and Andreas Rausch*
* Institute for Software and Systems Engineering
Technische Universität Clausthal, Clausthal-Zellerfeld, Germany
Email: adina.aniculaesei@tu-clausthal.de, andreas.vorwald@tu-clausthal.de, andreas.rausch@tu-clausthal.de

***Abstract*—Results of acceptance tests trigger various adaptations in the architecture and design of a complex software system. Several adaptation iterations are needed until all acceptance tests are successfully passed. Checking whether the adapted software system complies with an extensive catalogue of requirements is an elaborate task, which cannot be managed only via manual testing anymore. Over the years, model checking has established itself as an efficient method for the generation of requirements-based test cases. At the same time, the traction gained by model-based development tools, such as SCADE Suite, especially in the automotive and the avionics domains, facilitates the use of formal methods for the analysis and verification of complex software systems developed in these industries. This paper describes an approach which supports the generation of test cases from formalized requirements using the SCADE toolchain. In order to evaluate the applicability of our approach, we apply our concept on a simple system from the automotive domain and discuss outcomming results.**

Keywords–architecture adaptation; model-based development; requirements-based testing; model checking; automotive function; SCADE toolchain

I. INTRODUCTION

Control systems are installed in cars with the purpose to improve the driving experience and increase the safety of the vehicles and their passengers. Tasks which were previously carried out by the driver are now performed by complex software systems. An immediate consequence of this software complexity is that extensive catalogues of system requirements have become more common in the automotive industry [1].

Throughout their life cycle, automotive software systems are subjected to various modifications, which originate in different sources, e.g., change requests caused by defect removal or system enhancements triggered by end user demands. Once the changes have been implemented, the software system must pass the acceptance tests again in order to get into series production. This means that the software system must satisfy every requirement in the catalogue. Test results may expose further defects in the system design or in the system implementation. Thus, the architecture of the software system and its implementation may go through a series of adaptation iterations until the system has successfully passed all acceptance tests. These adaptations may further increase the complexity of the software system.

Software testing is a process which requires a lot of expert knowledge. Testing complex software systems against large requirements catalogue is a task which cannot be managed manually anymore. In the automotive industry, requirements specifications are often maintained as informal documents. In the best case scenario, they are broken down into lists of individual requirements, which are then maintained using a dedicated tool, e.g., IBM's Doors. The large number of requirements for every product version makes it impossible to guarantee consistency and to test the requirements in a rigorous manner. In the automotive domain, model-based development is used by software engineers to create formal models of the desired software system early in the development lifecycle and to test the software against these models, e.g., through back-to-back testing.

We have established the formal connection between system models and system requirements for the automotive domain in a previous work [2]. In [2], we used the approach presented in [3] and generated requirements-based test cases via model checking for a prototype of an adaptive cruise control system. Since model-based development has gained so much traction in the automotive industry, we are interested in finding out whether the approach developed in [2] is also applicable with software toolchains used in model-based development. In this paper, we focus on the SCADE toolchain [4] and we investigate the following research question:

RQ: *How can the SCADE toolchain be used to generate requirements-based test cases for an automotive function?*

As research methodology, we build an academic case study of a control system in the automotive domain. We apply requirements-based test case generation to a simple prototype of a door locking system using the SCADE Design Verifier as model checker. For the sake of simplicity, we formulate only one requirement for the door locking system. For this purpose, we use a controlled natural language with specific sentence patterns, showing which is the subject and which is the object targeted by the requirement [5]. Our work is meant to offer support to the test engineers, who need to develop meaningful and cost-efficient tests, but also to the software developers and software architects, who must decide on the basis of the test results whether any system adaptations are necessary.

Related Work. Using model checking for test-case generation is by now a well-known approach. The paper in [6] uses model checking to generate MC/DC model-based test sequences from the mode logic of a flight-guidance system. For the same type of system, Whalen et al. [3] use model checking to generate requirements-based test cases on the basis of three specific criteria: requirements coverage, antecedent coverage and unique first cause. In [7], the approach presented in [3] is evaluated on four industrial examples from the avionics domain. All four systems were modeled in the Simulink notation from Mathworks and then translated to the Lustre synchronous programming language for the purpose of test case generation.

Generating test cases from natural language requirements

is addressed among others in [8]. The approach uses NLP in order to generate knowledge graphs. Different graph traversing methods are used to construct the test cases. Other approaches use UML diagrams such as use-case or sequence diagrams for test generation [9] [10].

In [11], a translator framework is introduced which allows the translation of commercial modeling languages, e.g., SCADE, in the input languages of verification tools, e.g., Prover or PVS. This allows the integration of commercial model-based development tools with verification tools. The approach is demonstrated on several case studies from the avionics domain.

In this work, we provide a concept for a requirements-based test case generation, which is fully integrated with the SCADE toolchain. We apply it on an example system from the automotive domain. Some of the foundations of our approach are provided by the work of Whalen et al. in [3], [12], and [11].

Paper Outline. In Section II we describe preliminary notions, which are necessary to understand the approach presented in this work. In Section III, we give an overview of our concept. Section IV introduces our case study, while Section V describes the experiment carried out on the example system. In Section VI, we present the results of our experiment and discusses the lessons learned from this work. Section VII concludes the paper with a summary of our contribution and an overview of future work.

II. Preliminaries

In this section, we present the basic process of model checking and explain how this method can be used to generate test cases from system requirements. Furthermore, an overview of model-based development and formal verification with SCADE is given.

Basic Process of Model Checking. Given a system model and a system property to verify, a model checker builds a formal representation of the system model in the form of a finite state machine and explores its state space in search for states which falsify the system property. If the system property is falsified, the model checker returns a counter-example trace, showing how the state which falsifies the system property can be reached from the initial state of the system model.

Generation of Test Cases with Model Checking. Throughout the years, model checking has established itself as an efficient method to generate test cases from system requirements. One possibility to generate test cases using model checking is to build trap properties [3]. Trap properties are basically negations of the system properties, which are satisfied by the system model if the latter is correctly built. While verifying the system model against a trap property, the model checker searches for a counter-example to disprove the trap property. By the law of double negation in propositional logic, the counter-example which disproves the trap property is in fact an example showing how the original system property is satisfied. The counter-example is then used as a basis for building a requirements-based test case, which checks if the *System under Test (SuT)* satisfies the respective system requirement.

Model-based Development with SCADE. SCADE Suite is a development environment used for the model-based design and development of software system components.Software components are encapsulated in SCADE operators, which, in turn, are organised in SCADE projects. Each SCADE operator has inputs and outputs, which form the interface of the respective software component. The formal basis of the SCADE language is given by the declarative language Lustre and is defined in [4]. The systems of equations specific to the language Lustre are used to model the dataflow inside SCADE operators, connecting the input flows to the output flows of the operator. Hierarchical state machines are used to describe the control flow of SCADE operators.

Formal Verification with SCADE Design Verifier. In SCADE Suite, formal verification is performed using SCADE Design Verifier, a model checker based on a SAT-solver [13] [14]. The SCADE Design Verifier works on the basis of the SCADE observer principle. System properties which must be verified with the SCADE Design Verifier are first encapsulated as observers. An observer is a SCADE operator which takes as input both the input flows and the output flows of the system model. The observer produces a Boolean output flag. The system property is satisfied if the observer's output evaluates to *true* in every computation cycle. Should the flag evaluate to *false* in one computation cycle, the SCADE Design Verifier returns a counter-example which shows why this answer has been reached.

III. Test Case Generation from Requirements using the SCADE Toolchain

An overview of our approach is given in Figure 1. The concept illustrates the necessary steps for the generation and execution of requirements-based test cases.

System Model Construction and System Requirement Formalization. The system requirement is manually formalized as an obligation in *Linear Temporal Logic (LTL)*. The system model is designed with SCADE Suite on the basis of the system requirement, and therefore satisfies the LTL obligation. Both the system model and the system requirement are presented in Section IV.

Trap Property Generation. A trap property is the negation of an LTL obligation which is satisfied by the system model. Since the test case generation process using the SCADE toolchain is the focus of this paper, we limit ourselves to using only the *Requirements Coverage (RC)* criterium to build the trap property corresponding to the LTL obligation.

Test Case Generation using Model Checking. The system model and the trap property are given as input to the SCADE Design Verifier in order to generate traces. In the classical model checking process, the model checker explores the entire state space of the system model consisting of all the combinations of inputs and states in order to find violations of the LTL obligation. If found, then the model checker produces a conterexample trace which shows how the LTL obligation can be falsified. The trace is in turn transformed into a test case with which the SuT can be later executed.

Test Case Execution. The SuT, in our case the SCADE system model, is loaded in the SCADE Test Environment and then executed with the test input data specified in the generated test case.

IV. Case Study Exampple

Our case study is constructed around a simple prototype of a door locking system in an automobile. The door locking system is regarded as a safety feature for the vehicle, as its primary goal is to ensure that the doors do not open while the

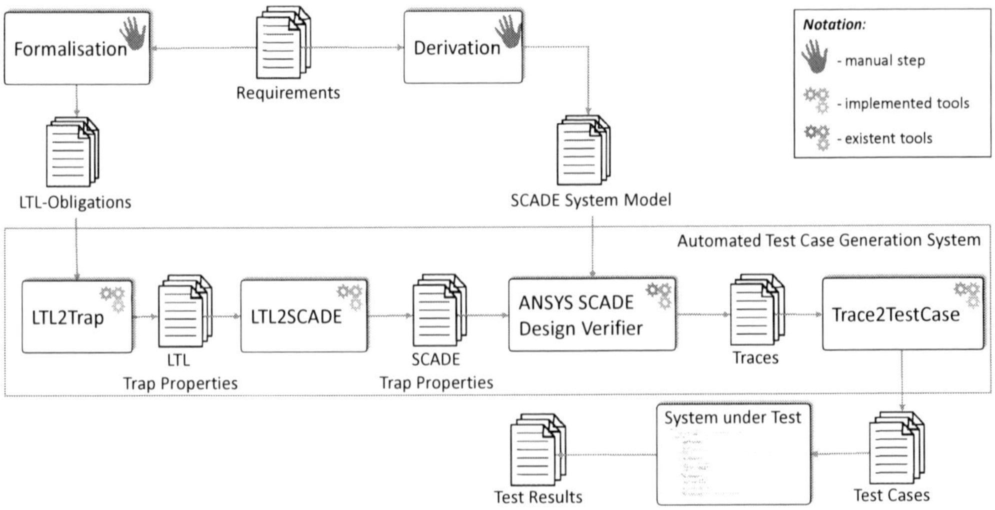

Figure 1. Test Case Generation from Requirements using the SCADE Toolchain.

vehicle is moving. Figure 2 depicts the implementation of the door locking system in the SCADE Suite.

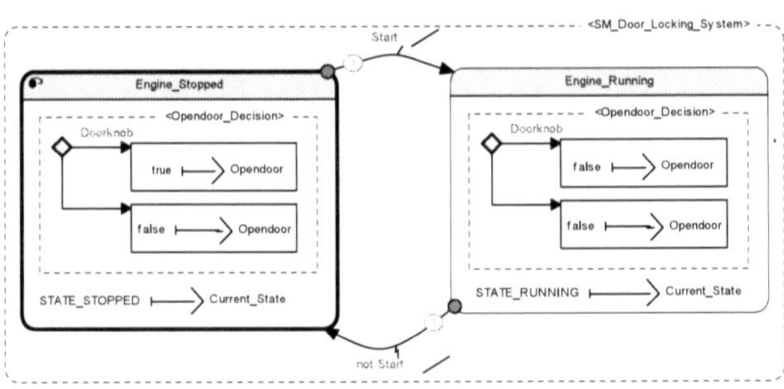

Figure 2. Case Study Example: A Simple Door Locking System.

A. System Model

We model the door locking system in strong correlation with the current vehicle status. Our example system is modeled as a state machine with two states which describe the vehicle status: state `Engine_Running` for the moving vehicle and state `Engine_Stopped` for the stillstanding vehicle. For the purpose of this case study, the functionality of the door locking system is kept rather simple. Thus, if a vehicle passenger operates the door handle while the engine is running, then the vehicle door stays closed. On the other side, if the engine is stopped and the vehicle passenger operates the door handle, then vehicle door opens.

The input interfaces of the door locking system consist of the boolean flags `Doorknob` and `Start`, which model the operation of the door handle by the vehicle passenger and respectively the start/stop of the vehicle engine. The output interfaces of the door locking system are represented by the boolean flag `Opendoor` and the enumeration variable `Current_State`. The former models the status of the door vehicle (opened/closed). The latter switches between the constants `STATE_STOPPED = 0` and `STATE_RUNNING = 1`, in order to keep track of the current state of the vehicle.

B. System Requirements

For the purpose of simplicity, we formulate one safety requirement for the door locking system. The system requirement, formulated in a controlled natural language [5], reads as follows:

***R1**. If the motor is running and the doorknob is pushed, then the door shall not be opened.*

V. Formalization and Test Case Generation

Our process for the generation of test cases from requirements has already been published in a previous work [2]. However, the purpose of this paper is to automatize this process using the SCADE toolchain. For the purpose of completeness, we present the steps of the test case generation process, highlighting the details specific for the work with the SCADE toolchain:

A. From System Requirements to LTL Obligations

We build the LTL obligation for the door locking system from the system requirement *R1*, presented in Section IV. The corresponding LTL obligation is written in (1):

$$\phi : G(Current\_State = STATE\_RUNNING \wedge Doorknob \rightarrow X(Opendoor = false)) \quad (1)$$

Observe that time model of LTL differs from the time model of the SCADE language, i.e., LTL looks from the present time point into the future while SCADE looks from the present point into the past. Therefore, the LTL obligation in (1) must be transformed using the `last` operator as shown in (2), so that it conforms to the SCADE time model:

$$\phi : G(last'Current\_State = STATE\_RUNNING \wedge Doorknob \rightarrow X(last'Opendoor = false)) \quad (2)$$

B. From LTL Obligations to Traces

In order to obtain a test case which satisfies the system requirement *R1*, the first step is to build a trap property by simply negating the LTL obligation shown in (2). Thus, the corresponding trap property for requirement *R1* is given in

(3):

$$\phi : \neg G(last' Current\_State = STATE\_RUNNING \wedge Doorknob \rightarrow X(last' Opendoor = false)) \quad (3)$$

The trap property is then transformed in SCADE code against which the SCADE system model can be verified using SCADE Design Verifier as model checker. Figure 3 gives an overview of the necessary steps for the transformation of the LTL trap property in SCADE code.

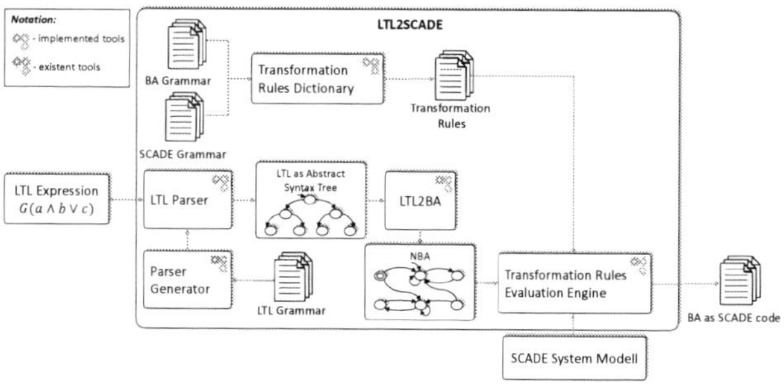

Figure 3. Transformation of LTL Obligations in SCADE Code.

LTL Parser Generation and AST Construction. We generate an LTL parser on the basis of the LTL grammar, in order ensure the correct parsing of the system requirements formalised in LTL with respect to operator priority rules. The operator precedence is encoded in the *Abstract Syntax Tree (AST)*. In our implementation of the LTL grammar, the logical and temporal operators of LTL, as well as the arithmetic operators are nonterminal symbols. As terminal symbols, our grammar allows the boolean constants, *true* and *false*, variable names and arithmetic constants in atomic propositions, e.g $a \leq 10$, but also the keyword `last`, which is specific to the SCADE language.

Büchi Automaton Construction. The common basis of LTL and SCADE is represented by automata. This is based on the fact that the concept of automata is integrated in the SCADE language [15] [4], and that nondeterministic Büchi automata (NBA) are an alternate representation of LTL formulae [16]. Figure 4 illustrates the steps needed to transform an LTL formula into an NBA. This transformation is based on the algorithm defined by Gerth et al. in [17]. The algorithm transforms an LTL formula expressed in positive normal form (PNF) into a generalized nondeterministic Büchi automaton (GNBA). Once this transformation is complete, only atomic propositions occur as transition guards. The atomic propositions are connected via the logical operator AND ($\wedge$), if there is more than one as transition guard on the same transition. Then, the GNBA is transformed into an NBA using the algorithm presented in [16]. The NBA constructed from the trap property of requirement *R1* is presented in Figure 5.

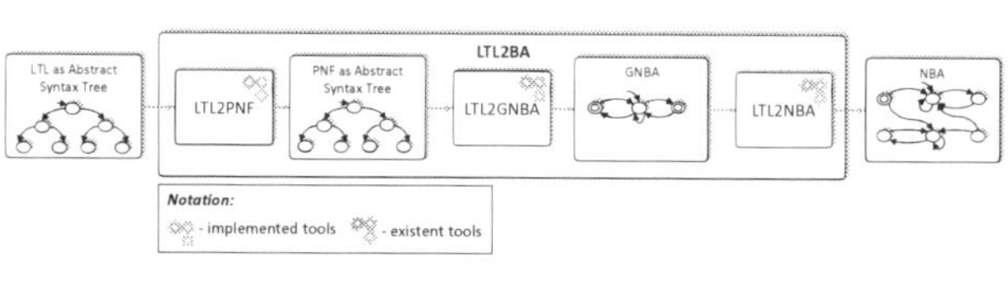

Figure 4. Transformation of LTL Obligations in Non-deterministic Büchi Automata.

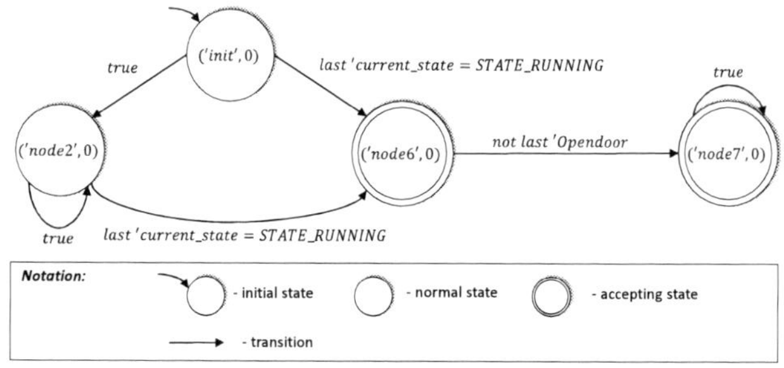

Figure 5. Büchi Automaton for Requirements *R1*.

SCADE Code Generation. The core idea of this process step is to create for each LTL trap property a new SCADE operator which has the same input as the SCADE system model. This SCADE operator is then used later to generate test cases. The inputs of the new SCADE operator are redirected to the SCADE system model to perform a computation cycle. Then, a unique output as observer for the LTL trap property and a corresponding state machine implementing the NBA of the LTL trap property are created. Furthermore, the name of the SCADE system model is used in order to build the name of the newly created SCADE operator: `<SCADE-system-model>_proof`. Figure 6 shows the SCADE Code generated for the system requirement *R1*.

```
node Doorlock_proof(Doorknob : bool; Start : bool)
returns (output0 : bool default = false)
var
Opendoor : bool last = false;
Current_State : uint8 last = 0;
_counter0 : uint64 default = 1 + last '_counter0 last = 0;
let
Opendoor, Current_State = Doorlock(Doorknob, Start);
_ = Opendoor;
_ = Current_State;
automaton SM0
initial state init_0
unless
if (last 'Current_State = STATE_RUNNING) and Start do
let
output0 = true;
_counter0 = 0;
tel
```

```
restart node6_0;
if true do
let
output0 = true;
_counter0 = 0;
tel
restart node2_0;
state node2_0
unless
if (last 'Current_State = STATE_RUNNING) and Start do
let
output0 = true;
_counter0 = 0;
tel
restart node6_0;
if true and last '_counter0 <= 1 do
let
output0 = true;
tel
```

```
restart node2_0;
state node6_0
unless
if (not last 'Opendoor) do
let
output0 = true;
_counter0 = 0;
tel
restart node7_0;
state node7_0
unless
if true do
let
output0 = true;
_counter0 = 0;
tel
restart node7_0;
returns .. ;
tel
```

Figure 6. SCADE code corresponding to the NBA generated from Requirement *R1*.

The SCADE Design Verifier is the model checker of the SCADE Suite and can be interfaced by using observers which are evaluated in each computation cycle during the state space exploration [15]. The model checker explores the state space in search of a trace which falsifies the trap property. It stops the state space exploration when it has exhausted the entire state space or when the observer of the trap property switches to *false*. When the latter occurs, a trace of input assignments is printed, which shows how the trap property can be falsified.

In SCADE, an NBA is represented by a statemachine. Automata are a feature of SCADE, and respectively of the Lustre language [15] [4]. Figure 7 illustrates the transformation of the NBA corresponding to the requirement *R1* in SCADE based on two transitions extracted from Figure 5. Every state of the NBA is represented in SCADE via the keyword `state`, while the initial state of the NBA is also marked by the keyword `initial`. A transition in the NBA is transformed into an *if*-statement within the state. In order to ensure optimal transition execution, the outgoing transitions of a state are sorted descending according to the number of transition guards. For example, if a state s_1 has two outgoing transitions, (s_1, a_0, s_2) and $(s_1, a_0 \wedge a_1, s_3)$, then the second one is prefered.

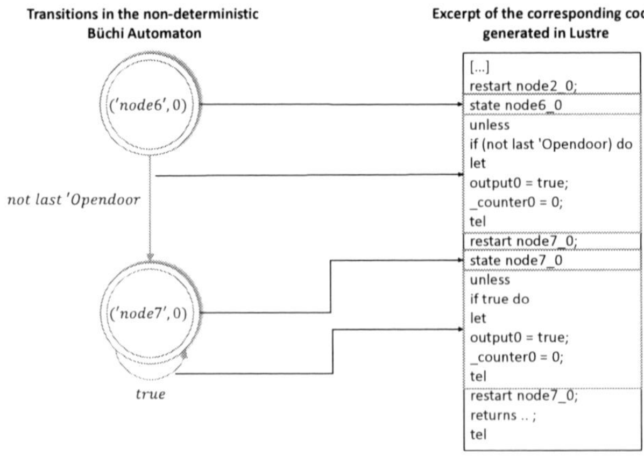

Figure 7. Excerpt of Transformation from non-deterministic Büchi Automata to Lustre code.

C. From Traces to Test Cases

The trace generated by the SCADE Design Verifer contains only test input data. However, in order to get the full test case, output data are also needed. Figure 8 displays the workflow used to obtain the test output data and generate test cases.

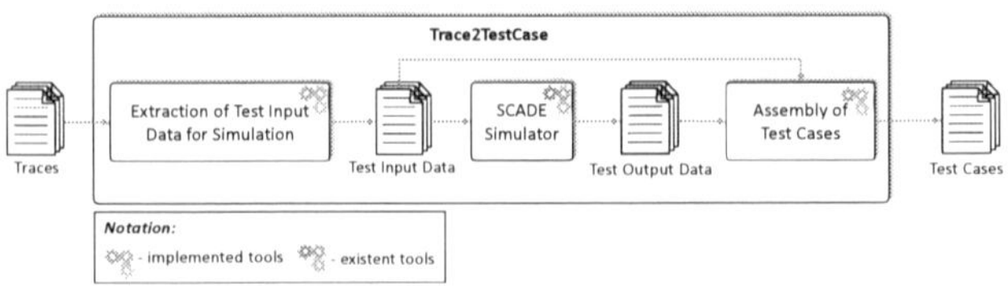

Figure 8. Transformation of Traces in Test Cases.

To begin with, the test input data is extracted from the trace. Then, the SCADE system model is run with the test input data in the SCADE Simulator. The test output data obtained from the simulation is assembled with the test input data extracted from the trace in a test case file (`.sss`-file), which can later be run in the SCADE Test Environment. A trace and the corresponding test case showing how requirement *R1* may be satisfied are shown in Figure 9.

VI. Evaluation

A. Setup

The system in Figure 2 was modeled in ANSYS SCADE 19.1 (build 20180327). To implement the workflow described in Figure 1, a Python 3.4 script using the Python-API of SCADE was created. The parser was then generated with the parser generator `ply` [18].

The SuT was then executed with the test case obtained from the system requirement *R1*. The results of the test case execution are displayed in Figure 10.

B. Lessons Learned

In order to successfully generate requirements-based test cases with the SCADE toolchain, test engineers must understand the innerworkings of SCADE state machines. According

```
# ----------------------------------------------------------
# Simulation scenario file for SCADE Simulator
# Task:  Doorlock_proof.output0
# Model: Verifier
# Node:  Doorlock
# ----------------------------------------------------------

SSM::set Doorlock_proof/Doorknob t
SSM::set Doorlock_proof/Start f
SSM::cycle

SSM::set Doorlock_proof/Doorknob t
SSM::set Doorlock_proof/Start t
SSM::cycle

SSM::set Doorlock_proof/Doorknob f
SSM::set Doorlock_proof/Start f
SSM::cycle

SSM::set Doorlock_proof/Doorknob f
SSM::set Doorlock_proof/Start f
SSM::cycle
```

(a)

```
SSM::set Doorlock/Doorknob t
SSM::set Doorlock/Start f
SSM::check Doorlock/Opendoor t
SSM::check Doorlock/Current_State 0
SSM::cycle

SSM::set Doorlock/Doorknob t
SSM::set Doorlock/Start t
SSM::check Doorlock/Opendoor f
SSM::check Doorlock/Current_State 1
SSM::cycle

SSM::set Doorlock/Doorknob f
SSM::set Doorlock/Start f
SSM::check Doorlock/Opendoor f
SSM::check Doorlock/Current_State 0
SSM::cycle

SSM::set Doorlock/Doorknob f
SSM::set Doorlock/Start f
SSM::check Doorlock/Opendoor f
SSM::check Doorlock/Current_State 0
SSM::cycle
```

(b)

Figure 9. a) Trace generated with the SCADE Design Verifier out of the System Requirement *R1*; b) Test Case generated from the Trace in a) with the SCADE Simulator.

Status	Step	Name	Actual Value	Expected Value
	1	Doorlock/Opendoor	true	t
	1	Doorlock/Current_State	0	0
	2	Doorlock/Opendoor	false	false
	2	Doorlock/Current_State	1	1
	3	Doorlock/Opendoor	false	false
	3	Doorlock/Current_State	0	0
	4	Doorlock/Opendoor	false	false
	4	Doorlock/Current_State	0	0

Figure 10. Execution of the System under Test with the Generated Test Case.

to their semantics, the data flow which connects the inputs to the outputs of a state in a SCADE state machine is executed synchronously in a single cycle, before any active transitions in the system model can be fired.

Often, it is necessary to know the state in which the computation of state variables used within a cycle originated. This is why it is often indispensable to make use of the `last` operator, especially for system requirements formulated over state variables. Take for example LTL formulae of the form $G(\mu \rightarrow X\psi)$ in which the logical formulae μ and ψ are expressed over state variables. In this case, the SCADE operator `last` is needed for the state variables in μ as well as for those in ψ, in order to get the state from which the calculation within a cycle starts. The use of the SCADE operator `last` can vary, depending on the system requirement and on the implementation of the system model. Since we found no sound way to normalize it, we decided to enable the use of this operator. Indeed, syntactically the `last` operator is considered as a terminal symbol, yet it has effect on LTL operators. To be more specific, the LTL formula $G(a \leq 10 \rightarrow X(\textbf{last}'\, b = 5))$ is semantically equivalent to the LTL formula $G(a \leq 10 \rightarrow b = 5)$, where b is a state variable in the current state. Here, the effect of the `last` operator on the LTL operator *X (neXt)* is similar to that of the absorbtion law in propositional logic. It is then up to the test engineers to decide whether the usage of the `last` operator is appropriate, depending on the system requirements and on the SCADE system model.

Furthermore, one has to consider that the link between SCADE and LTL is not perfect. Nondeterministic Büchi automata are usually used in automata-based LTL model checking to construct the product transition system of the negated property and the system model [16]. The SCADE Design Verifier is built on top of a SAT-Solver [13], with the property observer as its interface. This allowed us to use nondeterministic Büchi automata as a uniform approach to create chronological state sequences from LTL formulae. However, for LTL (sub-)formulae of the type $\mu\ U\ \psi$, the generated NBA contains non-accepting states. These states can have recursive transitions, which always fire. This behavior leads to endless loops, which in turn can generate wrong results. We solved this problem by adding a counter which increments up to a predefined maximum value everytime a recursive transition of a non-accepting state fires. The counter is then reset, if the next state is an accepting state. The maximum value can be defined by the test engineer. The defined value should not be too high, as it may cause long or indeterminate system runs, and not too low, so that correctness can be ensured.

VII. Conclusion and Future Work

In this paper, we implemented the concept defined by Aniculaesei et al. [2] on the industrial toolchain ANSYS SCADE, in order to generate test cases straight from the system requirements formalized in LTL and the SCADE system model. We used the SCADE Design Verifier as model checker to deliver test inputs in form of traces, which were then simulated to calculate the corresponding test outputs. The test cases, containing the test inputs and outputs, were assembled in SCADE scenario files (`.sss`-files). The scenario files are given as input to the SCADE Testing Environment in order to automatically execute the test cases on the System under Test, in this case the SCADE system model itself.

In order to connect LTL with SCADE, we needed to express chronological sequences of states over infinite time. For this purpose, we generated nondeterministic Büchi automata from formalised requirements in LTL by applying the algorithm defined by Gerth et al. in [17]. Here, we found out that this connection is not all-embracing when non-accepting states with recursive transitions occur in the generated NBA (see Section VI). Since we found no uniform concept for mapping of the LTL time model onto the SCADE time model, we enabled the use of `last` operator from SCADE in terminal symbols and we gave the user the liberty to decide upon the usage of this operator within LTL formulas. Based on our case study, valid test cases were generated (see Figure 9) and executed (see Figure 10).

In future work, we want to extend the concept for requirements-based test case generation developed for the SCADE toolchain with the approach in [2]. We plan to apply the extended concept on a more complex system in the automotive field. Here we plan to use construction methodologies for test case generation via model checking based on three different criteria, requirements coverage (RC), antecedent coverage (AC) and unique first cause coverage (UFC) as defined in [3] [7]. Furthermore, we plan to measure the quality of our test suites with respect to MC/DC Coverage [19] [20] by creating mutants on code level.

References

[1] M. Fockel, J. Holtmann, and M. Meyer, "Mit Satzmustern hochwertige Anforderungsdokumente effizient erstellen (*engl.*: Using Sentence Patterns to Efficiently Create High-quality Requirements Documents)," OBJEKTspektrum, no. RE/2014, jun 2014, pp. 1–4.

[2] A. Aniculaesei, F. Howar, P. Denecke, and A. Rausch, "Automated generation of Requirements-Based Test Cases for an Adaptive Cruise Control System," in 2018 IEEE Workshop on Validation, Analysis and Evolution of Software Tests (VST@SANER). IEEE, 2018, pp. 11–15.

[3] M. W. Whalen, A. Rajan, M. P. Heimdahl, and S. P. Miller, "Coverage metrics for requirements-based testing," in Proceedings of the 2006 international symposium on Software testing and analysis, L. Pollock and M. Pezzè, Eds. New York, NY: ACM, 2006, pp. 25–36.

[4] Esterel Technologies S.A.S., Scade Language Reference Manual. ANSYS, Inc., 2018.

[5] C. Rupp and SOPHISTen, "Schablonen für alle Fälle (*engl.*: Patterns for all Purposes)," SOPHIST GmbH, 2016. [Online]. Available: https://www.sophist.de/fileadmin/user_upload/Bilder_zu_Seiten/Publikationen/Wissen_for_free/MASTeR_Broschuere_3-Auflage_interaktiv.pdf

[6] S. Rayadurgam and M. P. E. Heimdahl, "Generating mc/dc adequate test sequences through model checking," in Proceedings of 28th Annual NASA Goddard Software Engineering Workshop. IEEE, 2003, pp. 91–96.

[7] M. Staats, M. W. Whalen, M. P. E. Heindahl, and A. Rajan, "Coverage metrics for requirements-based testing: Evaluation of effectiveness," in Proceedings of the Second NASA Formal Methods Symposium. NASA, april 2010, pp. 161–170.

[8] P. P. Kulkarni and Y. Joglekar, "Generating and Analyzing Test cases from Software Requirements using NLP and Hadoop," International Journal of Current Engineering and Technology, vol. 4, no. 6, 2014, pp. 3934–3937.

[9] N. Kosindrdecha and J. Daengdej, "A test case generation technique and process," Journal of Software Engineering, vol. 4, no. 4, 2010, pp. 265–287.

[10] C. Nebut, S. Pickin, Y. Le Traon, and J.-M. Jézéquel, "Automated Requirements-based Generation of Test Cases for Product Families," in Proceedings of 18th IEEE International Conference on Automated Software Engineering, 2003. Montreal, Quebec, Canada: IEEE, 2003, pp. 263–266.

[11] S. P. Miller, M. W. Whalen, and D. D. Cofer, "Software model checking takes off," Commununications of the ACM, vol. 53, no. 2, feb 2010, pp. 58–64. [Online]. Available: http://doi.acm.org/10.1145/1646353.1646372

[12] M. Whalen, D. Cofer, S. Miller, B. H. Krogh, and W. Storm, "Integration of Formal Analysis into a Model-based Software Development Process," in Proceedings of the 12th International Conference on Formal Methods for Industrial Critical Systems, ser. FMICS'07. Berlin, Heidelberg: Springer-Verlag, 2008, pp. 68–84. [Online]. Available: http://dl.acm.org/citation.cfm?id=1793603.1793612

[13] A. Bouali and B. Dion, "Formal verification for model-based development," SAE transactions, 2005, pp. 171–181.

[14] Esterel Technologies S.A.S., SCADE Suite User Manual. ANSYS, Inc., 2018, vol. SCS-UM-19 - DOC/rev/35771-03.

[15] ——, Scade Language Primer. ANSYS, Inc., 2018.

[16] C. Baier and J.-P. Katoen, Principles of model checking. Cambridge, Massachusetts, USA: MIT Press, 2008.

[17] R. Gerth, D. Peled, M. Y. Vardi, and P. Wolper, "Simple on-the-fly automatic verification of linear temporal logic," in Proceedings of the Fifteenth IFIP WG6.1 International Symposium on Protocol Specification, Testing and Verification XV. London, UK, UK: Chapman & Hall, Ltd., 1996, pp. 3–18. [Online]. Available: http://dl.acm.org/citation.cfm?id=645837.670574

[18] "PLY (Python Lex-Yacc)," accessed: 21.03.2019. [Online]. Available: https://www.dabeaz.com/ply/

[19] J. J. Chilenski and S. P. Miller, "Applicability of modified condition/decision coverage to software testing," Software Engineering Journal, vol. 9, no. 5, 1994, pp. 193–200.

[20] K. Hayhurst, D. S. Veerhusen, J. J. Chilenski, and L. K. Rierson, "A Practical Tutorial on Modified Condition/Decision Coverage," National Aeronautics and Space Administration, Langley Research Center, Tech. Rep., 2001. [Online]. Available: https://ntrs.nasa.gov/archive/nasa/casi.ntrs.nasa.gov/20010057789.pdf

A Controller Architecture for Anomaly Detection, Root Cause Analysis and Self-Adaptation for Cluster Architectures

Areeg Samir

Faculty of Computer Science
Free University of Bozen-Bolzano
Bolzano, Italy

Claus Pahl

Faculty of Computer Science
Free University of Bozen-Bolzano
Bolzano, Italy

***Abstract*—Service-based cloud computing allows applications to be deployed and managed through third-party provided services, making typically virtualised resources available. However, often there is no direct access to platform-level execution parameters of a provided service, and only some quality properties can be directly observed while others remain hidden from the service consumer. We introduce a controller architecture for autonomous, self-adaptive anomaly remediation in this semi-hidden setting. The controller determines the possible causes of consumer-observed anomalies in an underlying provider-controlled infrastructure. We use Hidden Markov Models to map observed performance anomalies into hidden resources, and to identify the root causes of the observed anomalies. We apply the model to a clustered computing resource environment that is based on three layers of aggregated resources.**

***Index Terms*—Cloud Computing; Container Clusters; Hidden Markov Model; Workload; Anomaly; Performance.**

I. Introduction

Cloud and Edge computing are examples of services being provided to allow applications to be deployed and managed by third-party providers that make shared virtualised resources accompanied by dynamic management facilities available [2],[3]. Due to the dynamic nature of loads in a distributed cloud and edge computing setting, consumers may experience anomalies (e.g., in our case variation in a resource performance) due to distribution, heterogeneity, or scale of computing that may lead to performance degradation and potential application failures. Furthermore, loads might vary over time: (i) changes of the load on individual resources, (ii) changing workload demand and prioritisation, (iii) reallocation or removal of resources in dynamic environments. These may affect the workload of current system components (container, node, cluster), and may require rebalancing their workloads. Recent studies [1],[4],[5] have looked at resource usage, rejuvenation, or analyzing the correlation between resource consumption and abnormal behavior of applications. Less attention has been given to the possibly hidden reason behind the occurrence of an observable performance degradation (root cause)[23], and how to deal with the degradation in a hierarchically organised cluster setting.

To handle these challenges in a shared virtualised environment, third party providers provide some factors that can be directly observed (e.g., the response time of service activations) while others remain hidden from the consumer (e.g., the reason behind the workload, the possibility to predict the future load behaviour, the dependency between the affected nodes and their loads in a cluster).

We differentiate between two types of observation in relation to workload and response time fluctuations: **System states (anomaly/fault)** that refer to anomalous or faulty behavior, which is hidden from the consumer. This indicates that the behavior of a system resource is significantly different from normal behavior. An anomaly in our case may point to an undesirable behavior of a resource such as overload, or to a desirable behavior like underload of a system resource, which can be used as a solution to reduce the load at overloaded resources. **Emission or Observation (observed failure from these states)**, which indicates the occurrence of failure resulting from a hidden state.

To address this problem, we use Hierarchical Hidden Markov Models (HHMMs) [8] as a stochastic model to map the observed failure behavior of a system resource to its hidden anomaly causes (e.g., overload) through tracking the detected anomaly to locate its root cause. We implement the proposed controller for a clustered computing resource environment. The contribution of this paper is a controller [7],[6] that automatically detects the anomalous behavior within a cluster of containers running on cluster nodes, where a sequence of observations is emitted by the system resource. The controller remedies the detected anomalies that occur at the container, node or cluster level. To achieve that this paper: (i) analysed the possible causes of observable anomalies in an underlying provider-controlled infrastructure; (ii) defined an anomaly detection, and analysis controller for a self-adaptive cluster environment, that automatically manages the resource workload fluctuations. The paper objective is to introduce the controller in terms of its architecture and processing activities.

The paper is organized as follows. Section II reviews related work. Section III explains the motivation behind our work. Section IV gives an overview of HHMM. Section V explains the mapping of failure and fault. Section VI explains the controller architecture. Section VII evaluates it.

II. RELATED WORK

There are a number of studies that have addressed workload analysis in dynamic environments [1],[4],[5]. They proposed various methods for analyzing and modeling workload.

Dullmann [13] provide an online performance anomaly detection approach that detects anomalies in performance data based on discrete time series analysis.

Peiris et al. [14] analyze root causes of performance anomalies by combining the correlation and comparative analysis techniques in distributed environments. Sorkunlu et al. [15] identify system performance anomalies through analyzing the correlations in the resource usage data. Wang et al. [5] propose to model the correlation between workload and the resource utilization of applications to characterize the system status.

Maurya and Ahmad [16] propose an algorithm that dynamically estimates the load of each node and migrates the task if necessary. The algorithm migrates the jobs from overloaded nodes to underloaded ones through working on pair of nodes, it uses a server node as a hub to transfer the load information in the network, which may result in overhead at the node.

Moreover, many literatures used HMM and its derivations to detect anomaly. In [17], the author proposed various techniques implemented for the detection of anomalies and intrusions in the network using HMM. In [19] the author detected faults in real-time embedded systems using HMM through describing the healthy and faulty states of a system's hardware components. In [21], HMM is used to find, which anomaly is part of the same anomaly injection scenarios.

The objective of this paper is to detect and locate the anomalous behaviour in containerized cluster environment [20] through considering the influence of dynamic workloads on their anomaly detection solutions. The proposed controller consists of: (1) *Monitoring*, that collects the performance data of (services, containers, nodes 'VM') such as CPU, memory, and network metrics; (2) *Detection*, that detects anomalous behaviour, which is observed in response time of a component; (3) *Identification*, which tracks the cause of the detected anomaly. (4) *Recovery*, that heals the identified anomalous components. (5) *Anomaly injection*, which simulates different anomalies, and gathers dataset of performance data representing normal and abnormal conditions.

III. MOTIVATING EXAMPLE

A failure is the inability of a component to perform its functions with respect to a specified (e.g., performance) requirements [18]. Faults (also called anomalies) are system properties that describe an exceptional condition occurring in the system operation that may cause one or more failures [24].

We assume that a failure is a kind of unexpected response time observed during system component runtime (i.e., observation), while fluctuations occurring during a resource execution of a component are considered as faults or anomalies (state of a hidden component). For example, fluctuations in workload such as overload faults may cause delay in a system response time (observed failure).

Generally, the observed metrics do not provide enough information to identify the cause of an observed failure. For example, the CPU utilization of a containerized application is about 30% with 400 users, and it increases to about 70% with 800 users in the normal situation. Obviously, the system is normal with 800 users. But probably the system shows anomalous behaviour with 400 users, when the CPU utilization is about 70%. Thus, it is hard to identify whether the system is normal or anomaly just based on the CPU utilization. Thus, specifying a threshold for the utilization of resource without considering the number of users, will raise anomalous behaviours. Consequently, it is important to integrate the data of workload into anomaly detection and identification solutions. Once provided with a link between faults (workloads) and failures (response time) emitted from components, we can also apply a suitable recovery strategy depending on the type of identified fault.

Thus, a self-adaptation controller will be introduced later in this paper to automatically manage faults through identifying the degradation of performance, determining the dependency between faults and failures, and applying recovery strategies. We can align the steps of the fault management with the Monitoring, Analysis, Planning, Execution, and Knowledge (MAPE-K) control loop as a conceptual framework.

IV. HIERARCHICAL HIDDEN MARKOV MODEL (HHMM)

Hierarchical Hidden Markov Model (HHMM) [8] is a generalization of the Hidden Markov Model (HMM) that is used to model domains with hierarchical structure (e.g., intrusion detection, plan recognition, visual action recognition). HHMM can characterize the dependency of the workload (e.g., when at least one of the states is heavy loaded). The states (cluster, node, container) in HHMM are hidden from the observer and only the observation space is visible (response time). The states of HHMM emit sequences rather than a single observation by a recursive activation of one of the substates (nodes) of a state (cluster). This substate might also be hierarchically composed of substates (containers). Each container has an application that runs on it. In case a node or a container emit observation, it will be considered a production state. The states that do not emit observations directly are called internal states. The activation of a substate by an internal state is a vertical transition that reflects the dependency between states. The states at the same level have horizontal transitions. Once the transition reaches to the End state, the control returns to the root state of the chain as shown in Figure 1. The edge direction indicates the dependency between states.

We choose HHMM as every state can be represented as a multi-levels HMM in order to: (1) show communication between nodes and containers, (2) demonstrate the impact of workloads on the resources, (3) track the anomaly cause, and (4) represent the response time variations that emit from nodes or containers.

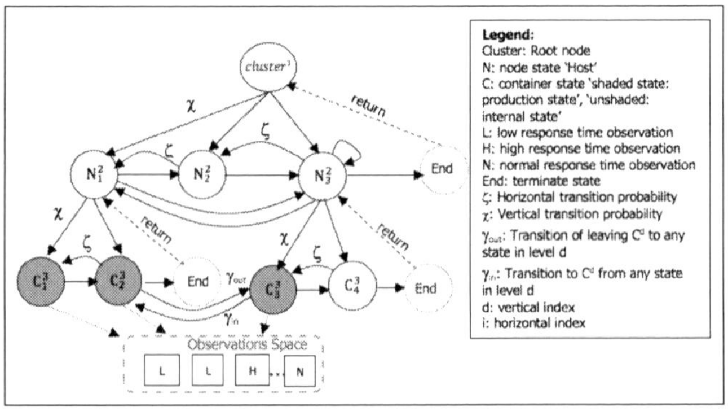

FIGURE 1. THE HHMM FOR WORKLOAD.

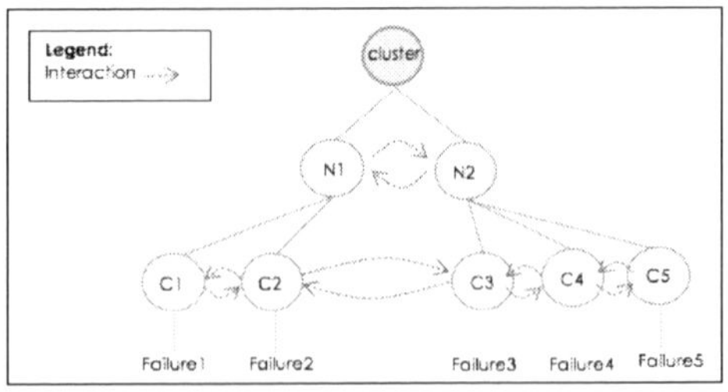

FIGURE 2. DEPENDENCIES BETWEEN CLUSTER, NODES AND CONTAINERS.

V. FAILURE-TO-FAULT MAPPING

Based on analyzing the log file and monitored metrics from existing systems, we can obtain knowledge regarding (1) the dependencies between containers, nodes and clusters; (2) response time fluctuations emitted from containers or nodes; (3) workload fluctuations that cause changes in response time. We need a mechanism that automatically maps a type of anomaly to its causes. We can identify different failure-fault cases that may occur at container, node or cluster level as illustrated in Figure 2. We focused on addressing the correlation between workload (overload) and the response time at container, node, and cluster.

A. Low Response Time Observed at Container Level

There are different reasons that may cause this:

- *Case 1.1. Container overload (self-dependency)*: means that a container is busy, causing low response times, e.g., c_1 in N_1 has entered into load loop as it tries to execute its processes while N_1 keeps sending requests to it, ignoring its limited capacity.
- *Case 1.2. Container sibling overloaded (internal container dependency)*: this indicates another container c_2 in N_1 is overloaded. This overloaded container indirectly affects the other container c_1 as there is a communication between them. For example, c_2 has an application that almost consumes all resources. The container has a communication with c_1. At such situation, when c_2 is overloaded, c_1 will go into underload. The reason is that c_2 and c_1 share the resources of the same node.
- *Case 1.3. Container neighbour overload (external container dependency)*: this happens when a container c_3 in N_2 is linked to another container c_2 in another node N_1. In another case, some containers c_3 and c_4 in N_2 dependent on each other, and container c_2 in N_1 depends on c_3. In both cases c_2 in N_1 is badly affected once c_3 or c_4 in N_2 are heavily loaded. This results in low response time observed from those containers.

B. Low Response Time Observed at Node Level

There are different reasons that cause such observations:

- *Case 2.1. Node overload (self-dependency)*: generally node overload happens when a node has low capacity, many jobs waited to be processed, or problem in network. Example, N_2 has entered into self load due to its limited capacity, which causes an overload at the container level as well c_3 and c_4.
- *Case 2.2. External node dependency*: occurs when low response time is observed at node neighbour level, e.g., when N_2 is overloaded due to low capacity or network problem, and N_1 depends on N_2. Such overload may cause low response time observed at the node level, which slow the whole operation of a cluster because of the communication between the two nodes. The reason behind that is N_1 and N_2 share the resources of the same cluster. Thus, when N_1 shows a heavier load, it would affect the performance of N_2.

C. Low Response Time Observed at Cluster Level

If a cluster coordinates between all nodes and containers, we may observe low response time at container and node levels that cause difficulty at the whole cluster level, e.g., nodes disconnected or insufficient resources.

- *Case 3.1. Communication disconnection* may happen due to problem in the node configuration, e.g., when a node in the cluster is stopped or disconnected due to failure or a user disconnect.
- *Case 3.2. Resource limitation* happens if we create a cluster with too low capacity which causing low response time observed at the system level.

The mapping between faults and failures needs to be formalised in a model that distinguishes observations and hidden states. Thus, HHMM is used to reflect the system topology.

VI. SELF-ADAPTIVE CONTROLLER ARCHITECTURE

This section explains the controller architecture (Figure 3).

A. Managed Component Pool

The system under observation consists of a cluster that is composed of a set of nodes that host containers as the application components. A node could be a virtual machine that has a given capacity. The main job of the node is to assign requests to its containers. Containers are stand-alone,

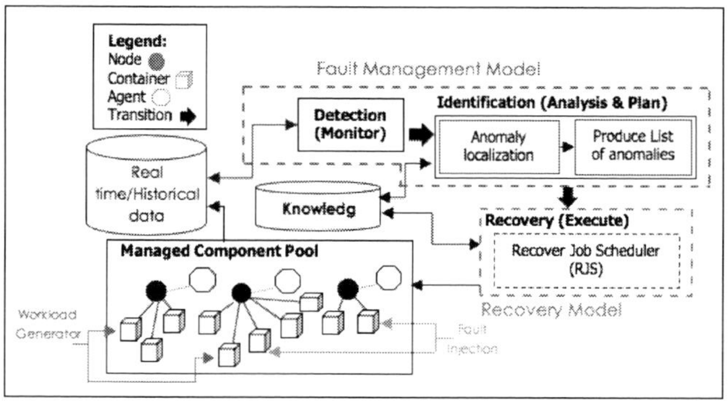

FIGURE 3. THE CONTROLLER ARCHITECTURE.

executable packages of software. Multiple containers can run on the same node, and share the operating environment with other containers. Each component either cluster, node, or container may emit observations. Observations are emissions of failure from a component resource.

We installed an agent on each node to collect metrics from the pool, and to expose log files of containers and nodes to Real-Time/Historical Data storage. The agent adds data interval function to determine the time interval at which the data collected belongs. The data interval function specifies the lower and upper limits for the data arrivals. The response time, and the state of the component are assigned to each interval. Moreover, the agent gathers data regarding the workload (i.e., no. of requests issued to component), and monitored metrics (i.e., CPU, Memory) to characterize the workload of components processed in an interval. The agent push the data to be stored in the Real time/Historical storage to be used by the Fault Management Model.

B. Fault Management Model

The model is based on the history of the overall system performance. This can be used to compare the predicted status with the currently observed one to detect anomalous behaviour. The fault management model consists of:

a) Detection (Monitor): To detect anomaly, the monitor collects system data from the Real time/Historical storage. Then, it checks if there is anomalous behaviour at the managed components through utilizing spearman's rank correlation coefficient to estimate the dissociation between the response time and the number of requests (workload). If there is a decrease in the correlation degree, then the metric is not associated with the increasing workload, which means the observed variation in performance isn't an anomaly. In case the correlation degree increase, this refers to the existence of anomaly occurred as the impact of dissociation between the workload and the response time exceeds a certain value. To achieve that we wrote an algorithm to be used as a general threshold to highlight the occurrence of anomaly in the managed pool under different workloads. We added a unique workload identifier to the group of workloads in the same period to achieve traceability through the entire system. We specified that the degree of dissociation (DD = 15) can be used as an indicator for performance degradation considering different response time, and different workloads. The value of DD will be compared against the monitored metrics (i.e., CPU, Memory utilization) to detect anomalous behaviour within the system. In case an anomaly is detected, the controller will move to the fault management to track the cause of anomaly in the system.

b) Identification (Analysis and Plan): Once there is appearance of anomaly, we built HHMMs to identify anomalies in system components as shown in Figure 1.

The HHMM vertically calls one of its substates $N_1^2 = \{C_1^3, C_2^3\}$, N_2^2, $N_3^2 = \{C_3^3, C_4^3\}$ with "vertical transition χ" and d index (superscript), where $d = \{1, 2, 3\}$. Since N_1^2 is abstract state, it enters its child HMM substates C_1^3 and C_2^3. Since C_2^3 is a production state, it emits observations, and may make horizontal transition γ, with i horizontal index (subscript), where $i = \{1, 2, 3, 4\}$, from C_1^3 to C_4^3. Once there is no another transition, C_2^3 transits to the end state End, which ends the transition for this substate, to return the control to the calling state N_1^2. Once the control returns to the state N_1^2, it makes a horizontal transition (if exist) to state N_2^2, which horizontally transits to state N_3^2. State N_3^2 has substates C_3^3 that transits to C_4^3 which may transit back to C_3^3 or transit to the End state. Once all the transitions under this node are achieved, the control returns to N_3^2. State N_3^2 may loop around, transit back to N_2^2, or enters its End state, which ends the whole process and returns control to the cluster. The model can't horizontally do transition unless it vertically transited. Further, the internal sates don't need to have the same number of substates. It can be seen that N_1^2 calls containers C_1^3 and C_2^3, while N_2^2 has no substates. The horizontal transition between containers reflect the request/reply between the client/server in our system under test, and the vertical transition refers to child/parent relationship between containers/node.

The observation O is denoted by $F_i = \{f_1, f_2, ..., f_n\}$ to refer to the response time observations sequence (failures). An observed low response time might reflect workload fluctuation. This fluctuation in workload is associated with a probability that reflects the state transition status from OL to NL ($PF_{OL \to NL}$) at a failure rate $\Re$, which indicates the number of failures for a N, C or $cluster$ over a period of time.

We used the generalized Baum-Welch algorithm [8] to train the model by calculating the probabilities of the model parameters: (1) the horizontal transitions from a state to another. (2) probability that the O is started to be emitted for $state_i^d$ at t. $state_i^d$ refers to container, node, or cluster. (3) the O of $state_i^d$ were emitted and finished at t. (4) the probability that $state^{d-1}$ is entered at t before O_t to activate state $state_i^d$. (5) the forward and backward transition from bottom-up.

The output of algorithm will be used to train Viterbi algorithm to find the anomalous hierarchy of the detected anomalous states. As shown in "(1)-(3)", we recursively calculate $\Im$ which is the ψ for a time set ($\bar{t} = \psi(t, t{+}k, C_i^d, C^{d-1})$), where ψ is a state list, which is the index of the most probable production state to be activated by C^{d-1} before activating C_i^d. $\bar{t}$ is the time when C_i^d was activated by C^{d-1}. The δ is the likelihood of the most probable state sequence generating $(O_t, \cdots, O_{(t+k)})$ by a recursive activation. The τ is the transition time at which C_i^d was called by C^{d-1}. Once all the recursive transitions are finished and returned to $cluster$, we get the most probable hierarchies starting from $cluster$ to the production states at T period through scanning the sate list ψ, the states likelihood δ, and transition time τ.

$$L = \max_{(1 \leq r \leq N_i^d)} \left\{ \delta(\bar{t}, t+k, N_r^{d+1}, N_i^d)\, a_{End}^{N_i^d} \right\} \quad (1)$$

$$\Im = \max_{(1 \leq y \leq N^{j-1})} \left\{ \delta(t, \bar{t}-1, N_i^d, N^{d-1}) a_{End}^{N^{d-1}} L \right\} \quad (2)$$

$$stSeq = \max_{cluster} \left\{ \delta(T, cluster), \tau(T, cluster), \psi(T, cluster) \right\} \quad (3)$$

Once we have a trained the model, we compare the detected hierarchies against the observed one to identify the type of workload. The hierarchies with the lowest probabilities will be considered anomaly. Once we detected and identified the workload type (e.g., OL), a hierarchy of faulty states (e.g., $cluster$, N_1^2, C_1^3 and C_2^3) that are affected by the anomalous component (C_1^3) is obtained that reflects observed anomalous behaviour. We repeat these steps until the probability of the model states become fixed. Each state is correlated with time that indicates: the time of it's activation, it's activated sub-states, and the time at which the control returns to the calling state. The result of the fault management model (anomalous components) is stored in Knowledge storage. This aid us in the recovery procedure as the anomalous state will be recovered first come-first heal.

C. Fault-Failure Recovery Cases

Based on the fault type, we apply a recovery mechanism that considers the dependencies between components, and the current component status. The recovery mechanism is specified based on historic and current observations of a response time for a container or node and the hidden states (containers or nodes). The following steps and concerns are considered by the recovery mechanism:

- Analysis: relies on current and historic observation.
- Observation (failure): indicates the type of observed failure (e.g., low response time).
- Anomaly (fault): reflects the fault type (e.g., overload).
- Reason: explains the causes of the problem.
- Remedial Action: explains different solutions that can be applied to solve the problem.
- Requirements: constraint that might apply.

We look at two anomaly cases and suitable recovery strategies, which exemplify recovery strategies for the fault-failure mapping cases 1.3 and 2.1. These strategies can be applied based on the observed response time (current and historic observations) and related faults (hidden states).

1) Container neighbour overload (external container dependency) **Analysis**: current/historic observations, hidden states
Observation (failure): low response time at the anomalous container and the dependent one.
Anomaly: overload in one or more containers results in underload for another container at different node.
Reason: heavily loaded container with external dependent one (communication)
Remedial Actions: *Option 1*: Separate the overloaded container and the external one depending on it from their nodes. Then, create a new node containing the separated containers considering the cluster capacity. Redirect other containers that in communication to these 2 containers in the new node. Connect current nodes with the new one and calculate the probability of the whole model to know the number of transitions (to avoid the occurrence of overload) and to predict the future behaviour. *Option 2*: For the anomalous container, add a new one to the node that has the anomalous container to provide fair workload distribution among containers considering the node resource limits. Or, if the node does not yet reach the resource limits available, move the overloaded container to another node with free resource limits. At the end, update the node. *Option 3*: create another (MM) node within the node with anomalous container behaviour. Next, direct the communication of current containers to (MM). We need to redetermine the probability of the whole model to redistribute the load between containers. Finally, update the cluster and the nodes. *Option 4*: distribute load. *Option 5*: rescale node. *Option 6*: do nothing, this means that the observed failure relates to regular system maintenance or update happened to the system. Thus, no recovery option will be applied.
Requirements: need to consider node capacity.

2) Node overload (self-dependency) **Analysis**: current and historic observations
Observation (failure): low response time at node level.
Anomaly: overloaded node.
Reason: limited node capacity.
Remedial Actions: *Option 1*: distribute load. *Option 2*: rescale node. *Option 3*: do nothing.
Requirements: collect information regarding containers and nodes, consider node capacity and rescale node(s).

D. Recovery Model

The recovery model (Execute stage in MAPE-K) receives an ordered list of faulty states from the identification step. It applies a recovery mechanism considering the type of the identified anomaly and the resource capacity. We have configured the fault management model to have a specific number of nodes and containers because increasing the number of nodes and containers will lead to a large amount of different recovery actions (Load balancing rules), which reduces model performance. We are mainly concerned with two workload anomalies: (1) overload as it reflects anomalous behavior,

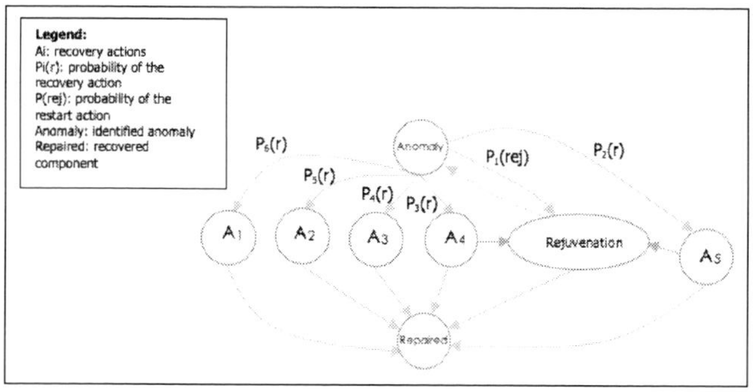

FIGURE 4. HMM FOR RECOVERY ACTIONS.

(2) underload category, as it is considered anomaly but it represents a solution to migrate load from heavy loaded component. We define different recovery actions for each fault-failure case. Consequently, for an identified anomaly case, we need to select the most appropriate action from the time and cost perspectives.

The Recover Job Scheduler (RJS) heals the identified anomaly based on first identified-first heal. It mitigates the anomalous state, by distributing the load to the underloaded components considering their status. The recovery actions are stored in the Knowledge storage to keep track of the number of applied actions to the identified anomalous component. Before applying any of the recovery option, "Restart" option will be applied to save the cost of trying multiple recovery options if the component doesn't reach its restart action number limit. In case a restart option doesn't enhance the situation, RJS checks the existence of underloaded component identified by the fault management model and stored in the knowledge storage. If there is underloaded component, the HMM is trained using the Forward-Backward algorithm to select the most probable action for the anomalous component as shown in Figure 4. The states A_i in the model refer to the hidden recovery actions. The $rejuventation$ hidden state refers to the restart action, and $P_i(r)$, is the probability of the recovery actions. We estimated $P_i(r)$ based on computing the maximum likelihood. The result of the HMM will be, for instance, the most probable action for anomalous state C_1^3 is 'distribute load'. The RJS apply the selected action to the fault component in the "Managed Component Pool". In case, RJS couldn't find underloaded components, the "pause" action will be applied. If the number of applied recovery actions for the anomalous component exceeds a predefined threshold, terminate action will be applied after backing up the component. For each component, we further keep a profile of the type of applied action to enhance the recovery procedure in the future.

a) Metrics for Recovery Plan Determination: In order to better capture the accuracy of the proposed fault identification, we estimated the Fault Rate to capture (1) the number of fault during system execution $\Re(FN)$, and (2) the overall length of failure occurrence $\Re(FL)$ as depicted in "(4)" and "(5)". This aids us later in reducing the fault/failure occurrence through providing the best suited recovery mechanism, for instance for frequent or long-lasting failures. The observed behaviour will be analysed in terms of failure rates for each state – e.g., low response times may result from overload states or normal load states – in order to determine the number of failures observed for each state and to estimate the total failure numbers for all the states. We define $\Re$ as follows:

$$\Re(FN) = \frac{No\ of\ Detected\ Faults}{Total\ No\ of\ Faults\ of\ Resource} \tag{4}$$

$$\Re(FL) = \frac{Total\ Time\ of\ Observed\ Failures}{Total\ Time\ of\ Execution\ of\ Resource} \tag{5}$$

The Average Failure Length (AFL), as in "(6)", might also be relevant to judge the relative urgency of recovery. Other relevant metrics that impact on the decision which strategy to use, but which we do not detail here, are resilience metrics addressing recovery times.

$$AFL = \frac{\sum Time\ of\ Failure\ Occurrence}{Number\ of\ Observed\ Failures} \tag{6}$$

VII. EVALUATION

The proposed framework is run on Kubernetes and Docker containers. We deployed TPC-W[1] benchmark on the containers to validate the framework. We focused on three types of faults CPU hog, Network packet loss/latency, and performance anomaly caused by workload congestion.

A. Environment Set-Up

To evaluate the effectiveness of the proposed framework, the experiment environment consists of three VMs. Each VM is equipped with LinuxOS, 3VCPU, 2GB VRAM, Xen 4.11 [2], and an agent. Agents are installed on each VM to collect the monitoring data from the system (e.g., host metrics, container, performance metrics, and workloads), and send them to the Real-Time/Historical storage to be processed by the Monitor. The VMs are connected through a 100 Mbps network. For each VM, we deployed two containers, and we run into them TPC-W benchmark.

TPC-W benchmark is used for resource provisioning, scalability, and capacity planning for e-commerce websites. TPC-W emulates an online bookstore that consists of 3 tiers: client application, web server, and database. Each tier is installed on VM. We didn't considered the database tier in the anomaly detection and identification, as a powerful VM should be dedicated to the database. The CPU and Memory utilization are gathered from the web server, while the Response time is measured from client's end. We ran TPC-W for 300 minutes. The number of records that we obtained from the TPC-W was 2000 records.

[1] http://www.tpc.org/tpcw/
[2] https://xenproject.org/

We further used docker *stats* command to obtain a live data stream for running containers. SignalFX Smart Agent[3] monitoring tool is used and configured to observe the runtime performance of components and their resources. We also used Heapster[4] to group the collected data, and store them in a time series database using InfluxDB[5]. The gathered data from the monitoring tool, and from datasets are stored in the Real-Time/Historical Data storage to enhance the future anomaly detection and identification. The gathered dataset is classified into training and testing datasets 50% for each. The model training last 150 minutes.

To simulate real anomaly scenarios, script is written to inject different types of anomalies. The anomaly injection for each component last 5 minutes. The anomaly scenarios are: (1) CPU Hog, consume all CPU cycles by employing infinite loops. (2) Memory Leak, exhausts the component memory. The stress[6] tool is used to create pressure on CPU and Memory.

Further, workload contention is generated to test the controller under different workloads. To generate workload, the TPC-W web server is emulated using client application, which generates workload (using Remote Browser Emulator) by simulating a number of user requests that is increased iteratively. Since the workload is always described by the access behavior, we consider the container is gradually workloaded within [30-2000] emulated users requests, and the number of requests is changed periodically. The client application reports response time metric, and the web server reports CPU and Memory utilization. To measure the number of requests and response (latency), HTTPing[7] is installed on each node. Also AWS X-Ray[8] is used to trace of the request through the system.

B. The Detection Assessment

The detection model is evaluated by Root Mean Square Error (RMSE), Mean Absolute Percentage Error (MAPE), and False Alarm Rate (FAR), which are the commonly used metrics [25] for evaluating the quality of detection. We further measured the Number of Correctly Detected Anomaly (CDA) and Accuracy of Detection (AD).

a) Root Mean Square Error (RMSE): It measures the differences between the detected value and the observed one by the model. A smaller RMSE value indicates a more effective detection scheme.

b) Mean Absolute Percentage Error (MAPE): It measures the detection accuracy of a model. Both RMSE and MAPE are negatively-oriented scores, which means lower values are better.

[3]https://www.signalfx.com/
[4]https://github.com/kubernetes-retired/heapster
[5]https://www.influxdata.com/
[6]https://linux.die.net/man/1/stress
[7]https://www.vanheusden.com/httping/
[8]https://aws.amazon.com/xray/

TABLE I. DETECTION EVALUATION.

Metrics	HHMM	DBN	HTM
RMSE	0.23	0.31	0.26
MAPE	0.14	0.27	0.16
CDA	96.12%	91.38%	94.64%
AC	0.94	0.84	0.91
FAR	0.27	0.46	0.31

c) Number of Correctly Detected Anomaly (CDA): It measures percentage of the correctly detected anomalies to the total number of detected anomalies in a given dataset. High CDA indicates the model is correctly detected anomalous behaviour.

d) Accuracy of Detection (AD): It measures the completeness of the correctly detected anomalies to the total number of anomalies in a given dataset. Higher AD means that fewer anomaly cases are undetected.

e) False Alarm Rate (FAR): The number of the normal detected component, which has been misclassified as anomalous by the model.

The efficiency of the model is compared with a Dynamic Bayesian network (DBN), see Table I. The results show that the HHMM and HTM model detects anomalous behaviour with promised results comparing to DBN.

C. The Identification Assessment

The accuracy of the results is compared with Dynamic Bayesian Network (DBN), and Hierarchical Temporal Memory (HTM), and it is evaluated based on different metrics such as: Accuracy of Identification (AI), Number of Correctly Identified Anomaly (CIA), Number of Incorrectly Identified Anomaly (IIA), and FAR.

a) Accuracy of Identification (AI): It measures the completeness of the correctly identified anomalies to the total number of anomalies in a given dataset. Higher AI means that fewer anomaly cases are un-identified.

b) Number of Correctly Identified Anomaly (CIA): It is the number of correct identified anomaly (NCIA) out of the total set of identification, which is the number of correct Identification (NCIA) + the number of incorrect Identification (NICI)). The higher value indicates the model is correctly identified anomalous component.

$$CIA = \frac{NCIA}{NCIA + NICI} \quad (7)$$

c) Number of Incorrectly Identified Anomaly (IIA): IIA is the number of the identified component, which represents an anomaly but misidentified as normal by the model. The lower value indicates that the model correctly identified anomaly component.

$$IIA = \frac{FN}{FN + TP} \quad (8)$$

TABLE II. Assessment of Identification.

Metrics	HHMM	DBN	HTM
AI	0.94	0.84	0.94
CIA	94.73%	87.67%	93.94%
IIA	4.56%	12.33%	6.07%
FAR	0.12	0.26	0.17

TABLE III. Recovery Evaluation.

Evaluation Metrics	*Results*
RA	99%
MTTR	60 seconds
OA	97%

d) False Alarm Rate (FAR): The number of the normal identified component, which has been misclassified as anomalous by the model.

$$FAR = \frac{FP}{TN + FP} \tag{9}$$

The false positive (FP) means the detection/identification of anomaly is incorrect as the model detects/identifies the normal behaviour as anomaly. True negative (TN) means the model can correctly detect and identify normal behaviour as normal.

As shown in Table II, HHMM and HTM achieved promising results for the identification of anomaly. While the results of the DBN a little bit decayed for the CIA with approximately 7% than HHMM, and 6% than HTM. Both HHMM and HTM showed higher identification accuracy as they are able to identify temporal anomalies in the dataset. The result interferes that the HHMM is able to link the observed failure to its hidden workload.

D. The Recovery Assessment

To assess the recovery decisions of the model, we measure: (1) the Recovery Accuracy (RA) to be the number of successfully recovered anomalies to the total number of identified anomalies, (2) Mean Time to Recovery (MTTR), the average time that the approach takes to recover starting from the anomaly injection until recovering it. (3) Over all Accuracy (OA) to be the number of correct recovered anomalies to the total number of anomalies. The results in Table III show that once HMM model is configured properly, it can efficiently recover the anomalies with an accuracy of 99%.

VIII. Conclusions

This paper presented a controller architecture for the detection, and recovery of anomalies in hierarchically organised clustered computing environments, that reflects recent container cluster orchestration tools like Kubernetes or Docker Swarm. The key objective was to provide an analysis feature, that maps observable quality concerns onto hidden resources in a hierarchical clustered environment, and their operation in order to identify the reason for performance degradations and other anomalies. From this, a recovery strategy that removes the workload anomaly, thus removing the observed performance failure is the second step.

We have proposed to use Hidden Markov Models (HMMs) to reflect the hierarchical nature of the unobservable resources, and to support the detection, identification, and recovery of anomalous behaviours. We have further analysed mappings between observations and resource usage based on a clustered container scenario.

The objective of this paper was to introduce the complete controller architecture with its key processing steps. In the future, we will complete the current controller prototype, carry out further experimental evaluations, and also address practical concerns such as the relevance for microservice architectures [10].

References

[1] X. Chen, C.-D. Lu, and K. Pattabiraman, "Failure prediction of jobs in compute clouds: A google cluster case study," *International Symposium on Software Reliability Engineering, ISSRE*, pp. 167–177, 2014.

[2] C. Pahl, P. Jamshidi, O. Zimmermann, "Architectural principles for cloud software," ACM Transactions on Internet Technology (TOIT) 18 (2), 17, 2018.

[3] D. von Leon, L. Miori, J. Sanin, N. El Ioini, S. Helmer, C. Pahl, "A Lightweight Container Middleware for Edge Cloud Architectures," Fog and Edge Computing: Principles and Paradigms, 145-170, 2019.

[4] G. C. Durelli, M. D. Santambrogio, D. Sciuto, and A. Bonarini, "On the design of autonomic techniques for runtime resource management in heterogeneous systems," Doctoral dissertation, Politecnico di Milano, 2016.

[5] T. Wang, J. Xu, W. Zhang, Z. Gu, and H. Zhong, "Self-adaptive cloud monitoring with online anomaly detection," *Future Generation Computer Systems*, vol. 80, pp. 89–101, 2018.

[6] P. Jamshidi, A. Sharifloo, C. Pahl, H. Arabnejad, A. Metzger, G. Estrada, "Fuzzy self-learning controllers for elasticity management in dynamic cloud architectures," 12th International ACM SIGSOFT Conference on Quality of Software Architectures, 2016.

[7] P. Jamshidi, A. Sharifloo, C. Pahl, A. Metzger, G. Estrada, "Self-learning cloud controllers: Fuzzy q-learning for knowledge evolution," Intl Conference on Cloud and Autonomic Computing, 208-211, 2015.

[8] S. Fine, Y. Singer, and N. Tishby, "The hierarchical hidden markov model: analysis and applications," *Machine Learning*, vol. 32, no. 1, pp. 41–62, 1998.

[9] R. Scolati, I. Fronza, N. El Ioini, A. Samir, C. Pahl, "A Containerized Big Data Streaming Architecture for Edge Cloud Computing on Clustered Single-Board Devices," CLOSER, 2019.

[10] D. Taibi, V. Lenarduzzi, C. Pahl, "Architecture Patterns for a Microservice Architectural Style," Springer, 2019.

[11] H. Arabnejad, C. Pahl, G. Estrada, A. Samir, F. Fowley, "A fuzzy load balancer for adaptive fault tolerance management in cloud platforms," European Conference on Service-Oriented and Cloud Computing, 109-124, 2017.

[12] H. Arabnejad, C. Pahl, P. Jamshidi, G. Estrada, "A comparison of reinforcement learning techniques for fuzzy cloud auto-scaling," 17th IEEE/ACM International Symposium on Cluster, Cloud and Grid Computing, 2017.

[13] T. F. Düllmann, "Performance anomaly detection in microservice architectures under continuous change," Master, University of Stuttgart, 2016.

[14] M. Peiris, J. H. Hill, J. Thelin, S. Bykov, G. Kliot, and C. Konig, "PAD: Performance anomaly detection in multi-server distributed systems," *Intl Conf on Cloud Computing, CLOUD*, 2014.

[15] N. Sorkunlu, V. Chandola, and A. Patra, "Tracking system behavior from resource usage data," in *International Conference on Cluster Computing, ICCC*, 2017.

[16] S. Maurya and K. Ahmad, "Load Balancing in Distributed System using Genetic Algorithm," *International Journal of Engineering and Technology (IJET)*, vol. 5, no. 2, pp. 139–142, 2013.

[17] H. Sukhwani, "A survey of anomaly detection techniques and hidden markov model," *Intl Journal of Computer Applications*, vol. 93, no. 18, 2014.

[18] R. Heinrich, A. van Hoorn, H. Knoche, F. Li, L.E. Lwakatare, C. Pahl, S. Schulte, J. Wettinger, "Performance engineering for microservices: research challenges and directions," ACM, 2017.

[19] N. Ge, S. Nakajima, and M. Pantel, "Online diagnosis of accidental faults for real-time embedded systems using a hidden Markov model," *Simulation*, vol. 91, no. 19, pp. 851–868, 2016.

[20] C. Pahl, A. Brogi, J. Soldani, P. Jamshidi, "Cloud container technologies: a state-of-the-art review," IEEE Transactions on Cloud Computing, 2018.

[21] G. Brogi, "Real-time detection of advanced persistent threats using information flow tracking and hidden markov," Doctoral dissertation, 2018.

[22] D. von Leon, L. Miori, J. Sanin, N. El Ioini, S. Helmer, C. Pahl, "A performance exploration of architectural options for a middleware for decentralised lightweight edge cloud architectures," CLOSER, 2018.

[23] A. Samir, C. Pahl, "Anomaly Detection and Analysis for Clustered Cloud Computing Reliability," Intl Conf on Cloud Computing, Grids, and Virtualization, 2019.

[24] IEEE, "IEEE standard classification for software anomalies (IEEE 1044 - 2009)," pp. 1–4, 2009.

[25] K. Markham, "Simple guide to confusion matrix terminology," 2014.

Real-Time Activity Recognition Utilizing Dynamically On-Body Placed Smartphones

Marc Kurz, Bernhard Hiesl, Erik Sonnleitner

University of Applied Sciences Upper Austria
Faculty for Informatics, Communications and Media
Department of Mobility and Energy
4232 Hagenberg, Austria
{firstname.lastname}@fh-hagenberg.at

Abstract—**This work-in-progress paper presents a project that deals with real-time recognition of people's activities by utilizing commercial smartphones. One important and crucial aspect is that the phone can be placed on various on-body positions (with different orientation and rotation), thus the system has to adapt autonomously to the current phone-location. There are many possibilities to purse the smartphone - for example, facing downwards to your body, facing up away from your body, left or right pocket or even back pocket. The application has to adapt to these variations of the on-body positions to fulfill the activity recognition task in real-time. The activities that are considered in this paper are five common modes of locomotion: (i) standing, (ii) walking, (iii) running, (iv) stairs-up and (v) stairs-down. The paper presents the problem definition, reflects related work on this topic, showing the relevance of the project, and discusses the intended approach, expected results and already conducted work.**

Keywords–Activity recognition; Mobile sensing; Self-adaptation; Adaptive application; Adaptive real-time strategies.

I. INTRODUCTION

Nowadays mobile phones are manufactured with strong processors, good cameras, sharp displays and precise sensors (e.g., accelerometer, gyroscope, magnetometer, GPS, etc.). The composition of these elements gives mobile platforms a vast playground for mobile developers to create applications in areas such as social media, entertainment and personal usage. More and more people tend to use their mobile phone on a daily basis, which transforms the device into a constant companion. Therefore, applications running on mobile phones could gather a huge amount of information about the user. For example, this might include the usage of the smartphone, current context or even the correct recognition of the activity the user is performing [1][2].

This paper presents a work-in-progress project dealing with the real-time recognition of people's activities utilizing a commercial smartphone. This idea is not new and has been subject to research in numerous previous publications (e.g., [3][4][5][6][7][8][9][10], see Section II - Related Work - for further details). The challenging and novel aspect is that the recognition of activities shall be rotation-, orientation- and position-independent - thus the system has to autonomously adapt to changes in the phone's position and orientation regarding the on-body placement. The five considered on-body positions for the smartphone are illustrated in Figure 1 (i.e., left-, right- front pocket, left-, right-, back-pocket, shirt-pocket). We have identified those five body positions since they are realistically used by users to carry the phone when not actively used. Furthermore, the phone could be rotated and oriented differently - thus the placement of the phone on the body of the user is very important. Common machine learning technologies are usually trained under laboratory conditions, presuming constant conditions (like position, location, etc.). This is the challenging aspect, since we also do not want to force the user to conduct a preliminary calibration - the system shall be able to self-adapt to the phone's position and orientation autonomously upon the recognition task. The relevant activities that are currently of interest are - for the sake of simplicity - reduced to five modes of locomotion: (i) standing, (ii) walking, (iii) running, (iv) stairs-up and (v) stairs-down. Possible real-world use cases and scenarios for such applications could be (i) personal logging (sports monitoring - e.g., answering questions whether the user has been physically active enough during a period of time), (ii) health-care, (iii) recommender systems, etc.

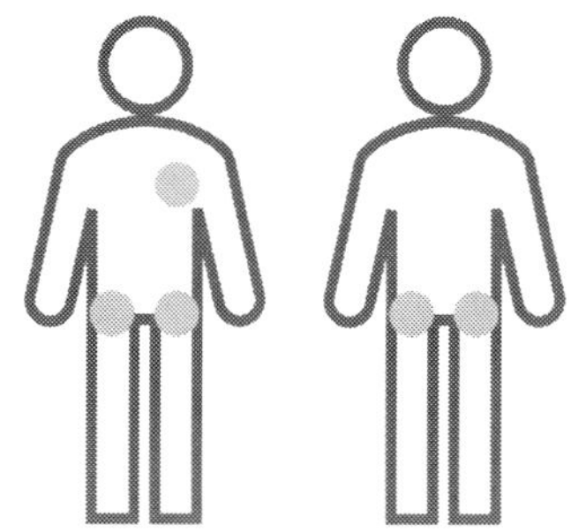

Figure 1. Possible on-body phone positions (i.e., left-, right- front pocket, left-, right-, back-pocket, shirt-pocket).

The research challenge can be summarized as follows:

> *How can highly accurate real-time activity recognition be realized utilizing a dynamically (i.e., rotation, position and orientation independent) on-body placed commercial smartphone?*

This paper provides a work-in-progress summary tackling this research challenge discussing related work (Section II), the methodological approach (Section III), an overview of the current status and preliminary results (Section IV). The paper closes with a conclusion and an outlook to future work in Section V.

II. Related Work

Prior investigations have proven that activity recognition using mobile phones or accelerometers placed on the body is feasible in a decent way [3][4][5]. However, nowadays there are countless variations of different implementations worldwide. In this paper distinction is made between activity recognition that is position and orientation dependent and activity recognition that is position and orientation independent.

Even though Bao and Intille [4] wrote their paper in 2004, it is still one of the most cited academic sources in the activity recognition domain. The reason for this is that they developed the first semi-naturalistic activity recognition system using five bi-axial acceleration sensors mounted on different body positions. Semi-naturalistic means that participants were not supervised executing the activities they were asked to perform. Therefore, activities were performed in a more natural way and it is possible that the execution of the activity varied as participants did not feel as subjects being observed. Furthermore, Bao and Intille [4] indicate that only two accelerometers and low-level features (mean, min, max) are sufficient to recognize an activity correctly using Decision Tree algorithms. Another approach worth mentioning is demonstrated by Ravi et al. [11], who use a single triaxial accelerometer near the pelvic region for the approach. Instead of decision trees, a meta level classifier classifies the activities. Other authors such as Kwapisz et al. [7], Anjum et al. [3] and Derawi and Bours [6] use mobile phones with built in tri-axial accelerometers in their position and orientation dependent activity recognition approaches. Kwapisz et al. [7], for example, provide only one position and orientation of the mobile phone. Furthermore, Anjum et al. [3] also stated that after evaluation of different classifiers including K-Nearest Neighbors (KNN), Support Vector Machines (SVM) and Naive Bayes, Decision Trees are performing best on single tri-axial accelerometers.

Similar approaches, which correspond to the topic of this paper, were developed by Yang [12], Sung et al. [13], Henpraserttae et al. [14] and Ustev and Durmaz Incel [15]. However, the solution of each investigation was implemented in a different unique way. To build a position and orientation independent system, Sun et al. [13], for example collected sensor data with varying positions and orientations using a mobile phone. Yang [12] instead extracts the vertical and horizontal movement of the mobile phone. Therefore, the application is no longer limited with respect to orientation. Additionally, Yang [12] used Decision Trees for the classification process. Henpraserttae et al. [14] have a more computational approach to achieve a position and orientation independent activity recognition system. They apply a projection-based method. The data acquisition transports each new record into the same coordinate system by applying a matrix multiplication with a reference matrix gathered with the magnetometer.

However, each of the named projects needs model updates when it comes to phone positions which have not been considered yet. The self-adaptiveness towards the orientation, position and location of the on-body phone placement is the novel aspect differentiating this research work from related work.

III. Methodology

Prior to implementation, machine learning technologies and suited algorithms are being evaluated with focus on the special purpose of adapting autonomously to the on-body sensor position. Furthermore, an Android app has been implemented for collecting data of subjects in order to analyse the specific activities and the corresponding algorithms for the different steps of the recognition process (i.e., signal processing, feature extraction, classification). This analysis has to be done with respect to the dynamic aspect of the sensor placement. The following Sections III-A to III-D summarize the methodology for the different relevant aspects. In Section IV, an overview of the current status and preliminary results is given.

A. Data Collection

Sensor data was collected for 15 subjects performing the 5 activities carrying the the smartphone on the five different on-body locations as illustrated in Figure 1, using 4 different orientations each. Since each recording took around 10 seconds, the total amount of recorded sensor data is approx. 4,5hrs. For recording, a simple phone application was implemented that allows for selecting the recorded activity (i.e., instant labelling of the sensor data is possible with this approach) and the on-body position of the phone (see Figure 2).

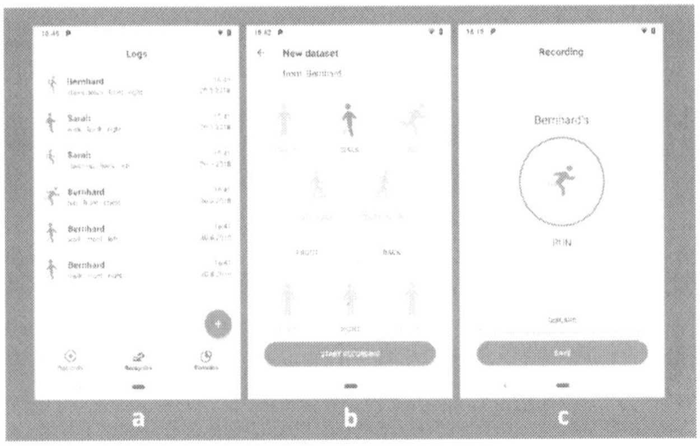

Figure 2. The application used for recording the data. (a) shows an overview of recorded data, (b) shows the selection of activity and phone-location prior to recording, (c) shows the screen to save or discard a recorded session.

The recorded modalities of the sensor data are (i) accelerometer, (ii) gyroscope and (iii) magnetometer at a rate of 100Hz. We did not consider further modalities since these three are so common that every commercial smartphone is capable of delivering these modalities. An example of raw recorded acceleration data for the activity *walk* is depicted in Figure 3.

B. Feature Extraction

As related work and projects show, low level features (which are easily computable) are significant enough to classify the correct activity [4][7][16]. For the feature extraction, a sliding window approach will be implemented and evaluated with the length of two seconds and an overlapping of 50%. Prior investigations show that this is a suitable sliding window size for activity recognition [4][13]. Usually, within two seconds at least one repetition of an activity should be completed. Inside of each window, the features as listed below will be extracted for each acceleration axis:

- **Mean:** The mean value of each window and each axis.
- **Max:** The max value of each window and each axis.

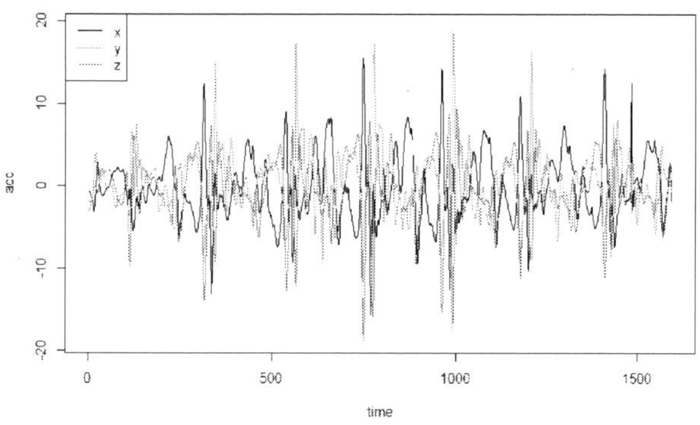

Figure 3. Exemplary data representing the activity *walk*.

- **Min:** The min value of each window and each axis.
- **Standard deviation, Variance:** The variance/standard deviation of each window and each axis.
- **Correlation:** The correlation between each pair of axes.
- **Energy:** The energy is calculated as the sum of the squared discrete Fast Fourier Transform (FFT).
- **Entropy:** The entropy is calculated as the normalized information entropy of the discrete FFT.

Subsequently, the feature vector will be used to train a machine learning model using Weka 3.8 [17]. Again, previous investigations regarding this topic show that low level features are significant enough to classify the correct activity [4][7][16].

C. Classification

The classification of activities combines the data collection and feature extraction and tries to map the recorded sensor data into an output class (i.e., the recognized activity). A first evaluation (related work research and first tryouts with the recorded dataset) of algorithms for classification shows that the following seem to be promising methods for our approach:

- K-Nearest Neighbors (KNN)
- Decision Tree (J48)
- Naive Bayes
- Support Vector Machines (SVM)

Since we have two crucial requirements for our application, namely (i) real-time recognition of activities, and (ii) adaptation to the dynamic placement of the smartphone, the algorithms for feature extraction and classification shall be robust, easily implementable and performant. Furthermore, the models that build the base for the classification process need to be small enough to be processed and calculated on mobile devices. This is the reason why we consider rather "classical" approaches (e.g., KNN, SVM, etc.) rather than recent methods like neural networks [18].

Once the classification models are created, they will be integrated into the system. As already mentioned, the classification process shall be executed in real-time. Therefore, recording and feature extraction will be needed in this process as well. In order to achieve this, the sliding window was used again. After the user starts the automatic recognition of the application, the sliding window algorithm calculates and extracts all required features of the recorded acceleration data. Due to the window size of the algorithm, it takes about two seconds to recognize the activity in real-time.

D. Dynamic Adaptation

The dynamic adaptation of the system tackles the problem of different positions, locations and orientations of the on-body placed smartphone. Every person might carry the phone differently, meaning that the sensor data might look different. This is obviously a problem for classification algorithms since supervised learning methods work in a way that they compare trained models with the real-time (preprocessed) sensor data. To achieve highly accurate real-time activity recognition with data coming from dynamically placed phones, the system has to be capable of adapting to this position-, location-, and orientation-dynamic. Compared with the previously mentioned algorithms for feature extraction and classification the following approaches seem to be promising for dynamic adaptation:

(i) Magnitude of acceleration data.
(ii) 2D projection of sensor data, respectively horizontal/vertical acceleration.
(iii) Matrix multiplication to normalize the sensor data.
(iv) Quaternions as representation of rotations in 3D space compared with Euler angles [19].

Again, it is important to achieve the activity recognition task in real-time (i.e. getting instant feedback within 1-2 seconds) and that the user is not being forced to artificially mount the smartphone at a previously defined position. Furthermore, forcing the user to execute a calibration task prior to the recognition of activities is not desired.

IV. Current Status & Preliminary Results

The current status of the project is that the sensor data from 15 subjects (8 male, 7 female, all between 22 and 30 years old) has been recorded and analysed. Feature extraction and classification methodologies have been analysed and we were able to limit the number of suitable algorithms. We have learnt that for our specific use cases of real-time recognition and dynamic adaptation, computationally expensive algorithms like neural networks [18] are not suited.

We have implemented and used a recording app (see Figure 2), which collected sensor data from a smartphone. Subjects participating in this study were asked to put the phone in their pockets in different positions and orientations while performing the five varying activities (modes of locomotion). To achieve the best approach concerning performance and recognition, different classifiers such as KNN, Naive Bayes, SVM and Decision Tree were developed using the machine learning program Weka 3.8 [17]. The trained models were compared with each other. After evaluation it became evident that Decision Tree was the most suitable model applicable to this project. The reason for this assumption is based on the model's overall result of 94% accuracy. Nevertheless, KNN, SVM and Naive Bayes will be further evaluated and considered since related work shows that these algorithms are also performing well. Evaluations of the real-time approach have shown that this will be realized with the help of the sliding window procedure, which has a fixed size of two seconds and an overlapping of 50%.

The flow of recognizing activities (see Figure 4) is currently being developed and evaluated in order to achieve the real-time requirement. As already mentioned, by not considering the dynamic-aspect of on-body phone placement, the accuracy of the recognition task utilizing standard features and rather easy classification algorithms is around 94%. We are currently in the process of fine-tuning our models, algorithms and other parameters (like the sliding window approach) to further increase the accuracy.

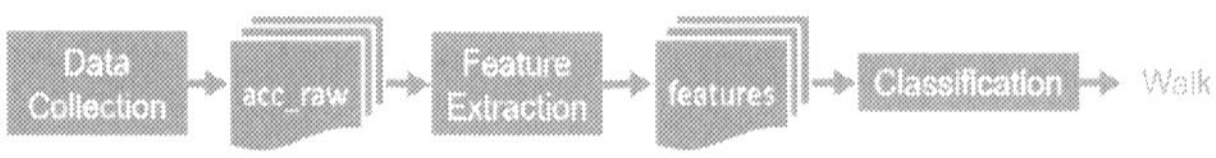

Figure 4. The subsequent steps of the real-time activity recognition task [1].

In parallel, work on the dynamic aspect has been started to achieve the system's self-adaptiveness regarding the dynamic placement of the smartphone. As mentioned, some promising approaches are currently being investigated (i.e., (i) magnitude, (ii) 2D projection, (iii) normalization of sensor data, and (iv) quaternions).

V. Conclusion and Outlook

This work-in-progress paper presents a project for recognizing people's activities at real-time utilizing nothing more than a commercial smartphone. For the sake of simplicity, the activities are reduced to the five most common modes of locomotion, which are (i) standing, (ii) walking, (iii) running, (iv) stairs-up and (v) stairs-down. Besides the requirement of recognizing the activities in real-time, another crucial aspect is the fact that the smartphone does not need to be mounted on the body of persons at a special location/position with a specific orientation. The placement of the phone shall be done in a natural way in whatever pocket the user is comfortable with. The system shall be capable of autonomously adapting to the dynamic on-body placement of the smartphone to achieve highly accurate activity recognition. Preliminary results and evaluations towards the real-time capability are promising. In order to evaluate methods and algorithms, a dataset consisting of 15 subjects performing the activities has been recorded and analysed. The dynamic placement aspect is currently subject to research, whereas different methodological approaches seem to be promising: (i) magnitude of acceleration data, (ii) 2D projection of sensor data, (iii) normalization of data by applying matrix manipulations, and (iv) quaternions as representation of rotations.

Besides future work to investigate the research challenge it is intended to extend the application further. Particularly, it is intended to include a higher number of activities, which can be considered in recording and recognition as well as to integrate more customer oriented activities. Furthermore, the current implementation only uses offline trained models. In the future, users could be able to train their personal model. In other words, future aims include the modification of the current implementation, which should allow the user to record activities, label activities and train personal models on the mobile phone.

References

[1] M. Kurz, "Opportunistic activity recognition methodologies," Ph.D. dissertation, Johannes Kepler University Linz, Jun. 2013.

[2] M. Kurz, G. Hölzl, and A. Ferscha, "Dynamic adaptation of opportunistic sensor configurations for continuous and accurate activity recognition," in Fourth International Conference on Adaptive and Self-Adaptive Systems and Applications (ADAPTIVE 2012), Nice, France, 2012.

[3] A. Anjum and M. U. Ilyas, "Activity recognition using smartphone sensors," 2013 IEEE 10th Consumer Communications and Networking Conference (CCNC), 2013, pp. 914–919. [Online]. Available: http://ieeexplore.ieee.org/lpdocs/epic03/wrapper.htm?arnumber=6488584

[4] L. Bao and S. S. Intille, "Activity recognition from user-annotated acceleration data," in International Conference on Pervasive Computing. Springer, 2004, pp. 1–17.

[5] G. Bieber, J. Voskamp, and B. Urban, "Activity recognition for everyday life on mobile phones," in International Conference on Universal Access in Human-Computer Interaction. Springer, 2009, pp. 289–296.

[6] M. Derawi and P. Bours, "Gait and activity recognition using commercial phones," computers & security, vol. 39, 2013, pp. 137–144.

[7] J. R. Kwapisz, G. M. Weiss, and S. A. Moore, "Activity recognition using cell phone accelerometers," ACM SigKDD Explorations Newsletter, vol. 12, no. 2, 2011, pp. 74–82.

[8] M. del Rosario, S. Redmond, and N. Lovell, "Tracking the evolution of smartphone sensing for monitoring human movement," Sensors, vol. 15, no. 8, 2015, pp. 18 901–18 933.

[9] K. Kunze, P. Lukowicz, H. Junker, and G. Tröster, "Where am i: Recognizing on-body positions of wearable sensors," in International Symposium on Location-and Context-Awareness. Springer, 2005, pp. 264–275.

[10] Y. He and Y. Li, "Physical activity recognition utilizing the built-in kinematic sensors of a smartphone," International Journal of Distributed Sensor Networks, vol. 9, no. 4, 2013, p. 481580.

[11] N. Ravi, N. Dandekar, P. Mysore, and M. M. L. Littman, "Activity Recognition from Accelerometer Data," Proc. The 17th Conference on Innovative Applications of Artificial Intelligence (IAAI'05), vol. 3, 2005, pp. 1541–1546. [Online]. Available: http://www.aaai.org/Papers/IAAI/2005/IAAI05-013

[12] J. Yang, "Toward physical activity diary: motion recognition using simple acceleration features with mobile phones," in Proceedings of the 1st international workshop on Interactive multimedia for consumer electronics. ACM, 2009, pp. 1–10.

[13] L. Sun, D. Zhang, B. Li, B. Guo, and S. Li, "Activity recognition on an accelerometer embedded mobile phone with varying positions and orientations," in International conference on ubiquitous intelligence and computing. Springer, 2010, pp. 548–562.

[14] A. Henpraserttae, S. Thiemjarus, and S. Marukatat, "Accurate activity recognition using a mobile phone regardless of device orientation and location," in Body Sensor Networks (BSN), 2011 International Conference on. IEEE, 2011, pp. 41–46.

[15] Y. E. Ustev, O. Durmaz Incel, and C. Ersoy, "User, device and orientation independent human activity recognition on mobile phones: Challenges and a proposal," in Proceedings of the 2013 ACM conference on Pervasive and ubiquitous computing adjunct publication. ACM, 2013, pp. 1427–1436.

[16] X. Su, H. Tong, and P. Ji, "Activity recognition with smartphone sensors," Tsinghua science and technology, vol. 19, no. 3, 2014, pp. 235–249.

[17] M. Hall, E. Frank, G. Holmes, B. Pfahringer, P. Reutemann, and I. H. Witten, "The WEKA data mining software," ACM SIGKDD Explorations Newsletter, vol. 11, no. 1, 2009, p. 10. [Online]. Available: http://portal.acm.org/citation.cfm?doid=1656274.1656278

[18] J. Yang, M. N. Nguyen, P. P. San, X. Li, and S. Krishnaswamy, "Deep convolutional neural networks on multichannel time series for human activity recognition." in Ijcai, vol. 15, 2015, pp. 3995–4001.

[19] S. Sempena, N. U. Maulidevi, and P. R. Aryan, "Human action recognition using dynamic time warping," in Electrical Engineering and Informatics (ICEEI), 2011 International Conference on. IEEE, 2011, pp. 1–5.

Consistent Persistence of Context-Dependent Runtime Models

Thomas Kühn and Christopher Werner
Software Technology Group
Technische Universität Dresden
Dresden, Germany
Email: {thomas.kuehn3, christopher.werner}@tu-dresden.de

Tobias Jäkel
Database Systems Group
Technische Universität Dresden
Dresden, Germany
Email: tobias.jaekel@tu-dresden.de

***Abstract*—Today's complex software systems act in various situations and contexts and thus, have to adapt themselves correspondingly during runtime. To model and represent the underlying context-dependent domain knowledge, contextual modeling languages, such as the Compartment Role Object Model (CROM), can be employed. However, these models and their instances become unwieldy rather quickly and are subject to many adaptations. Especially, when persisting a runtime model of a self-adaptive system this becomes a huge performance bottleneck. Notably, though not all elements of a context-dependent domain model have to be persisted to save the overall state of the application. Yet, simply removing information can easily lead to inconsistent models and instances in the database. To remedy too much or too less data saving and maintain adaptation processes, the persistent elements of a context-dependent domain model have to be annotated, such that the persisted domain model and instance is consistent with the runtime domain model and instance. For our solution, we introduce a formal approach to derive a persistent CROM from an arbitrary CROM model with persistence annotations, such that the persistent CROM is well-formed and consistent to the domain model and instance at runtime. In conclusion, this will allow context-aware systems to persist partial runtime model instances of context-dependent domain models while guaranteeing their consistency and the automatic adaptation of the persistent model after adapting the domain model.**

***Keywords*–CROM; RSQL; context-dependent domain model; persistency; transformation function.**

I. INTRODUCTION

Self-adaptive Systems (SaS) have been conquering a lot of areas in automation, like robotics, control systems, or even home automation [1]. In recent years, several definitions of SaS arose, as shown in [1][2]. Notably, all definitions share the characteristic that SaS monitor themselves, their environment, and/or related components to adjust their behavior accordingly, e.g., dynamic production systems, autonomous mobile robots, and smart home solutions. To represent SaS' knowledge bases, current SaS employ context-dependent domain models [3][4], like CROM [5]. These domain models capture the system's situational state by means of contexts [2], as well as its context-dependent relations and constraints. Moreover, they are adapted and extended over time. For instance, a self-adaptive smart home, which monitors itself and features two basic contexts: a regular context and an emergency context. In the emergency context, for example, the front door is unlocked, such that the rescue team may enter faster, or the connected smart devices emit alarm sounds to alert the residents. However, such context-dependent domain models become unwieldy rather quickly, because all environmental information, as well as the system's context-dependent structure is modeled. This, especially, holds true for the resulting instances of such models at runtime. Considering persistence, this will result in a huge database containing potentially unnecessarily stored information, such as auxiliary sensor data. Yet, simply removing this unnecessary information can easily lead to inconsistent, invalid models and instances in the database [5]. Moreover, in case of system failure and recovery, this leads to invalid model instances at runtime. Especially, in case of context-dependent domain models, such as CROM [6], invalid instances can ultimately lead to unanticipated system behavior [7, p. 58]. For instance, persisting empty contexts or contextually unassigned behavior violates CROM's validity, as shown in [8]. To remedy this, the persistent elements of a context-dependent domain model must be annotated, such that the persisted domain model and instance is consistent with the runtime domain model and instance. The adaptation, like modification of running contexts and integration of new contexts, of the context-dependent domain models leads to an adaptation of the underlying database schema and the created persistency annotations. To manage this adaptation scenario, like adding a new context-aware application to a smart home, an automated transformation algorithm is needed that maps the update of the domain model to the evolution of the persisted domain model and underlying database schema. We employ CROM [5] as modeling language for context-dependent domain models and provide a formal approach for deriving both a well-formed persistence model, as well as a valid, reduced instance from an arbitrarily annotated CROM model and corresponding instances. Moreover, we utilize the role-based contextual database system (RSQL) [9] as the corresponding target database system for the resulting persistent models and instances. Finally, we demonstrate our algorithm utilizing a small example scenario within a smart home setting, and prove that our method guarantees the consistency of the resulting persistence models and reduced instances [10]. In sum, this will allow SaS to persist partial runtime model instances of context-dependent domains models before and after adaptation steps while guaranteeing their consistency.

The paper is organized as follows: Before delving into the formal definitions, Section II introduces a simple smart home scenario as our running example. Afterwards, Section III presents a brief introduction to both CROM and RSQL. In Section IV, our formal transformation algorithm is defined. Moreover, it is proven that this algorithm ensures well-formedness and validity persisted context-dependent domain models and instances. To illustrate the application of our approach, Section V applies the transformation algorithm to the running example. Related work is discussed in Section VI and the paper is concluded in Section VII.

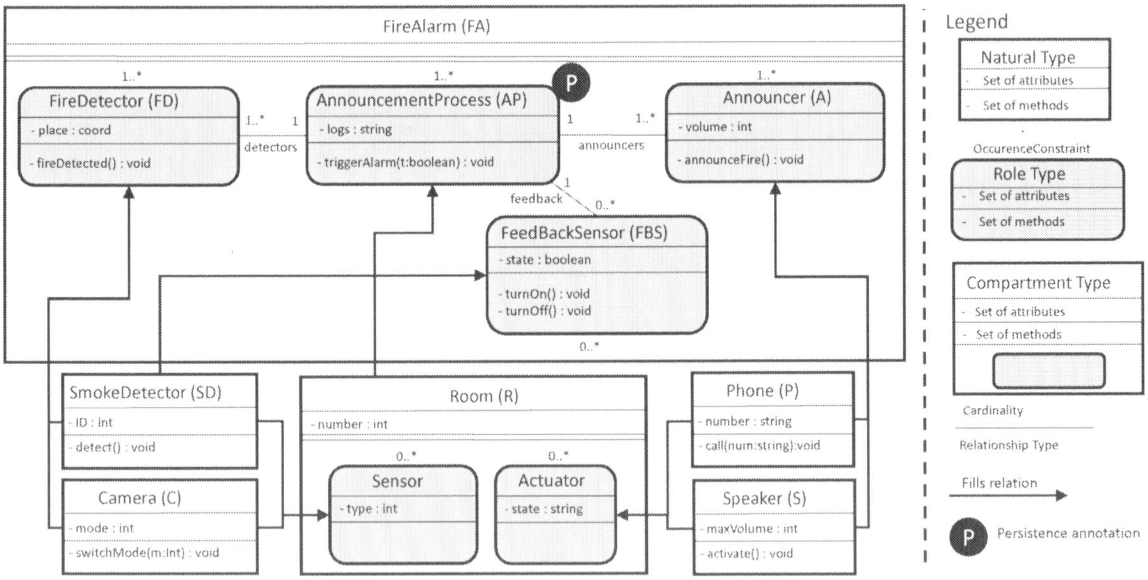

Figure 1. Annotated CROM Model of a Fire Alarm Scenario.

II. Running Example

Emergencies usually require SaS behavior and consequently utilize context-dependent domain models, because typical behavior is substituted with an adequate emergency response. Henceforth, we focus on fire as an emergency within a smart home, illustrated in Figure 1. Like any regular house, the smart home setting features *Rooms (R)*. Additionally, we assume that each *R* may contain several *Sensors* and *Actuators*. A *Sensor* can be either a *SmokeDetector (SD)* or a *Camera (C)*. As player type for the *Actuator* role type, we assume Phones (P), as well as *Speakers (S)*. While speakers are stationary, phones have the tendency to move around with their owner. In each room, with at least one sensor and actuator, the *FireAlarm (FA)* compartment is created. The available sensors and actuators of the room will start playing the *FireDetector (FD)* and *Announcer (A)* role type, respectively. In case a fire is detected by a fire detector, the *AnnouncementProcess (AP)* is triggered, which announces the fire alarm via all actuators playing the announcer role. For example, a smart speaker could announce the fire by activating noisy sounds or notifying the fire fighter department via Internet. All the detection and announcement procedures are coordinated by the *AP* role type, which also holds the log information. Additionally, our scenario requires the system to store the log information of each fire alarm persistently in a database system. Thus, the most basic annotation is the *AP* role type, which is in fact an invalid model with respect to the CROM metamodel. In case of restoring the system after a breakdown, an *AP* role could not be situated in any compartment, since this information will not be persistently stored. However, applying the *Persistency Transformation* algorithm φ will ensure a consistent database model by adding additional types to the database schema.

III. Preliminaries

Before describing our method to restrict a context-dependent domain model to a consistent partial persistence model, we first introduce CROM and RSQL to model respectively persistent context-dependent domain models.

A. Compartment Role Object Model

CROM [5] permits modeling dynamic, context-dependent domains by introducing *compartment types* to represent an objectified context, i.e., containing *role types* and *relationship types*. *Natural types*, in turn, fulfill role types in multiple compartment types. The following definitions are retrieved from [5], where a more detailed discussion can be found.

Definition 1 (Compartment Role Object Model). *Let* NT, RT, CT, *and* RST *be mutual disjoint sets of Natural Types, Role Types, Compartment Types, and Relationship Types. Then,* $\mathcal{M} = (\mathsf{NT}, \mathsf{RT}, \mathsf{CT}, \mathsf{RST}, \mathsf{fills}, \mathsf{rel})$ *is a* CROM, *where* $\mathsf{fills} \subseteq \mathsf{T} \times \mathsf{CT} \times \mathsf{RT}$ *is a relation and* $\mathsf{rel} : \mathsf{RST} \times \mathsf{CT} \to (\mathsf{RT} \times \mathsf{RT})$ *is a partial function. Here,* $\mathsf{T} := \mathsf{NT} \cup \mathsf{CT}$ *denotes the set of all rigid types. A CROM is* well-formed *if it holds that:*

$$\forall rt \in \mathsf{RT}\ \exists\, t \in \mathsf{T}\ \exists! ct \in \mathsf{CT} : (t, ct, rt) \in \mathsf{fills} \tag{1}$$

$$\forall ct \in \mathsf{CT} : (t, ct, rt) \in \mathsf{fills} \tag{2}$$

$$\forall rst \in \mathsf{RST}\ \exists ct \in \mathsf{CT} : (rst, ct) \in \boldsymbol{domain}(\mathsf{rel}) \tag{3}$$

$$\forall (rt_1, rt_1)\ \in \boldsymbol{codomain}(\mathsf{rel}) : rt_1 \neq rt_2 \tag{4}$$

$$\forall (rst, ct)\ \in \boldsymbol{domain}(\mathsf{rel}) : \mathsf{rel}(rst, ct) = (rt_1, rt_2) \wedge (\_, rt_1, ct), (\_, rt_2, ct) \in \mathsf{fills} \tag{5}$$

In detail, fills denotes that rigid types can play roles of a certain role type in which compartment type and rel capture the two role types at the respective ends of each relationship type. The well-formedness rules ensure that the fills relation is surjective (1); each compartment type has a nonempty, disjoint set of role types as its parts (2, 3); and rel maps each relationship type to exactly two distinct role types of the same compartment type (4, 5). For a given function $f : A \to B$, $\boldsymbol{domain}(f) = A$ returns the domain and $\boldsymbol{codomain}(f) = B$ the range of f. For comprehensibility, we use subscripts to indicate the model a set, relation or function belongs to, e.g., $\mathsf{RT}_{\mathcal{M}}$ denotes the set of role types of the CROM $\mathcal{M}$. Accordingly, a CROM can be constructed for the fire alarm scenario, depicted in Figure 1.

Example 1 (Fire Alarm Model). *Let* $\mathcal{F} = (\mathsf{NT}, \mathsf{RT}, \mathsf{CT}, \mathsf{RST}, \mathsf{fills}, \mathsf{parts}, \mathsf{rel})$ *be the model of the fire alarm scenario, where the components are defined as:*

$$\mathsf{NT} := \{\mathsf{SD}, \mathsf{C}, \mathsf{P}, \mathsf{S}\} \qquad \mathsf{CT} := \{\mathsf{FA}, \mathsf{R}\}$$
$$\mathsf{RT} := \{\mathsf{FD}, \mathsf{AP}, \mathsf{A}, \mathsf{FBS}, \mathsf{Sensor}, \mathsf{Aktuator}\}$$
$$\mathsf{RST} := \{\mathsf{detectors}, \mathsf{announcers}, \mathsf{feedback}\}$$
$$\mathsf{fills} := \{(\mathsf{SD}, \mathsf{FA}, \mathsf{FD}), (\mathsf{C}, \mathsf{FA}, \mathsf{FD}), (\mathsf{A}, \mathsf{FA}, \mathsf{AP}), (\mathsf{S}, \mathsf{FA}, \mathsf{A}), \dots\}$$
$$\mathsf{rel} := \{(\mathsf{detectors}, \mathsf{FA}) \to (\mathsf{FD}, \mathsf{AP}), (\mathsf{feedback}, \mathsf{FA}) \to (\mathsf{AP}, \mathsf{FBS}), (\mathsf{announcers}, \mathsf{FA}) \to (\mathsf{AP}, \mathsf{A}), \dots\}$$

Unsurprisingly, a well-formed CROM can directly encode concepts of context-dependent domains. A CROM instance features naturals, roles, compartments and relationships.

Definition 2 (Compartment Role Object Instance). *Let* $\mathcal{M} = (\mathsf{NT}, \mathsf{RT}, \mathsf{CT}, \mathsf{RST}, \mathsf{fills}, \mathsf{rel})$ *be a well-formed CROM and* N, R, *and* C *be mutual disjoint sets of Naturals, Roles and Compartments, respectively. Then, a* Compartment Role Object Instance (CROI) *of* $\mathcal{M}$ *is a tuple* $\mathrm{i} = (N, R, C, \mathsf{type}, \mathsf{plays}, \mathsf{links})$, *where* $\mathsf{type} : (N \to \mathsf{NT}) \cup (R \to \mathsf{RT}) \cup (C \to \mathsf{CT})$ *is a labeling function,* $\mathsf{plays} \subseteq (N \cup C) \times C \times R$ *a relation, and* $\mathsf{links} : \mathsf{RST} \times C \to \mathcal{P}(R \times R)$ *is a total function. Moreover,* $O := N \cup C$ *denotes the set of all objects in* i. *To be* compliant *to the model* $\mathcal{M}$ *the instance* i *must satisfy the following conditions:*

$$\forall (o, c, r) \in \mathsf{plays} : (\mathsf{type}(o), \mathsf{type}(c), \mathsf{type}(r)) \in \mathsf{fills} \tag{6}$$
$$\forall (o, c, r), (o, c, r') \in \mathsf{plays} : r \neq r' \Rightarrow \mathsf{type}(r) \neq \mathsf{type}(r') \tag{7}$$
$$\forall r \in R\ \exists ! o \in O\ \exists ! c \in C : (o, c, r) \in \mathsf{plays} \tag{8}$$
$$\begin{aligned} \forall rst \in \mathsf{RST} \forall c \in C\ \forall (r_1, r_2) \in \mathsf{links}(rst, c) :& \\ (rst, \mathsf{type}(c)) \in \boldsymbol{domain}(\mathsf{rel}) \wedge& \\ \mathsf{rel}(rst, \mathsf{type}(c)) = (\mathsf{type}(r_1), \mathsf{type}(r_2)) \wedge& \\ (\_, c, r_1), (\_, c, r_2) \in \mathsf{plays}& \end{aligned} \tag{9}$$

The type function assigns a distinct type to each instance, plays identifies the objects (either natural or compartment) playing a certain role in a specific compartment, and links captures the roles currently linked by a relationship type in a certain compartment. A compliant CROI guarantees the consistency of both the plays relation and the links function with the model $\mathcal{M}$. Axioms (6), (7) and (8) restrict the plays relation, such that it is consistent to the types defined in the fills relation and the parts function, an object is prohibited to play instances of the same role type multiple times in the same compartment, and each role has one distinct player in one distinct compartment, respectively. In contrast, Axiom (9) ensures that the links function only contains those roles, which participate in the same compartment c as the relationship and whose types are consistent to the relationship's definition in the rel function.

Admittedly, neither Definition 1 nor 2 captures constraints of context-dependent domains. Hence, two context-dependent constraints, i.e., *occurrence constraints* and *relationship cardinalities* are introduced. Henceforth, cardinalities are given as $\mathsf{Card} \subset \mathbb{N} \times (\mathbb{N} \cup \{\infty\})$ with $i \leq j$, whereas elements of Card are written as $i..j$.

Next, the *Constraint Model* is defined to collect all constraints imposed on a particular CROM $\mathcal{M}$.

Definition 3 (Constraint Model). *Let* $\mathcal{M} = (\mathsf{NT}, \mathsf{RT}, \mathsf{CT}, \mathsf{RST}, \mathsf{fills}, \mathsf{rel})$ *be a well-formed CROM. Then* $\mathcal{C} = (\mathsf{occur}, \mathsf{card})$ *is a* Constraint Model *over* $\mathcal{M}$, *where* $\mathsf{occur} : \mathsf{CT} \to \mathcal{P}(\mathsf{Card} \times \mathsf{RT})$ *and* $\mathsf{card} : \mathsf{RST} \times \mathsf{CT} \to (\mathsf{Card} \times \mathsf{Card})$ *are partial functions. A Constraint Model is* compliant *to* $\mathcal{M}$, *iff:*

$$\begin{aligned} \forall ct \in \boldsymbol{domain}(\mathsf{occur})\ \forall (\_, rt) \in \mathsf{occur}(ct) :& \\ (\_, ct, rt) \in \mathsf{fills}& \end{aligned} \tag{10}$$
$$\boldsymbol{domain}(\mathsf{card}) \subseteq \boldsymbol{domain}(\mathsf{rel}) \tag{11}$$

In detail, occur collects a cardinality limiting the occurrence of the given role type in each compartment. Moreover, card assigns a cardinality to each relationship type. Notably, all these constraints are defined context-dependent, i.e., no constraint crosses the boundary of a compartment type. In contrast to [5], our definition excludes empty counter roles ε and *Role Groups*. Similar to the CROM $\mathcal{F}$, the corresponding compliant constraint model is easily derived, from Figure 1:

Example 2 (Fire Alarm Constraints). *Let* $\mathcal{F}$ *be the fire alarm from Example 1. Then* $\mathcal{C}_{\mathcal{F}} = (\mathsf{occur}, \mathsf{card})$ *is the compliant constraint model with the following components:*

$$\mathsf{occur} := \{\mathsf{FA} \to \{(1..\infty, \mathsf{FD}), (1..\infty, \mathsf{AP}), (1..\infty, \mathsf{A})\}\}$$
$$\begin{aligned} \mathsf{card} := \{&(\mathsf{detectors}, \mathsf{FA}) \to (1..\infty, 1..1), \\ &(\mathsf{announcers}, \mathsf{FA}) \to (1..1, 1..\infty), \\ &(\mathsf{feedback}, \mathsf{FA}) \to (1..1, 0..\infty)\} \end{aligned}$$

Finally, the validity of a given CROI is defined with respect to a CROM and corresponding constraint model.

Definition 4 (Validity). *Let* $\mathcal{M} = (\mathsf{NT}, \mathsf{RT}, \mathsf{CT}, \mathsf{RST}, \mathsf{fills}, \mathsf{rel})$ *be a well-formed CROM,* $\mathcal{C} = (\mathsf{occur}, \mathsf{card})$ *a constraint model on* $\mathcal{M}$, *and* $\mathrm{i} = (N, R, C, \mathsf{type}, \mathsf{plays}, \mathsf{links})$ *a CROI compliant to* $\mathcal{M}$. *Then* i is valid with respect to $\mathcal{C}$ *iff the following conditions hold:*

$$\forall c \in C\ \forall (i..j, rt) \in \mathsf{occur}(\mathsf{type}(c)) : i \leq \left| R^c_{rt} \right| \leq j \tag{12}$$
$$\begin{aligned} \forall c \in C \forall rst \in \mathsf{RST} :\ & \mathsf{rel}(rst, \mathsf{type}(c)) = (rt_1, rt_2) \wedge \\ & \mathsf{card}(rst, \mathsf{type}(c)) = (i..j, k..l) \wedge \\ & \left(\forall r_2 \in R^c_{rt_2} : i \leq \left| \mathsf{pred}(rst, c, r_2) \right| \leq j \right) \wedge \\ & \left(\forall r_1 \in R^c_{rt_1} : k \leq \left| \mathsf{succ}(rst, c, r_1) \right| \leq l \right) \end{aligned} \tag{13}$$

Here, $R^c_{rt} := \{ r \in R \mid (o, c, r) \in \mathsf{plays} \wedge \mathsf{type}(r) = rt \}$ *denotes the set of roles of type* rt *played in a compartment* c; $\mathsf{pred}(rst, c, r) := \{ r' \mid (r', r) \in \mathsf{links}(rst, c) \}$ *and* $\mathsf{succ}(rst, c, r) := \{ r' \mid (r, r') \in \mathsf{links}(rst, c) \}$ *collects all predecessors respectively successors of a given role* r *with respect to an* rst.

Each axiom verifies a particular set of constraints. Axiom (12) validates the occurrence of role types. In essence, it checks the number of roles of the given type played in a constrained compartment. In contrast, (13) checks whether relationships respect the imposed cardinality constraints. In conclusion, the formal model easily captures the context-dependent concepts and constraints. Moreover, it allows for checking the well-formedness of CROMs and validity of CROIs. Although a database schema can be generated for a CROM (including the Constraint Model), due to the lack of persistence annotations, the full model must be stored for compliance and validity.

B. Role-Based Contextual Database System (RSQL)

RSQL directly addresses the persistence of context-dependent information in a database system [9]. In particular, RSQL combines a metatype distinction in the database model, an adapted query language on the database model's basis, and finally a proper result representation [11]. The database model, including the metatype distinction, consists of two levels, (i) the schema level and (ii) the instance level. On the schema level, RSQL introduces Dynamic Data Types (DDT) that combine the notion of an entity type with the notion of roles while fully implementing the metatype distinction on the basis of CROM [11, p. 72]. On the instance level, the database model introduces *Dynamic Tuples* (DT) [11, p. 78], that are defined to allow for dynamic structure adaptations during runtime without changing an entity's overall type [9]. Hence, DDTs define the space in which DTs might expand or shrink their structure, depending on the context they are acting in. Also, RSQL features a set of formal operators to process context-dependent information on the basis of DTs [11, p. 84].

The query language, as external database system interface, features an individual data definition (DDL), data manipulation (DML), and data query language (DQL) [9]. As the database model, the query language implements a metatype distinction on the basis of CROM as first class citizen. The list of DDL statements and grammar, DML statements, and DQL statement grammar are shown in [11, p. 116, p. 122, p. 127].

Finally, to complete the database integration of context-dependent information, RSQL returns *RSQL Result Nets*. These represent a novel data structure for results, which feature various functionalities to navigate through players, their roles, compartments, and relationships [11, p. 147].

IV. Persistence Algorithm

Henceforth, we present an algorithm that transforms an annotated CROM model into a dedicated CROM model for persistence. In detail, we first introduce persistence annotations to annotate CROM model elements. Afterwards, the transformation algorithm is presented. Finally, we prove that given a well-formed CROM model with persistence annotations and a valid CROM instance, the resulting limited CROM model is well-formed and the restricted CROI is valid.

A. Persistence Annotation

Accordingly, the following definition extends CROM by introducing annotations for modeling elements.

Definition 5 (Persistence Annotation). *Let* $\mathcal{M} = (\mathsf{NT}, \mathsf{RT}, \mathsf{CT}, \mathsf{RST}, \mathsf{fills}, \mathsf{rel})$ *be an arbitrary CROM, then* $P = (\mathsf{NT}, \mathsf{RT}, \mathsf{CT}, \mathsf{rel})$ *denotes a persistence annotation of* $\mathcal{M}$, *whereas* $\mathsf{NT}_P \subseteq \mathsf{NT}_\mathcal{M}$, $\mathsf{RT}_P \subseteq \mathsf{RT}_\mathcal{M}$, $\mathsf{CT}_P \subseteq \mathsf{CT}_\mathcal{M}$, *and* $\mathsf{rel}_P \subseteq \textbf{\textit{domain}}(\mathsf{rel}_\mathcal{M})$

In general, this definition permits to select a subset of natural types, role types, compartment types, and context-dependent relationship types. For the sake of simplicity, we excluded attributes, because persisting attributes does not add any complexity to the proposed method. In case of the fire alarm scenario (Figure 1), the persistence annotation for the CROM $\mathcal{F}$ could be defined as $P = (\emptyset, \{AP\}, \emptyset, \emptyset)$. As the transformation must be aware of compartment types, which are existentially dependent on at least one of its containing role types, we define the following auxiliary definitions.

Definition 6 (Existential Parts). *Let* $\mathcal{M} = (\mathsf{NT}, \mathsf{RT}, \mathsf{CT}, \mathsf{RST}, \mathsf{fills}, \mathsf{parts}, \mathsf{rel})$ *be an arbitrary CROM,* $\mathcal{C} = (\mathsf{occur}, \mathsf{card})$ *a constraint model on* $\mathcal{M}$, *and* $ct \in \mathsf{CT}$ *an arbitrary compartment type in* $\mathcal{M}$. *Then* $\textbf{ext}(ct) := \{rt \mid (t, ct, rt) \in \mathsf{fills} \wedge (i..j, rt) \in \mathsf{occur}(ct) \wedge i \geq 1\}$ *collects the set of* existential parts *of the compartment type* ct.

In general, this definition introduces the **ext** function to determine the existential parts of the given compartment type, i.e., contain a role type with an occurrence constraint $(i..j)$ with $i \geq 1$. For instance, while the room R has no existential parts, the fire alarm compartment type FA has three, i.e., $\textbf{ext}(\mathsf{FA}) = \{\mathsf{FD}, \mathsf{AP}, \mathsf{A}\}$.

B. Transformation Algorithm

After defining persistence annotations over CROM models, it is possible to define the *Persistency Transformation* for arbitrary CROM models and corresponding constraint models, as follows:

Definition 7 (Persistency Transformation). *Let* $\mathcal{M}$ *be a well-formed CROM,* $\mathcal{C}$ *a constraint model compliant to* $\mathcal{M}$, *and* $P = (\mathsf{NT}_P, \mathsf{RT}_P, \mathsf{CT}_P, \mathsf{rel}_P)$ *a persistence annotation over* $\mathcal{M}$. *Then* $(\mathcal{N}, \mathcal{D}) = \varphi(\mathcal{M}, \mathcal{C}, P)$ *constructs the persistence model* $\mathcal{N} = (\mathsf{NT}, \mathsf{RT}, \mathsf{CT}, \mathsf{RST}, \mathsf{fills}, \mathsf{rel})$ *and respective constraint model* $\mathcal{D} = (\mathsf{occur}, \mathsf{card})$ *from the given CROM, constraint model, and persistence annotation.* φ *first computes the* $\mathsf{fills}_\mathcal{N}$ *relation and* $\mathsf{rel}_\mathcal{N}$ *function by applying the inference rules depicted in Figure 2. From them, the sets* $\mathsf{NT}_\mathcal{N}$, $\mathsf{RT}_\mathcal{N}$, $\mathsf{CT}_\mathcal{N}$, $\mathsf{RST}_\mathcal{N}$ *can be determined as:*

$$\mathsf{T}_\mathcal{N} := \{t \mid (t, ct, rt) \in \mathsf{fills}_\mathcal{N}\} \tag{14}$$

$$\mathsf{CT}_\mathcal{N} := \{ct \mid (t, ct, rt) \in \mathsf{fills}_\mathcal{N}\} \tag{15}$$

$$\mathsf{RT}_\mathcal{N} := \{rt \mid (t, ct, rt) \in \mathsf{fills}_\mathcal{N}\} \tag{16}$$

$$\mathsf{NT}_\mathcal{N} := \mathsf{NT}_P \cup (\mathsf{T}_\mathcal{N} \setminus \mathsf{CT}_\mathcal{N}) \tag{17}$$

$$\mathsf{RST}_\mathcal{N} := \{rst \mid (rst, ct) \in \textbf{\textit{domain}}(\mathsf{rel}_\mathcal{N})\} \tag{18}$$

Finally, the partial function occur *and* card *can be restricted to the model* $\mathcal{N}$, *as showcased in Figure 2.*

To put it succinctly, the *Persistency Transformation* first constructs the CROM $\mathcal{N}$ for persistence by inductively creating the $\mathsf{fills}_\mathcal{N}$ relation and the $\mathsf{rel}_\mathcal{N}$ partial function before creating the carrier sets $\mathsf{NT}_\mathcal{N}$, $\mathsf{RT}_\mathcal{N}$, $\mathsf{CT}_\mathcal{N}$, $\mathsf{RST}_\mathcal{N}$. Lastly, the constraint model $\mathcal{D}$ is constructed by restricting the $\mathsf{occur}_\mathcal{D}$ and $\mathsf{card}_\mathcal{D}$ functions accordingly. In case of fills, the axioms (19), (20), (25), and (26) initialize $\mathsf{fills}_\mathcal{N}$ with respect to the annotated compartment types, role types, and relationships types, respectively. Afterwards, $\mathsf{fills}_\mathcal{N}$ is inductively extended in three ways. First, (23) checks all compartment types that fulfill a previously selected role type and adds all of its existential parts (role types), if any exist. Likewise, (24) checks all previously selected compartment types and includes all of its existential parts (role types), if any exist. Third, (25) and (26) check if a previously selected role type has a relationship to another role type with a cardinality $(i..j)$ with $i \geq 1$. By contrast, rel is initialized only with relationships either directly annotated (27) or contained in an annotated compartment type (28). Afterwards, this partial function is inductively expanded, if a previously selected role type has a relationship to another role type with a cardinality greater than zero. Consequently, the components of $\mathcal{N}$ are derived from the contents of both $\mathsf{fills}_\mathcal{N}$ and $\mathsf{rel}_\mathcal{N}$.

Inductive definition of $\mathsf{fills}_{\mathcal{N}}$:

$$\text{CTSel}\frac{ct \in \mathsf{CT}_P \quad (t,ct,rt) \in \mathsf{fills}_{\mathcal{M}}}{(t,ct,rt) \in \mathsf{fills}_{\mathcal{N}}} \tag{19}$$

$$\text{RTSel}\frac{rt \in \mathsf{RT}_P \quad (t,ct,rt) \in \mathsf{fills}_{\mathcal{M}}}{(t,ct,rt) \in \mathsf{fills}_{\mathcal{N}}} \tag{20}$$

$$\text{RelSelLeft}\frac{(rst,ct) \in \mathsf{rel}_P \quad \mathsf{rel}_{\mathcal{M}}(rst,ct) = (rt_1,rt_2) \quad (t,ct,rt_1) \in \mathsf{fills}_{\mathcal{M}}}{(t,ct,rt_1) \in \mathsf{fills}_{\mathcal{N}}} \tag{21}$$

$$\text{RelSelRight}\frac{(rst,ct) \in \mathsf{rel}_P \quad \mathsf{rel}_{\mathcal{M}}(rst,ct) = (rt_1,rt_2) \quad (t,ct,rt_2) \in \mathsf{fills}_{\mathcal{M}}}{(t,ct,rt_2) \in \mathsf{fills}_{\mathcal{N}}} \tag{22}$$

Induction cases for $\mathsf{fills}_{\mathcal{N}}$:

$$\text{CTExt}\frac{(ct_1,ct_2,\_) \in \mathsf{fills}_{\mathcal{N}} \quad (t,ct_1,rt) \in \mathsf{fills}_{\mathcal{M}} \quad ct_1 \in \mathsf{CT}_{\mathcal{M}} \quad rt \in \mathbf{ext}_{\mathcal{M}}(ct_1)}{(t,ct_1,rt) \in \mathsf{fills}_{\mathcal{N}}} \tag{23}$$

$$\text{OccurExt}\frac{(s,ct,rt') \in \mathsf{fills}_{\mathcal{N}} \quad rt \in \mathbf{ext}_{\mathcal{M}}(ct) \quad (t,ct,rt) \in \mathsf{fills}_{\mathcal{M}}}{(t,ct,rt) \in \mathsf{fills}_{\mathcal{N}}} \tag{24}$$

$$\text{RelExtRight}\frac{\begin{array}{c}(s,ct,rt_1) \in \mathsf{fills}_{\mathcal{N}} \quad (t,ct,rt_2) \in \mathsf{fills}_{\mathcal{M}} \quad (rst,ct) \in \mathbf{domain}(\mathsf{card}_{\mathcal{C}}) \\ \mathsf{rel}_{\mathcal{M}}(rst,ct) = (rt_1,rt_2) \quad \mathsf{card}_{\mathcal{C}}(rst,ct) = (i..j,k..l) \quad k \geq 1\end{array}}{(t,ct,rt_2) \in \mathsf{fills}_{\mathcal{N}}} \tag{25}$$

$$\text{RelExtLeft}\frac{\begin{array}{c}(t,ct,rt_2) \in \mathsf{fills}_{\mathcal{N}} \quad (s,ct,rt_1) \in \mathsf{fills}_{\mathcal{M}} \quad (rst,ct) \in \mathbf{domain}(\mathsf{card}_{\mathcal{C}}) \\ \mathsf{rel}_{\mathcal{M}}(rst,ct) = (rt_1,rt_2) \quad \mathsf{card}_{\mathcal{C}}(rst,ct) = (i..j,k..l) \quad i \geq 1\end{array}}{(s,ct,rt_1) \in \mathsf{fills}_{\mathcal{N}}} \tag{26}$$

Inductive definition of $\mathsf{rel}_{\mathcal{N}}$:

$$\text{RelSel}\frac{(rst,ct) \in \mathsf{rel}_P}{\mathsf{rel}_{\mathcal{N}}(rst,ct) := \mathsf{rel}_{\mathcal{M}}(rst,ct)} \tag{27}$$

$$\text{RelInCT}\frac{ct \in \mathsf{CT}_P \quad (rst,ct) \in \mathbf{domain}(\mathsf{rel}_{\mathcal{M}})}{\mathsf{rel}_{\mathcal{N}}(rst,ct) := \mathsf{rel}_{\mathcal{M}}(rst,ct)} \tag{28}$$

Induction case for $\mathsf{rel}_{\mathcal{N}}$:

$$\text{RelExt}\frac{\begin{array}{c}(s,ct,rt_1),(t,ct,rt_2) \in \mathsf{fills}_{\mathcal{N}} \quad (rst,ct) \in \mathbf{domain}(\mathsf{card}_{\mathcal{C}}) \quad \mathsf{rel}_{\mathcal{M}}(rst,ct) = (rt_1,rt_2) \\ \mathsf{card}_{\mathcal{C}}(rst,ct) = (i..j,k..l) \quad (i \geq 1 \vee k \geq 1)\end{array}}{\mathsf{rel}_{\mathcal{N}}(rst,ct) := \mathsf{rel}_{\mathcal{M}}(rst,ct)} \tag{29}$$

Definition of $\mathsf{occur}_{\mathcal{D}}$ and $\mathsf{card}_{\mathcal{D}}$:

$$\text{OccurIn}\frac{(t,ct,rt) \in \mathsf{fills}_{\mathcal{N}} \quad (i..j,rt) \in \mathsf{occur}_{\mathcal{C}}(ct)}{(i..j,rt) \in \mathsf{occur}_{\mathcal{D}}(ct)} \tag{30}$$

$$\text{CardIn}\frac{(rst,ct) \in \mathbf{domain}(\mathsf{rel}_{\mathcal{N}}) \quad (rst,ct) \in \mathbf{domain}(\mathsf{card}_{\mathcal{C}})}{\mathsf{card}_{\mathcal{D}}(rst,ct) := \mathsf{card}_{\mathcal{C}}(rst,ct)} \tag{31}$$

Figure 2. Inductive definition of $\mathsf{fills}_{\mathcal{N}}$, $\mathsf{rel}_{\mathcal{N}}$, $\mathsf{occur}_{\mathcal{D}}$, and $\mathsf{card}_{\mathcal{D}}$.

Besides the CROM $\mathcal{N}$, the components of the constraint model $\mathcal{D}$ are defined inductively, as well. In detail, (30) and (31) restrict the occurrence respectively cardinality constraints of $\mathcal{C}$ to those compliant to the target model $\mathcal{N}$, i.e., include all rules from $\mathsf{occur}_{\mathcal{C}}$ for all compartment types and role types in $\mathcal{N}$ and the cardinality from $\mathsf{card}_{\mathcal{C}}$ for all relationship types defined in $\mathsf{rel}_{\mathcal{N}}$. In conclusion, φ generates both a CROM $\mathcal{N}$ and a corresponding $\mathcal{D}$ from the given CROM $\mathcal{M}$, the constraint model $\mathcal{C}$, and persistence annotation P.

Up to this point, this definition is only applicable to the type level, and has no direct effect on the instance level. However, to store an instance of an annotated CROM model, it must be reduced, as well.

Definition 8 (Instance Restriction). *Let* $\mathcal{M} = (\mathsf{NT}, \mathsf{RT}, \mathsf{CT}, \mathsf{RST}, \mathsf{fills}, \mathsf{rel})$ *be a well-formed CROM and* $\mathfrak{i}$ *an arbitrary CROI. Then* $\mathfrak{p} := \Psi(\mathcal{M}, \mathfrak{i})$ is a restriction of $\mathfrak{i}$ with respect to $\mathcal{M}$. *In detail,* $\mathfrak{p} = (N, R, C, \mathsf{type}, \mathsf{plays}, \mathsf{links})$ *is determined by first applying the induction rules, shown in Figure 3, to determine* $\mathsf{plays}_{\mathfrak{p}}$ *and* $\mathsf{links}_{\mathfrak{p}}$. *Afterwards, the other components are defined as follows:*

$$N_{\mathfrak{p}} := \{o \mid (o,c,r) \in \mathsf{plays}_{\mathfrak{p}} \wedge \mathsf{type}_{\mathfrak{i}}(o) \in \mathsf{NT}_{\mathcal{M}}\} \tag{32}$$

$$R_{\mathfrak{p}} := \{r \mid (o,c,r) \in \mathsf{plays}_{\mathfrak{p}}\} \tag{33}$$

$$\begin{aligned} C_{\mathfrak{p}} := \{o \mid (o,c,r) \in \mathsf{plays}_{\mathfrak{p}} \wedge \mathsf{type}_{\mathfrak{i}}(o) \in \mathsf{CT}_{\mathcal{M}}\} \\ \cup \{c \mid (o,c,r) \in \mathsf{plays}_{\mathfrak{p}}\} \end{aligned} \tag{34}$$

$$\mathsf{type}_{\mathfrak{p}} := \mathsf{type}_{\mathfrak{i}} \tag{35}$$

Inductive definition of $\mathsf{plays_p}$:

$$\frac{(o,c,r)\in\mathsf{plays_i} \qquad (\mathsf{type_i}(o),\mathsf{type_i}(c),\mathsf{type_i}(r))\in\mathsf{fills}_{\mathcal{M}}}{(o,c,r)\in\mathsf{plays_p}} \tag{36}$$

Inductive definition of $\mathsf{links_p}$:

$$\frac{(rst,c)\in\mathbf{domain}(\mathsf{links_i}) \qquad (r_1,r_2)\in\mathsf{links_i}(rst,c) \qquad (rst,\mathsf{type_i}(c))\in\mathbf{domain}(\mathsf{rel}_{\mathcal{M}}) \qquad \mathsf{rel}_{\mathcal{M}}(rst,\mathsf{type_i}(c))=(\mathsf{type_i}(r_1),\mathsf{type_i}(r_2))}{(r_1,r_2)\in\mathsf{links_p}(rst,c)} \tag{37}$$

Figure 3. Definitions of the restriction of $\mathsf{plays_p}$ and $\mathsf{links_p}$.

In fact, the restriction of a CROI $\mathfrak{i}$ with respect to a CROM $\mathcal{M}$ is derived by only including elements from $\mathsf{plays_i}$ whose types correspond to $\mathsf{fills}_{\mathcal{M}}$ (36) and by only including relationships from $\mathsf{links_i}$ that have been defined in $\mathcal{M}$ including the correct types of the left and right side (37). Afterwards, the carrier sets N, R, C are computed simply based on $\mathsf{plays_p}$. Notably, $\mathsf{type_i}$ is passed as is, because the typing of entities must be retained after restricting the CROI. In conclusion, both the *Persistency Transformation* φ and the *instance restriction* ψ work in concert. While φ generates the persistence CROM model $\mathcal{N}$ and constraints $\mathcal{D}$ from a given CROM model $\mathcal{M}$ with constraints $\mathcal{C}$, ψ can be employed to restrict a CROI instance $\mathfrak{i}$ of $\mathcal{M}$ to the persistence CROM model $\mathcal{N}$, ultimately, constructing the persistence CROI instance.

C. Well-formedness, Compliance, and Validity

Although, both transformations were designed thoroughly, their suitability for persisting context-dependent domain models is determined by their ability to retain the well-formedness, compliance, and validity of the created models and instances. In detail, this entails that given a well-formed CROM $\mathcal{M}$ and compliant constraint model $\mathcal{C}$, φ will always generate a well-formed CROM $\mathcal{N}$ and compliant constraint model $\mathcal{D}$ for persistence. Moreover, given an arbitrary CROI $\mathfrak{i}$ compliant to $\mathcal{M}$ and valid with respect to $\mathcal{C}$, then ψ will always create a restricted CROI $\mathfrak{p}$ that is compliant to $\mathcal{N}$ and valid with respect to $\mathcal{D}$. Thus, the resulting partial domain model can be safely stored in and loaded from a database system.

Conversely, we henceforth discuss three main theorems. First, we show that the *Persistency Transformation* ensures well-formedness of the model and compliance of the constraints. Second, we extend this result to the compliance and validity of instances of such CROM models. Finally, we show that each restricted instance is also a compliant and valid instance of the original model. Consequently, this guarantees the consistency of stored partial runtime model instances of context-dependent domains models. For brevity, the full proofs are omitted, but will be presented in a separate technical report.

Theorem 1 (Well-formedness and Compliance)**.** *Let $\mathcal{M}$ be a well-formed CROM, $\mathcal{C}$ a constraint model compliant to $\mathcal{M}$, and P a persistence annotation of $\mathcal{M}$. Then $(\mathcal{N},\mathcal{D}) := \varphi(\mathcal{M},\mathcal{C},P)$ constructs a well-formed persistence model $\mathcal{N}$ and corresponding constraint model $\mathcal{D}$ compliant to $\mathcal{N}$.*

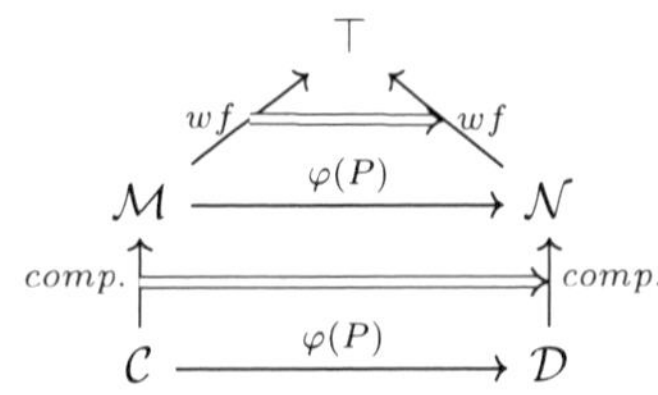

Figure 4. Commutative diagram for well-formedness and compliance.

Proof: Before proving this theorem, we can make the following observations when investigating the inference rules (cf. Figure 2). Specifically, from the structure of (19–29) we can deduce the following relations between a given CROM $\mathcal{M}$ and the resulting $\mathcal{N}$:

$$\mathsf{fills}_{\mathcal{N}} \subseteq \mathsf{fills}_{\mathcal{M}}$$
$$\mathbf{domain}(\mathsf{rel}_{\mathcal{N}}) \subseteq \mathbf{domain}(\mathsf{rel}_{\mathcal{M}})$$
$$\forall (rst,ct)\in\mathbf{domain}(\mathsf{rel}_{\mathcal{N}}):\ \mathsf{rel}_{\mathcal{N}}(rst,ct)=\mathsf{rel}_{\mathcal{M}}(rst,ct)$$

Similarly, the structure of (30–31) entails the following relations between the constraint model $\mathcal{C}$ and $\mathcal{D}$:

$$\mathbf{domain}(\mathsf{occur}_{\mathcal{D}}) \subseteq \mathbf{domain}(\mathsf{occur}_{\mathcal{C}})$$
$$\forall ct\in\mathbf{domain}(\mathsf{occur}_{\mathcal{C}}):\ \mathsf{occur}_{\mathcal{D}}(ct)\subseteq\mathsf{occur}_{\mathcal{C}}(ct)$$
$$\mathbf{domain}(\mathsf{card}_{\mathcal{D}}) \subseteq \mathbf{domain}(\mathsf{card}_{\mathcal{C}})$$
$$\forall (rst,ct)\in\mathbf{domain}(\mathsf{card}_{\mathcal{D}}):\ \mathsf{card}_{\mathcal{D}}(rst,ct)=\mathsf{card}_{\mathcal{C}}(rst,ct)$$

Finally, Theorem 1 can be shown to hold for well-formed CROMs $\mathcal{M}$ and corresponding compliant constraint models $\mathcal{C}$ following the commutative diagram in Figure 4. To show that the well-formedness of $\mathcal{N}$ is implied by $\mathcal{M}$, we successively apply the relations between $\mathcal{N}$ and $\mathcal{M}$ to the axioms (1–5). Likewise, the compliance of $\mathcal{D}$ to $\mathcal{N}$ can be entailed from the compliance of $\mathcal{C}$ to $\mathcal{M}$ by applying the relations between $\mathcal{D}$ and $\mathcal{C}$ to axioms (10) and (11). ■

After proving that φ preserves the well-formedness and compliance of the generated persistence CROM and constraint model, the final step is to prove that ψ restricts a CROI $\mathfrak{i}$ compliant to $\mathcal{M}$ and valid with respect to $\mathcal{C}$ to a persistence CROI $\mathfrak{p}$, which is itself compliant and valid to the persistence CROM of $\mathcal{M}$ and $\mathcal{C}$, respectively.

Theorem 2 (Validity)**.** *Let $\mathcal{M}$ be a well-formed CROM, $\mathcal{C}$ a constraint model compliant to $\mathcal{M}$, P a persistence annotation of $\mathcal{M}$, as well as $\mathfrak{i}$ a CROI compliant to $\mathcal{M}$ and valid with respect to $\mathcal{C}$. Then the construction $(\mathcal{N},\mathcal{D}) := \varphi(\mathcal{M},\mathcal{C},P)$ and the restriction $\mathfrak{p} := \psi(\mathcal{N},\mathfrak{i})$ entails that $\mathfrak{p}$ is compliant to $\mathcal{N}$ and valid with respect to $\mathcal{D}$.*

Proof: Again, to prove Theorem 2 major conclusions can already be drawn from Definition 8 (cf. Figure 3) and the fact that $\mathfrak{i}$ is compliant to the well-formed CROM $\mathcal{M}$. Thus, the following relations between $\mathfrak{p}$ and $\mathfrak{i}$ can be deduced:

$$\mathsf{plays_p} \subseteq \mathsf{plays_i}$$
$$\mathbf{domain}(\mathsf{links_p}) \subseteq \mathbf{domain}(\mathsf{links_i})$$
$$\forall (rst,c)\in\mathbf{domain}(\mathsf{links_i}) :\ \mathsf{links_p}(rst,c)=\mathsf{links_i}(rst,c)$$

To show that Theorem 2 holds for all $\mathfrak{i}$ compliant to $\mathcal{M}$ and valid wrt. $\mathcal{C}$, we need to show the compliance of $\mathfrak{p}$ to $\mathcal{N}$ and the validity to $\mathcal{D}$ (cf. Figure 5).

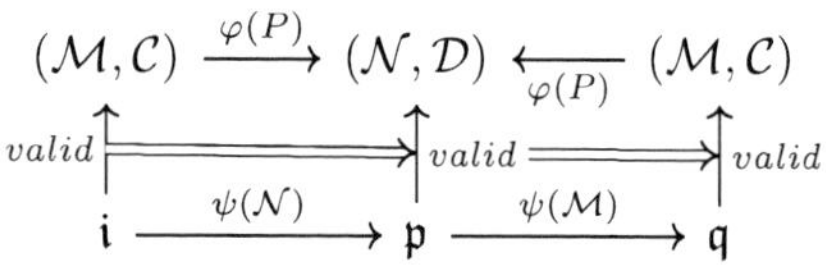

Figure 5. Commutative diagram for validity and lifted validity.

The compliance of $\mathfrak{p}$ to $\mathcal{N}$ can be shown by applying the relations between $\mathfrak{p}$ and $\mathfrak{i}$ to the axioms (6–9) assuming that $\mathfrak{i}$ is compliant to $\mathcal{M}$. Conversely, the validity of $\mathfrak{p}$ with respect to $\mathcal{D}$ is entailed from the validity of $\mathfrak{i}$ with respect to $\mathcal{C}$, as well as from Definition 8. Especially, it holds that if a role type is persisted $rt \in \mathsf{RT}_{\mathcal{N}}$ then all corresponding role (instances) are retained from $\mathfrak{i}$ in $\mathfrak{p}$, such that $R^c_{rt,\mathfrak{p}} = R^c_{rt,\mathfrak{i}}$ holds for all $c \in C_\mathfrak{i}$. Applying these entailments to (12) and (13), we can show that $\mathfrak{p}$ is valid with respect to $\mathcal{D}$. ■

While this proves the consistency of stored partial context-dependent domain models and instances, the question arises whether the persistent partial runtime model can be safely used as starting point after a system breakdown. To show this, we extend the notion of compliance and validity of a persisted CROI $\mathfrak{p}$ to the original CROM $\mathcal{M}$ and corresponding $\mathcal{C}$. Yet, the persisted CROI $\mathfrak{p}$ must first be lifted to the original CROM $\mathcal{M}$, i.e., $\psi(\mathcal{M}, \mathfrak{p})$. This leads to the following theorem:

Theorem 3 (Lifted Validity). *Let $\mathcal{M}$ be a well-formed CROM, $\mathcal{C}$ a constraint model compliant to $\mathcal{M}$, P a persistence annotation of $\mathcal{M}$, as well as $\mathfrak{i}$ a CROI compliant to $\mathcal{M}$ and valid with respect to $\mathcal{C}$. Then the construction $(\mathcal{N}, \mathcal{D}) := \varphi(\mathcal{M}, \mathcal{C}, P)$ and the restriction $\mathfrak{q} := \psi(\mathcal{M}, \psi(\mathcal{N}, \mathfrak{i}))$ entails that $\mathfrak{q}$ is compliant to $\mathcal{M}$ and valid with respect to $\mathcal{C}$.*

Proof: As a consequence of Theorem 2, it also holds that $\mathfrak{p} := \psi(\mathcal{N}, \mathfrak{i})$ is compliant to $\mathcal{N}$ and valid with respect to $\mathcal{D}$. Thus, to prove Theorem 3, we need to show that $\mathfrak{q} := \psi(\mathcal{M}, \mathfrak{p})$ is compliant to $\mathcal{M}$ and valid with respect to $\mathcal{C}$, as the right side of Figure 5 indicates. Moreover, though from Definition 7 it follows, that $\mathcal{N}$ might contain natural types, which where defined as compartment types in $\mathcal{M}$. Accordingly, $\mathfrak{q} := \psi(\mathcal{M}, \mathfrak{p})$ leaves the CROI as is and only moves affected instances form $N_\mathfrak{p}$ to $C_\mathfrak{q}$, in short, transforming natural instances back to compartment instances. However, as both rules (23) and (24) ensure that only compartment types without existential parts (cf. Definition 6) will be persisted as natural type, consequently, for each compartment instance $c \in C_\mathfrak{q}$ with $\mathsf{type}_\mathfrak{q}(c) \in (\mathsf{CT}_\mathcal{M} \cap \mathsf{NT}_\mathcal{N})$, its type has no existential parts $\mathbf{ext}(\mathsf{type}_\mathfrak{q}(c)) = \emptyset$ and $R^c_{rt,\mathfrak{q}} = \emptyset$ for all $rt \in \mathsf{RT}_\mathcal{M}$. As a result, the compliance of $\mathfrak{q}$ to $\mathcal{M}$ immediately follows from the compliance of $\mathfrak{p}$ to $\mathcal{N}$. In contrast, the validity of $\mathfrak{q}$ with respect to $\mathcal{C}$ can be easily entailed from the emptiness of $R^c_{rt,\mathfrak{q}}$ (see above) applied to axioms (12) and (13). ■

In conclusion, these theorems prove that the transformation algorithm guarantees well-formedness, compliance and validity of the generated persistent context-dependent domain model and their instance. This does not only entail correct storage, but also retrieval after a system breakdown. Simply put, the transformation ensures that the persisted instance model p can also be loaded back as a valid instance model q of the runtime domain model $(\mathcal{M}, \mathcal{C})$. To put it succinctly, the transformation guarantees that any persisted instance model is also valid wrt. the complete domain model and constraints.

V. Illustrative Case Study

A. Model Transformation

The *Persistency Transformation* will produce the persistence model depicted in Figure 6. As it can be seen, the *FBS* role type is gone, as well as *R* has been transformed into a natural type, because it has no existential parts that will not be persisted in the database schema. All other role types and natural types are necessary for compliance and consistency to the domain model. However, in the following we will demonstrate the algorithm step by step and explain how the algorithm extends the model and why.

We start with the source model $\mathcal{F}$ and the constraint model $\mathcal{C}_\mathcal{F}$ as defined in Example 1 and 2, respectively. Additionally, we assume the persistence annotation $P = (\emptyset, \{AP\}, \emptyset, \emptyset)$. Henceforth, we define the persisted CROM model $\mathcal{P} = (\mathsf{NT}_\mathcal{P}, \mathsf{RT}_\mathcal{P}, \mathsf{CT}_\mathcal{P}, \mathsf{RST}_\mathcal{P}, \mathsf{fills}_\mathcal{P}, \mathsf{rel}_\mathcal{P})$. At first, the $\mathsf{fills}_\mathcal{P}$ and $\mathsf{rel}_\mathcal{P}$ relations are constructed by the rules given in Figure 2. By applying Rule (20), $\mathsf{fills}_\mathcal{P}$ is extended by $(\mathrm{R}, \mathrm{FA}, \mathrm{AP})$ with all their respective player types. Next, Rule (24) must be applied, resulting in four new entries in $\mathsf{fills}_\mathcal{P}$. Specifically, all role types with an occurrence constraint greater than 0 are added, which applies to *FD* and *A*. Consequently, the resulting $\mathsf{fills}_\mathcal{P}$ is populated with the following triples:

$$\mathsf{fills}_\mathcal{P} = \{(R, FA, AP), (SD, FA, FD), (C, FA, FD), (P, FA, A), (S, FA, A)\}$$

Additionally, the $\mathsf{rel}_\mathcal{P}$ is populated by the rules (27–29), whereas rules (27) and (28) do not apply here, since neither a relationship type is annotated nor a compartment type. Hence, the relationship types *detectors* and *announcers* are collected by Rule (29), because they link role types that are already in $\mathsf{fills}_\mathcal{P}$ and have a cardinality constraint of at least 1. As a result, the $\mathsf{rel}_\mathcal{P}$ is populated as following:

$$\mathsf{rel}_\mathcal{P}(detectors, FA) = (FD, AP)$$
$$\mathsf{rel}_\mathcal{P}(announcer, FA) = (AP, A)$$

Out of these two relations, the corresponding type sets are created by employing rules (15–18) and are the following:

$$\mathsf{CT}_\mathcal{P} = \{FA\} \qquad \mathsf{RST}_\mathcal{P} = \{detectors, announcers\}$$
$$\mathsf{RT}_\mathcal{P} = \{AP, FD, A\} \qquad \mathsf{NT}_\mathcal{P} = \{SD, C, P, S, R\}$$

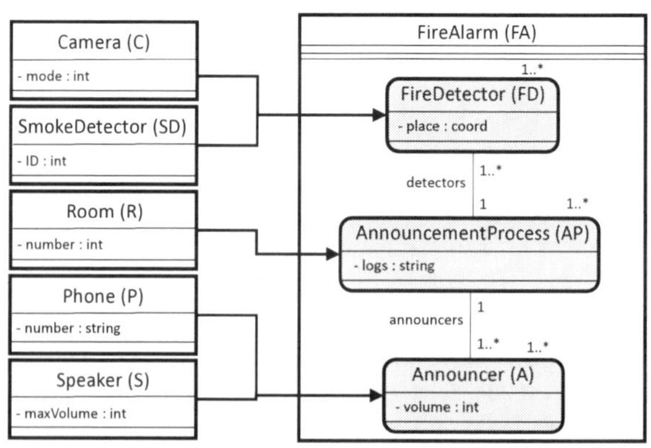

Figure 6. The resulting persisted CROM model.

```
CREATE CT FA (ID Int PRIMARY KEY);
CREATE RT FD (place Coord,ID Int PRIMARY KEY)
    ↪ PLAYED BY (SD,C) PART OF FA WITH OCC (1,⋆);
CREATE RT A (loud Int,ID Int PRIMARY KEY)
    ↪ PLAYED BY (P,S) PART OF FA WITH OCC (1,⋆);
CREATE RT AP (logs Text,ID Int PRIMARY KEY)
    ↪ PLAYED BY (R) PART OF FA WITH OCC (1,⋆);
CREATE RST detectors CONSISTING OF
    ↪ FD BEING (1..⋆) AND AP BEING (1..1);
CREATE RST announcers CONSISTING OF
    ↪ AP BEING (1..1) AND A BEING (1..⋆);
```

Listing 1. RSQL Data Definition Language Statements to Create $\mathcal{N}$.

After inductively defining the persisted CROM $\mathcal{P}$, the constraint model $\mathcal{D_P} := \{\mathsf{occur}, \mathsf{card}\}$ is computed from $\mathcal{C_F}$ by applying (30) and (31). This results in the following partial function definitions, where the feedback cardinality constraint is removed.

$$\begin{aligned}\mathsf{occur}_{\mathcal{D_P}} &:= \{\mathsf{FA} \to \{(1..\infty, \mathsf{FD}), (1..\infty, \mathsf{AP}), (1..\infty, \mathsf{A})\}\} \\ \mathsf{card}_{\mathcal{D_P}} &:= \{(\mathsf{detectors}, \mathsf{FA}) \to (1..\infty, 1..1), \\ &\qquad (\mathsf{announcers}, \mathsf{FA}) \to (1..1, 1..\infty)\}\end{aligned}$$

Finally, the CROM $\mathcal{P}$ and constraint model $\mathcal{D_P}$ is used to create a database schema and persist valid instances of the fire alarm model.

B. Database Schema

As aforementioned, the persistence CROM model $\mathcal{P}$ will be stored in an RSQL database that preserves the context-dependent semantics and information [9]. RSQL is able to directly store CROM-based models, thereby avoiding the need to transfer runtime semantics onto traditional database semantics. Listing 1 lists the RSQL data definition language statements to create the schema for $\mathcal{P}$. Please note, for the sake of brevity, we assume that all natural types have already been created. In practice, this schema can be generated from a given CROM and corresponding constraint model [12]. Additionally, queries directly leverage the context-dependent information during query processing. This allows the SaS to consistently persist, i.e., insert, update, delete and query, parts of the context-dependent knowledge base into the RSQL database system.

VI. Related Work

The Unified Modeling Language (UML) lacks expressive power to model context-dependent domains and while some approaches extended UML in this regard [13][14][15][16], their semantics is usually more ambiguous.

The *Metamodel for Roles* [14] tries to be the most general formalization of context-dependent roles. Similar to CROM, it distinguishes between *Players*, *Roles*, and *Context* on the type and the instance level. Yet, the metamodel is too general to be useful, because the sets of entities are not required to be disjoint (on both the type and instance level) [5]. Similarly, the *Information Networking Model* (INM) [17] is a data modeling approach designed to overcome the inability of data models to capture context-dependent information. While this approach allows to model nested *Contexts* with attributes containing *Roles*, the various kinds of relations cannot be constrained [17]. By extension, the few hybrid models are presented in the *HELENA* approach [16]. It features *Ensembles* as compartments to capture a collaborative task by means of roles that are played by *Components*. In particular, *HELENA* provides formal definitions for both type and instance level, as well as an operational semantics based on sets and labeled transition systems [16]. Furthermore, *HELENA* only supports occurrence constraints on roles, and no cardinality constraints on relationships. In contrast to them, CROM has a well-defined, formal semantics [5], has graphical editing support [12][18] and supports reasoning [6]. A more detailed comparison of context-dependent modeling and programming languages can be found in [19][8].

To persist context-dependent domain models, several approaches are proposed. Generally, these can be classified by their implemented technique. In detail, we distinguish the following techniques: (i) mapping engines, (ii) persistent programming languages, and (iii) full DBS implementation.

Firstly, mapping engines, as technique to bridge the transient application and persistent database world, are well-known from the object-relational impedance mismatch [20]. However, mapping engines like DAMPF [21], ObjectTeams JPA [22], or ConQuer [23] store the transient runtime information in traditional database systems, which does not preserve the context-dependent semantics and thus, cannot be leveraged for storing or querying. Additionally, in multi-application scenarios the database system cannot ensure the metamodel constraints, because the mapping engines hide these constraints from the database system. Secondly, persistent programming languages like the Dynamic Object-Oriented Database Programming Language with Roles (DOOR) [24] or Fibonacci [25] unify the transient application world with the persistent database world. Unfortunately, these approaches help in single application scenarios only, because the persistent data storage is part of the individual applications and thus, not shared with other applications. Especially for self-adaptive software systems, several applications need to share their information, not only directly, but also using a persistent database system, which makes persistent programming language inappropriate for such systems. Finally, the last class of approached comprises the integration of contextual semantics with a database system. The conceptual model of INM has been implemented into a database system and features a dedicated query language [17], [26]. However, INM misses the constraints of relations between the classes. However, none of them considers to partially persist a context-dependent domain model while ensuring its well-formedness and validity.

VII. Conclusion and Future Work

SaS rely on context-dependent domain models at runtime to reason about their environmental situations and system state. Considering persistence, not all information captured in the knowledge base needs to be stored persistently. Yet, finding a valid partial model that is consistent with the original domain model is a daunting task, as the model's well-formedness and validity depends on the well-formedness rules, constraints, and instances of the model itself and also changes after an adaptation of the original domain model. To remedy this, we proposed the *Persistency Transformation* φ, an algorithm that computes a minimal valid partial runtime model given a set of annotated model elements. In fact, we employed CROM, a dedicated, formalized modeling language for context-dependent domain models. Based on CROM, we were able to show that our transformation ensures both the well-formedness of the partial CROM model (including the compliance of the partial constraint model). Moreover, we showed that arbitrary valid instances of a CROM model can be automatically restricted (Instance Restriction ψ) with respect to the partial CROM model, ultimately, yielding valid partial instances of the partial CROM model. Furthermore, we proved that such a valid partial instance can be lifted (Instance Restriction ψ) to the complete CROM model retaining its validity and compliance. Conversely, we can ensure, in case of restoring, such context-dependent information will result in a valid and well-formed runtime model. While the proposed transformation is independent of the underlying database system, our case study employed RSQL, a dedicated database system for storage and retrieval of context-dependent knowledge bases. Regardless of the underlying database system, our approach does not only automate finding a viable partial model, but also guarantees the consistency of this partial model and runtime instances. This reduces the requirements for databases persisting context-dependent knowledge bases of SaS by reducing the memory footprint and avoiding unintended system behavior after a system restore. Notably, the presented algorithm relies on the formal underpinning of CROM and thus might not be applicable to other context-dependent domain models. Moreover, the performance and complexity of the algorithm was not considered in this work. Furthermore, the presented approach explicitly excludes *role groups*, as they can express arbitrary propositional logic formulas [5], thus significantly increasing the expressiveness of CROM.

In the future, we want to fully evaluate the feasibility of our approach by developing a reference implementation and evaluating its performance in more realistic application scenarios. Moreover, we want to introduce role groups by extending the *Persistency Transformation* and investigating the resulting time complexity in the presence of arbitrary role groups. Ultimately, we want to set up a persistence framework for context-dependent domain models. Such an integrated framework would combine modeling the SaS graphically, adding persistence annotations, computing the valid partial persistence model, as well as creating the corresponding RSQL schema statements. Finally, the designed SaS could directly utilize this framework to consistently persist partial context-dependent domain models.

ACKNOWLEDGMENT

This work has been funded by the German Research Foundation within the Research Training Group "Role-based Software Infrastructures for continuous-context-sensitive Systems" (GRK 1907).

REFERENCES

[1] F. D. Macías-Escrivá, R. Haber, R. del Toro, and V. Hernandez, "Self-adaptive Systems: A Survey of current Approaches, Research Challenges and Applications," Expert Systems with Applications, vol. 40, no. 18, 2013, pp. 7267–7279.

[2] C. Krupitzer, F. M. Roth, S. VanSyckel, G. Schiele, and C. Becker, "A survey on engineering approaches for self-adaptive systems," Pervasive and Mobile Computing, vol. 17, 2015, pp. 184 – 206.

[3] C. Hoareau and I. Satoh, "Modeling and processing information for context-aware computing: A survey," New Generation Computing, vol. 27, no. 3, May 2009, pp. 177–196.

[4] T. Jäkel, M. Weissbach, K. Herrmann, H. Voigt, and M. Leuthäuser, "Position Paper: Runtime Model for Role-Based Software Systems," in International Conference on Autonomic Computing, ICAC. Wuerzburg, Germany: IEEE, Jul. 2016, pp. 380–387.

[5] T. Kühn, S. Böhme, S. Götz, C. Seidl, and U. Aßmann, "A Combined Formal Model for Relational Context-Dependent Roles," in International Conference on Software Language Engineering. ACM, 2015, pp. 113–124.

[6] S. Böhme and T. Kühn, "Reasoning on context-dependent domain models," in 7th Joint International Conference on Semantic Technology. Springer, November 2017, pp. 69–85.

[7] Y. Brun et al., "Engineering self-adaptive systems through feedback loops," in Software engineering for self-adaptive systems. Springer, 2009, pp. 48–70.

[8] T. Kühn, "A family of role-based languages," Ph.D. dissertation, Technische Universität Dresden, 2017.

[9] T. Jäkel, T. Kühn, H. Voigt, and W. Lehner, "Towards a Role-Based Contextual Database," in 20th East European Conference on Advances in Databases and Information Systems. Springer International Publishing, 2016, pp. 89–103.

[10] T. Kühn, "Persistence transformation," 2019. [Online]. Available: https://github.com/Eden-06/formalCROM/tree/master/persistency

[11] T. Jäkel, "Role-based data management," Ph.D. dissertation, Technische Universität Dresden, 2017.

[12] T. Kühn, K. Bierzynski, S. Richly, and U. Aßmann, "Framed: Full-fledge role modeling editor (tool demo)," in International Conference on Software Language Engineering. ACM, 2016, pp. 132–136.

[13] Q. Z. Sheng and B. Benatallah, "ContextUML: a UML-based Modeling Language for Model-driven Development of Context-aware Web Services," in International Conference on Mobile Business. IEEE, 2005, pp. 206–212.

[14] V. Genovese, "A Meta-Model for Roles: Introducing Sessions," in 2nd Workshop on Roles and Relationships in Object Oriented Programming, Multiagent Systems, and Ontologies, 2007, pp. 27–38.

[15] G. Guizzardi and G. Wagner, "Conceptual Simulation Modeling with onto-UML," in Winter Simulation Conference. Winter Simulation Conference, 2012, pp. 5:1–5:15.

[16] R. Hennicker and A. Klarl, "Foundations for Ensemble Modeling–The Helena Approach," in Specification, Algebra, and Software. Springer, 2014, pp. 359–381.

[17] M. Liu and J. Hu, "Information Networking Model," in International Conference on Conceptual Modeling. Springer, 2009, pp. 131–144.

[18] T. Kühn, K. I. Kassin, W. Cazzola, and U. Aßmann, "Modular feature-oriented graphical editor product lines," in 22th International Software Product Line Conference. Gothenburg, Sweden: ACM, 10th-14th of September 2018, pp. 76–86.

[19] T. Kühn, M. Leuthäuser, S. Götz, C. Seidl, and U. Aßmann, "A Metamodel Family for Role-based Modeling and Programming Languages," in 7th International Conference on Software Language Engineering. Springer, 2014, pp. 141–160.

[20] C. Ireland, D. Bowers, M. Newton, and K. Waugh, "A Classification of Object-relational Impedance Mismatch," in Advances in Databases, Knowledge, and Data Applications. IEEE, 2009, pp. 36–43.

[21] S. Götz, "Dampf - Dresden Auto-Managed Persistence Framework," Technische Universität Dresden, Diploma Thesis, 2010.

[22] O. Otto, "Development of a Persistence Solution for Object Teams based on the Java Persistence API (dt: Entwicklung einer Persistenzlösung für Object Teams auf Basis der Java Persistence API)," Technische Universität Berlin, Diploma Thesis, 2009.

[23] A. Bloesch and T. Halpin, "Conceptual Queries using ConQuer-II," in International Conference on Conceptual Modeling. Springer, 1997, pp. 113–126.

[24] R. Wong, L. Chau, and F. Lochovsky, "A Data Model and Semantics of Objects with Dynamic Roles," in International Conference on Data Engineering. IEEE, Apr 1997, pp. 402–411.

[25] A. Albano, G. Ghelli, and R. Orsini, "Fibonacci: A Programming Language for Object Databases," The VLDB Journal, vol. 4, no. 3, 1995, pp. 403–444.

[26] J. Hu, Q. Fu, and M. Liu, "Query Processing in INM Database System," in Web-Age Information Management. Springer, 2010, pp. 525–536.

Adapting a Web Application for Natural Language Processing to Odd Text Representation Formats

Bart Jongejan

Department of Nordic Studies and Linguistics
University of Copenhagen, Denmark
Email: bartj@hum.ku.dk

***Abstract*—Users of Natural Language Processing (NLP) are best helped if that technology has a low threshold. Therefore, there is a niche for NLP infrastructures that can adapt to the notations used in scholarly projects, instead of requiring that projects adapt to the notation prescribed by a particular NLP infrastructure. The Text Tonsorium is a web application that fits in that niche, because it is not married to any notation and therefore can integrate tools that are tailored to the needs and notations of projects. There are no costs involved related to manually modelling project specific tools into workflow templates, since the Text Tonsorium automatically computes those templates.**

Keywords–Natural Language Processing; NLP workflows; digital edition; medieval diplomas.

I. Introduction

A. Notations, encodings, file formats

Researchers use notations to express their thoughts and findings in ways that can be understood by their peers. Examples are Venn diagrams, staff notation (for music), Arabic numerals, and notations for regular expressions. Incompatible notations, such as Arabic and Roman numerals, can and do live alongside each other. That is neither good nor bad, but just a reality. The use of different notations for the same thing is sometimes a precondition for progress.

In the computer age, the related concepts of encoding and file format have also become prominent. For software to be able to automatically add annotations to a scholarly document, say, the software has to "understand" the encoding, the file fomat, as well as the notation of the input. In this paper, the distinctions between these three concepts are not important. "Notation" will be used as the generic term for all the conventions that have to be adhered to in order to make successful use of software.

B. NLP infrastructures prescribe notation

There is a tendency in Natural Language Processing (NLP) infrastructure projects to strive for notations that are adhered to by all who want to use the services of those infrastructures. The adoption of widely used notations is probably good for a large number of projects. However, there are also scholarly projects that decide to use notations that primarily achieve other goals than the option to use NLP, for example, that it must be possible to make manual annotations in a visually attractive way, or that project participants do not have to be retrained. In addition, adopting the notation prescribed by an NLP infrastructure has a risk. The project may bet on the wrong notation by choosing a specific NLP infrastructure: notations promoted by infrastructures proliferate at the same rate as projects implementing those infrastructures and can become obsolete after a short time. Universal notations that can replace all other notations and that are not only safe to use now, but also in the foreseeable future, do not exist. Conversely, not adhering to the notation required by an NLP infrastructure excludes scholarly projects from the use of that infrastructure.

C. Mapping between notations

When making NLP tools available to a scholarly project that uses its own notation, there is a need for a technical mediation between the notation employed in that project and the notations required by the NLP tools that currently are in the toolbox. Ideally, the mapping between the notation employed by the project and the notation used by existing NLP tools goes both ways, so that results from the NLP infrastructure appear in the notation employed by the project.

One way to realize a mapping is to let the scholarly project be responsible for the necessary conversions, so that no adaptation of the NLP infrastructure is necessary. This approach was, for example, adopted in the DK-Clarin project [1]. The goals of this project were twofold: a repository with many Danish linguistic resources, and an on-line NLP service for the Danish language. In order to optimize the usefulness of shared resources, users of the DK-Clarin repository were requested to only contribute text resources that complied with a particular schema, called "TEIP5 DK-CLARIN", that followed the Text Encoding Initiative guidelines, version P5 (TEI P5). This notation was agreed on by the users who participated in the DK-Clarin project. The expectation was that other users would also adopt this notation. To nudge users in the right direction, it was decided that the NLP tools could only be applied to resources that had been deposited in the repository. The idea was that the cost of transition from non-conforming notations to the "TEIP5 DK-CLARIN" notation would be outweighed by the advantage of being able to use the NLP tools. In that way, the infrastructure would not have to carry the cost of conversion of notation, but could turn that over to the users.

D. Structure of the paper

The structure of the remaining part of this paper is as follows. Section II presents a workflow management system, the Text Tonsorium (TT), that does not prescribe the use of any particular notation and therefore can be used in projects that use their own notation. Section III presents related work. Section IV presents a use case that illustrates how the TT can adapt to a project that uses its own notation. This is done step by step in four subsections: upload of data, specification of the desired output, computation and selection of workflows, and tracking the execution of the selected workflow as it progresses through its job steps. Section V describes how the Directional Acyclic Graph (DAG) structure of workflows makes it possible to handle both common and project specific notations. That section also describes in a few words how the TT computes workflows. Section VI gives a short outline of the human efforts that are needed to integrate a tool. The concluding remarks and future plans are drawn in Section VII.

II. The Text Tonsorium

This paper exposes the benefits of an approach that is almost opposite to the approach that gives users of an NLP infrastructure the sole responsibility for necessary notation conversions. Both projects and the NLP infrastructure gain something by supplementing an existing and evolving NLP infrastructure with project specific tools for handling project specific notations. Projects thus have the advantage that the notation mapping problem is solved by the NLP infrastructure, while, in the wake of the adaptations for project specific purposes, the infrastructure may very well be enriched with tools that are also useful for a general public. Also the quality of the output from the NLP tools may improve, since the cooperation between a project and the NLP infrastructure may produce new or improved linguistic resources with which NLP tools like Part of Speech taggers and lemmatizers can be (re-)trained.

A precondition for the viability of this approach is that the cost of extending the infrastructure with project specific tools is manageable. Most importantly, the cost per extension should stay more or less constant. The TT is a workflow manager for NLP that supports this approach and does so at a cost that is manageable, because the cost of integration of a new tool does not depend on the number of already integrated tools.

The cost of integration of a new tool would hardly remain the same as the number of already integrated tools grows if existing, preconfigured workflow templates would have to be copied and manually adapted to new notations, since the number of such workflow templates very likely also would grow and the average workflow template would become more complex. The TT eliminates the manual construction of workflow templates. Instead, it creates workflow templates automatically, basing its computations on the features of the actual input, the user's requirements with respect to the output, and the metadata of the tools that are registered in the infrastructure.

The TT was built during the DK-Clarin project as the NLP component of the Clarin.dk [2] infrastructure. Two requirements determined the architecture of this component. Both requirements had the purpose of minimizing the maintenance effort needed to run the infrastructure, so that it could continue to be available and growing in times of low funding.

The first requirement was that if a user of the Clarin.dk infrastructure would like to share a tool with other users, the registration and integration of that tool had to be done by the user, and not by the maintainers of the TT. The second requirement was that the maintainers of the TT should not be involved in the construction of workflow templates.

The second requirement could have been fulfilled by just not offering facilities for workflows at all or by offering a facility that would enable users to construct workflows by hand. The choice fell on a solution that required a user interface with only few fields and controls, and a back-end that computed viable workflow templates automatically, using the characteristics of the input and the desired output as the boundary conditions for the computation of workflow templates.

The possibility to handle other notations than the "TEIP5 DK-CLARIN" notation was a fortuitous side effect of this architecture, but it was not a publicly accessible feature until, in 2017, the NLP component became a web application [3] independent of the Clarin.dk repository, under the new name "Text Tonsorium".

A detailed technical description that explains how the TT computes workflow templates and why most of the implementation was done in a domain specific programming language for Symbolic Mathematics, Bracmat, is in [4]. More about the user perspective of the TT is in [5]. The TT is open source [6].

III. Related Work

Most NLP workflow management systems require (expert) users for the construction of workflow templates and either have elaborate graphical interfaces and tool-profile matching algorithms to assist the user, or require that the user does some scripting.

Weblicht [7] offers NLP workflows that can take a range of file formats as input but no resources that already have some structure, such as metadata and manually created annotations in the text that should not get lost in the NLP workflow. The exception are resources expressed in the Text Corpus Format (TCF) [8], which combines several stand-off annotation layers in a single file. The TCF is the native file format in Weblicht and is used for all data interchange between the tools.

The Nextflow system [9][10] powers the Dutch Philosophical Integrator of Computational and Corpus Libraries (PICCL) [11] portal. The Format for Linguistic Annotation (FoLiA) [12] is the standard notation in PICCL.

Other systems that require the manual construction of workflow templates are, for example (in alphabetical order): Galaxy [13], Gate [14], Kathaa [15], Kepler [16], Taverna [17], TextGrid [18], UIMA [19], and zymake [20].

Curator [21] is a workflow management system with a limited set of NLP tools. Some of these tools depend on outputs from other tools, yet manual construction of workflow templates is not necessary. Workflows are implicitly and uniquely defined in Curator because there is exactly one tool for each type of annotation layer.

Universal Dependencies (UD) is an international effort to develop parsers for many languages. Software contributions must conform to the notation defined for the Conference on Computational Natural Language Learning (CoNLL). [22]

IV. Use case: add PoS tags and lemmas to transcriptions of medieval diplomas

This section shows how the TT adds Part of Speech tags and lemmas to documents that use a project specific notation. The project, *Script and Text in Space and Time* (STST) [23], has the goal, among other things, to provide dynamic and interactive digital editions of medieval diplomas.

The TT is in a way similar to software that computes routes between two addresses on a map. From the user's perspective, there are four steps. On the front page, the user is invited to upload input for NLP processing. On the second page, the user specifies the output. On the third page, the user selects a workflow from a list of possible workflows. On the fourth and final page, the user can follow the execution of the workflow as it progresses, and see the outputs.

The enhancements to the TT that were made for the sake of the STST project will be pointed out as we discuss each of the four steps.

A. First step: upload data

The front page of the TT is shown in Figure 1. The user has three options to send input to the TT: by upload of files, by listing Universal Resource Locators (URLs), and by direct text entry. These methods can in principle be combined, but the TT currently assumes that all uploaded sources have the same language, file type, type of content, etc. The upload starts when the user presses the *Specify the required result* button.

Since, in principle, data that is uploaded to the TT could pass through NLP tools that are monitored by third parties, the user is asked not to upload sensitive data.

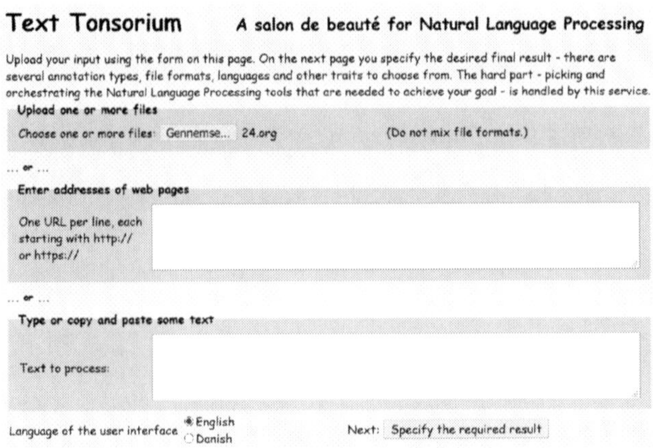

Figure 1. Front page of Text Tonsorium with three input modes.

In this example, the user uploads a single file, "24.org" [24]. This file contains a header and a table, and utilizes Org-mode [25], a notation native to the editor of choice in the STST project, Emacs. The project uses a GitHub repository as shared work space for this and hundreds of other transcriptions of diplomas. For the STST project, an extra benefit of using GitHub is that it has provisions for visualizing Org-mode files in an attractive way.

B. Second step: specify the desired output

When the input is uploaded, the TT's first action is to find out what it is. In this example, the input is uploaded with the media type "application/x-download", "application/octet-stream", or "text/plain", depending on the user's browser. Since these media types are very general, the file is opened by the TT and its content analyzed. The TT ascertains, for example, whether a text file conforms to the aforementioned project's notation. About 360 characters of code are dedicated to this specific analysis. The result of the analysis is shown in the upper part of the second window, see Figure 2. In the shown example, the TT was able to fill out all fields. In general, the TT does not know the language of the input and leaves that field empty, but in this case the language, Latin, is revealed in the header section of the uploaded file.

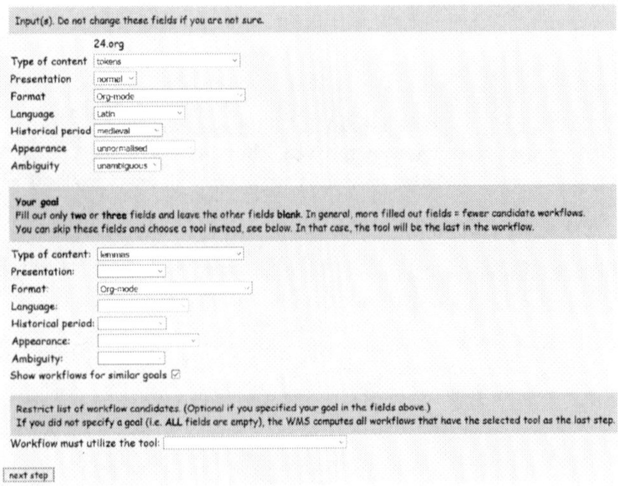

Figure 2. Window where the user specifies the output: lemmas, Org mode. The input features are set by the Text Tonsorium.

The lower part of the window in Figure 2 is where the user specifies the goal. The goal, like the input, is specified in terms of one or more features.

Currently seven features can be specified, and that number can change in the future. Originally, there were only three features, namely those for *language*, *file format* and *type of content*. Later came *presentation* (indicating whether or not a result was sorted, and if yes, alphabetically or according to frequency), *appearance* (whether a result was "noisy", "human readable" or just "clean and concise"), *historical period* ("classical", "medieval", "early modern", "late modern" and "contemporary"), and *ambiguity* ("unambiguous", "ambiguous", or "pruned, but not necessarily unambiguous").

Some feature values can subsume other values as well. For example, the *type of content* called "lemmas" also includes the combination "segments, lemmas", which means that sentence structure of the input is still intact in the output.

The user is advised to leave some fields empty in the goal specification. A very detailed specification decreases the chances that any workflow can fulfil the goal. A good strategy is always to specify the language (this can also be done in the input) and the type of content, and perhaps also the format.

More expert users of the TT can optionally specify a tool that the workflow has to contain. If the output fields are empty, then the output specifications of the selected tool are taken as the goal, and the selected tool will be the last in the workflow. If some of the output fields are also filled out, then the selected tool can be anywhere in the workflow.

In this example the user specifies that the output must have lemmas and that it must have the Org-mode file format. Because the *Show workflows for similar goals* field is checked, the TT will also try to fulfil goals that offer Part of Speech tags besides lemmas, and a few other goals.

C. Third step: workflow templates are computed and user selects one

When the user presses the *next step* button on the output specification page, the TT starts to compute workflow templates that, given the current input, lead to the goal specified by the user. If no workflow template exists that can fulfil the goal with the tools that are currently integrated, then the TT

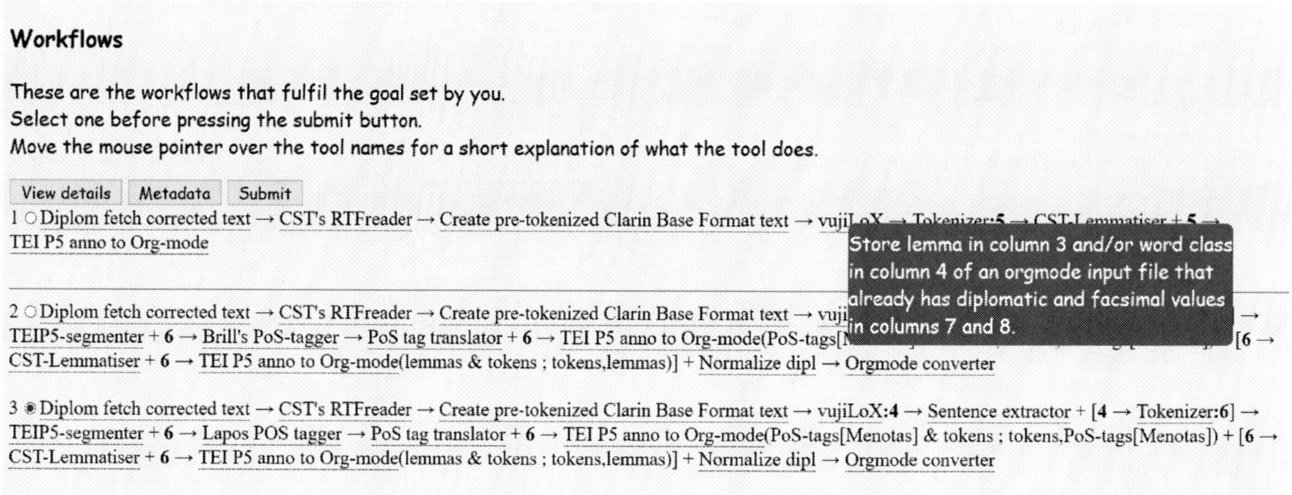

Figure 3. The three workflows that lead to the user's goal. The user has already chosen the third workflow. The "Orgmode converter" tool is explained.

will quickly tell the user that. On the other hand, if there are workflows, then the best ones will be listed.

The list can be quite long. If that is the case, the user is perhaps able to see that the list in part is populated by workflows that are meant for the wrong historical period, or that deliver ambiguous output, or that have other undesirable common features. She can then go back to the output specification window and specify the output in more detail by leaving fewer fields empty. In that way, it is often possible to reduce the presented list to such a degree that the user gets a well organized overview over the possibilities.

Quite often the user will see workflows that are the same apart from different styles of some feature values. For example, the *content type* called "tags" has several tag styles, such as "Universal" and "Penn Treebank" (provided that the language is English). Another example are the two different styles of the "html" value of the *format* feature, one style saying that the body uses the traditional `h`, `p`, `table`, `br`, etc. elements, and another style that does not involve these elements. The latter style is hard to process in an NLP workflow, but defines the text layout to an extremely high degree, as in a PDF document. Normally style values are kept out of sight of the user. Styles are hard to specify for non-specialist users and would add a lot of unintelligable clutter to the user interface.

In this example, the TT lists three workflows, see Figure 3. The first workflow does not involve a Part of Speech tagger, so the user can discard it. The second and third workflows are very similar. The only difference is the Part of Speech tagger. The second workflow involves a Brill POS-tagger, while the third workflow involves the Lapos POS-tagger.

Common to all three workflows and specifically implemented to meet the special needs in the STST project are the tools "Diplom fetch corrected text", "Normalize dipl" and "Orgmode converter". These three tools handle Org mode files that have the internal organization used in the project. The tools "vujiLoX" and "TEI P5 anno to Org-mode" were also created for the sake of this project but are of a general nature. The "vujiLoX" tool lowercases all characters in the input and also converts all *v* to *u* and all *j* to *i*. This tool prepares Latin texts for the lemmatiser. The "TEI P5 anno to Org-mode" tool combines two stand-off annotations into a single two-column table in Org-mode notation. These two tools show that the TT's involvement in a project not only helps the project but can also be useful for users outside that project.

D. Fourth step: execution of the selected workflow and viewing the output

Once the user has selected a workflow and pressed the *next step* button, the TT will execute the selected workflow for all the inputs that the user has uploaded.

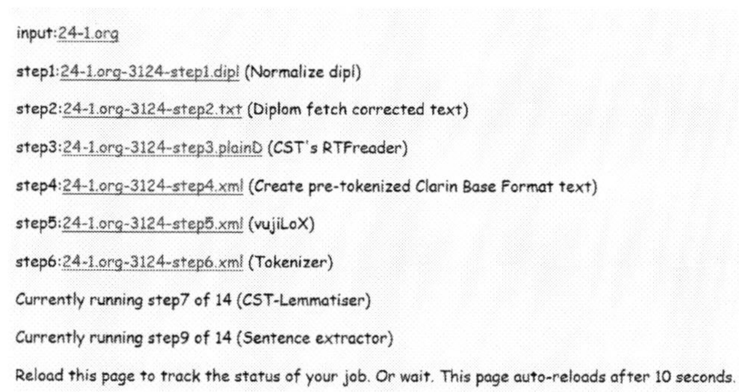

Figure 4. The third workflow halfway being executed.

The output of a tool can be viewed as soon as the tool finishes. The user can reload the page where the workflow unfolds or wait for the automatic page refresh that comes every 10 seconds, see Figure 4.

When all processes in a workflow have been executed, all results can be downloaded in a single zip file. The results can be downloaded again, but after a few days, they are deleted from the server. The output of the workflow is, in this example, the input file enriched with values in columns that were originally empty, see Figure 5.

V. The Structure and Computation of Workflows in the Text Tonsorium

The TT follows the dataflow programming paradigm, which means that a workflow template computed by the TT has the layout of a DAG (See Figure 6) and that NLP tools in mutually independent paths of the graph can be executed at the same time. For example, in Figure 4, the "CST-lemmatiser"

```
| :m:          |                          |
| Text number  | 24                       |
| Shelfmark    | AM dipl dan fasc LI 11   |
| Year         | 1257                     |
| Date         | Jan 13                   |
| Place        | Lateranet                |
| Language     | lat                      |
| Scribe       |                          |
| Material     | perg                     |
| Sender       | Pave Alexander 4.        |
| Jexlev       | 9                        |
| Rep.         | 247                      |
| Dipl. Dan.   | 2 rk. I nr. 205          |
| Reg. Dan.    |                          |
| Ea.          | 580                      |
| SDHK         |                          |

*** Notes

*** Transcription
| :s: |       |             |        |  |             |               |             
| pm  |    1r |             |        |  |             |               |             
| lm  | 24-01 |             |        |  |             |               |             
| PE  |     b |             |        |  |             |               |             
| w   |       | alexander   | PROPN  |  |alexander    | ALEXANDER     | ALEXANDER   
| PE  |     e |             |        |  |             |               |             
| w   |       | episcopus   | NOUN   |  |episcopus    | ep(iscopu)s   | ep&pk;s     
| w   |       | seruus      | NOUN   |  |seruus       | seruus        | feruus      
| w   |       | seruus      | NOUN   |  |seruorum     | seruor(um)    | feruoꝝ      
| w   |       | deus        | NOUN   |  |dei          | dei           | ðei         
| p   |       | /           | X      |  |/            | /             | /           
| w   |       | dilectus    | VERB   |  |dilectis     | Dilectis      | Dilectis    
| w   |       | in          | ADP    |  |in           | in            | in          
| w   |       | christus    | PROPN  |  |christo      | (Christ)o     | xp&pk;o     
| w   |       | filia       | NOUN   |  |filiabus     | filiab(us)    | filiabȝ     
| p   |       | ..          | PUNCT  |  |..           | ..            | ..          
| w   |       | abbato      | VERB   |  |abbatisse    | Abbatisse     | Abbatiffe   
| w   |       | et          | CCONJ  |  |et           | et            | et          
| w   |       | conuentus   | VERB   |  |conuentui    | Conuentui     | Conuentui   
| w   |       | monasterium | NOUN   |  |monasterii   | Monasterij    | (M)onafterij
```

Figure 5. Part of the output in Org-mode. Columns 3, 4 and 6 contain results from three tools. All other content is copied from the input.

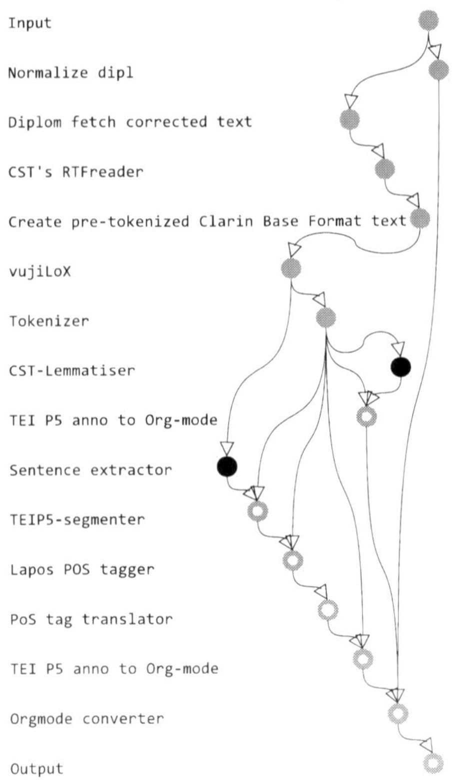

Figure 6. Topological ordering of the third workflow. The black nodes are the currently running steps in Figure 4.

and the "Sentence extractor" are both being executed. These two tools are marked with black filled circles in Figure 6.

The TT computes DAGs by dynamic programming, followed by a pruning step. It starts by fulfilling the user's goal by the output specifications of some tool. It then defines the specifications of that tool's input(s) as the new goal(s). The process is repeated until all goals are satisfied by the specifications of the user's input. Any DAG that leads from the user input to an intermediate goal is memoized, saving both memory and time if the same intermediate goal is needed to satisfy the needs of another tool in the completed workflow template. After a complete DAG is found, the TT backtracks and does an exhaustive search for alternative DAGS, using different tools or the same tools with different settings. The number of found DAGs, which can run in the thousands, is afterwards reduced by excluding those DAGs that have characteristics that users very likely would regard as erroneous, such as multiple occurrences of a particular tool that have different parameter settings for no good reason.

Before presenting the pruned list of workflow template candidates for the user, the TT suppresses details that are not essential for seeing the differences between the candidates. For example, in Figure 3, information about the language, which is Latin in all three workflows, is not shown.

Before a workflow is executed, the corresponding workflow template is instantiated with the actual input provided by the user, and expressed as a list of job steps. Each step comprises the URL of the tool to run, the specification of the necessary input(s) (user provided input or output from other steps), and the actual values of the input and output parameters. Each time new output becomes available, the TT activates job steps for which all required inputs are available.

A huge advantage of DAG-structured workflows is that they can involve both tools that are aware of special notations and tools that are not. Though not impossible, this is hard to achieve with workflows that have a strictly linear structure, as is the case with workflows that use TCF, CoNLL, FoLiA, or other notations that accumulate annotations while traversing a sequence of tools.

The DAG structure has the additional quality that processes in different branches can be executed synchronously.

VI. Integration of Tools

There are some limitations as to which types of tool can be integrated in the TT. The tool must run from the command line and may not require any user interaction while running. Also, all parameters to the tool must either be fixed or take values from a nominal scale [26]. This makes it hard or impossible to integrate, for example, Deep Learning scripts that require that the user experiments with several settings of real-valued parameters.

If a candidate tool fulfils these requirements, the TT offers an easy way of embedding it in an ecosystem of already existing tools.

Once a tool is integrated, users of the TT can see that the new tool is taken into consideration when the TT computes workflow templates.

Integration of a new tool starts in the administrative page of the TT. The registration form is in two parts. One part stores name, description, creator, etc., and, most importantly, the URL where the webservice that wraps around the tool can be found. The second part specifies the input and output profile(s) of the tool in terms of features and feature value subspecifications.

After the registration of a new tool, the TT can create a PHP script for the new web service that is already tailored to the new command line tool to be integrated. This PHP script parses the HTTP parameters that the TT will set when the tool is called and fetches all the input files from the TT server that the tool needs. To wrap the script around the tool, the programmer must look for the pieces of PHP code marked "TODO" and follow the instructions. Dummy code is present that makes it possible to test that the script is callable over HTTP.

VII. CONCLUSION AND FUTURE WORK

Three features of an NLP infrastructure are key to being adaptable to scholarly projects that have chosen a notation that is unknown to the NLP infrastructure. The first feature is that it must be cheap to create workflow templates, so that many different projects, each with their own traditions and requirements, can be served at affordable cost. The second feature is that the NLP infrastructure must not impose a notation on projects that want to use the NLP tools, but rather should open up for "odd" notations. The third feature is that the workflow templates should be composable of tools that require varying notations, so that tools that are tailored to specific projects can cooperate with tools that use different notations.

The TT fulfils these three requirements. (1) The cost of integration of new tools is not influenced by the tools that are already integrated, since workflow templates containing many steps are automatically created at no cost. (2) The TT can handle a wide variety of notations in input and in output. (3) The workflow templates that the TT produces are directed acyclic graphs. That makes it straightforward to pass notation around tools that cannot handle it. In the example given in this paper, all the layout and content in the input is reproduced in the output, which is hard to achieve in linear pipelines of NLP tools.

In the future, we want to speed up processing of large amounts of documents by exporting TT's automatically computed workflow templates to faster workflow execution platforms. We also want to improve the user interface by providing much more context sensitive guidance.

REFERENCES

[1] L. Offersgaard, B. Jongejan, and B. Maegaard, "How Danish users tried to answer the unaskable during implementation of clarin.dk," Nov. 2011, [retrieved: April, 2019]. [Online]. Available: https://cst.dk/dighumlab/publications/dkclarin_SDH_nov2011.pdf

[2] "Clarin.dk," https://clarin.dk/, [retrieved: April, 2019].

[3] "Text tonsorium," https://cst.dk/WMS/, 2017, [retrieved: April, 2019].

[4] B. Jongejan, "Implementation of a workflow management system for non-expert users," in Proceedings of the Workshop on Language Technology Resources and Tools for Digital Humanities (LT4DH). Osaka, Japan: The COLING 2016 Organizing Committee, December 2016, pp. 101–108, [retrieved: April, 2019]. [Online]. Available: http://aclweb.org/anthology/W16-4014

[5] ——, "Workflow management in CLARIN-DK," in Proceedings of the workshop on Nordic language research infrastructure at NODALIDA 2013; May 22-24; 2013; Oslo; Norway. NEALT Proceedings Series 20, no. 89. Linköping University Electronic Press; Linköpings universitet, 2013, pp. 11–20.

[6] "Text tonsorium (source code repository)," https://github.com/kuhumcst/DK-ClarinTools, 2017, [retrieved: April, 2019].

[7] E. W. Hinrichs, M. Hinrichs, and T. Zastrow, "Weblicht: Web-based LRT services for German," in ACL 2010, Proceedings of the 48th Annual Meeting of the Association for Computational Linguistics, July 11-16, 2010, Uppsala, Sweden, System Demonstrations. The Association for Computer Linguistics, 2010, pp. 25–29, [retrieved: April, 2019]. [Online]. Available: http://www.aclweb.org/anthology/P10-4005

[8] U. Heid, H. Schmid, K. Eckart, and E. Hinrichs, "A corpus representation format for linguistic web services: The D-SPIN text corpus format and its relationship with iso standards," in Proceedings of the 7th International Conference on Language Resources and Evaluation, 2010, pp. 494–499.

[9] "Nextflow," https://www.nextflow.io/, [retrieved: April, 2019].

[10] P. Di Tommaso et al., "Nextflow enables reproducible computational workflows," Nature Biotechnology, vol. 35, Apr 2017, pp. 316–319, [retrieved: April, 2019]. [Online]. Available: https://doi.org/10.1038/nbt.3820

[11] "PICCL: Philosophical integrator of computational and corpus libraries," https://github.com/LanguageMachines/PICCL, [retrieved: April, 2019].

[12] M. van Gompel and M. Reynaert, "FoLiA: A practical XML format for linguistic annotation - a descriptive and comparative study," Computational Linguistics in the Netherlands Journal, vol. 3, 2013, pp. 63–81, [retrieved: April, 2019]. [Online]. Available: https://www.clinjournal.org/clinj/article/view/26/22

[13] B. Giardine et al., "Galaxy: A platform for interactive large-scale genome analysis," Genome Res, vol. 15, 2005, pp. 1451–1455, [retrieved: April, 2019]. [Online]. Available: https://www.ncbi.nlm.nih.gov/pmc/articles/PMC1240089/

[14] H. Cunningham, D. Maynard, K. Bontcheva, and V. Tablan, "GATE: An architecture for development of robust hlt applications," in Proceedings of the 40th Annual Meeting on Association for Computational Linguistics, ser. ACL '02. Stroudsburg, PA, USA: Association for Computational Linguistics, 2002, pp. 168–175, [retrieved: April, 2019]. [Online]. Available: https://doi.org/10.3115/1073083.1073112

[15] S. P. Mohanty, N. J. Wani, M. Srivastava, and D. M. Sharma, "Kathaa: A visual programming framework for NLP applications," in Proceedings of the 2016 Conference of the North American Chapter of the Association for Computational Linguistics: Demonstrations. San Diego, California: Association for Computational Linguistics, June 2016, pp. 92–96, [retrieved: April, 2019]. [Online]. Available: http://www.aclweb.org/anthology/N16-3019

[16] A. Goyal et al., "Natural language processing using Kepler workflow system: First steps," Procedia Computer Science, vol. 80, 2016, pp. 712 – 721, international Conference on Computational Science 2016, ICCS 2016, 6-8 June 2016, San Diego, California, USA.

[17] K. Wolstencroft et al., "The Taverna workflow suite: designing and executing workflows of web services on the desktop, web or in the cloud," Nucleic Acids Research, vol. 41, 2013, pp. W557–W561.

[18] H. Neuroth, F. Lohmeier, and K. M. Smith, "TextGrid - virtual research environment for the humanities," IJDC, vol. 6, no. 2, 2011, pp. 222–231, [retrieved: April, 2019]. [Online]. Available: http://dx.doi.org/10.2218/ijdc.v6i2.198

[19] D. Ferrucci and A. Lally, "Building an Example Application with the Unstructured Information Management Architecture," IBM Syst. J., vol. 43, no. 3, Jul. 2004, pp. 455–475, [retrieved: April, 2019]. [Online]. Available: http://dx.doi.org/10.1147/sj.433.0455

[20] E. Breck, "zymake: A computational workflow system for machine learning and natural language processing," in Software Engineering, Testing, and Quality Assurance for Natural Language Processing. Columbus, Ohio: Association for Computational Linguistics, June 2008, pp. 5–13, [retrieved: April, 2019]. [Online]. Available: https://www.aclweb.org/anthology/W08-0503

[21] J. Clarke, V. Srikumar, M. Sammons, and D. Roth, "An NLP curator (or: How I learned to stop worrying and love NLP pipelines)," in Proceedings of the Eight International Conference on Language Resources and Evaluation (LREC'12), pp. 3276–3282, [retrieved: April, 2019]. [Online]. Available: http://lrec-conf.org/proceedings/lrec2012/pdf/664_Paper.pdf

[22] "Universal Dependencies," http://universaldependencies.org/, [retrieved: April, 2019].

[23] "Script and text in space and time," https://humanities.ku.dk/research/digital-humanities/projects/writing-and-texts-in-time-and-space/, [retrieved: April, 2019].

[24] "Diploma 24.org," https://github.com/Clara-Kloster/Guldkorpus/blob/master/transcriptions/org/working/24.org, 2018, [retrieved: April, 2019].

[25] C. Dominik, The Org-Mode 7 Reference Manual: Organize Your Life with GNU Emacs. UK: Network Theory, 2010, with contributions by David O'Toole, Bastien Guerry, Philip Rooke, Dan Davison, Eric Schulte, and Thomas Dye.

[26] S. S. Stevens, "On the Theory of Scales of Measurement," Science, vol. 103, Jun. 1946, pp. 677–680.

Just-In-Time Delivery for NLP Services in a Web-Service-Based IT Infrastructure

Soheila Sahami

Natural Language Processing Group
University of Leipzig, Germany
Email: sahami@informatik.uni-leipzig.de

Thomas Eckart

Natural Language Processing Group
University of Leipzig, Germany
Email: teckart@informatik.uni-leipzig.de

Abstract—**Just-In-Time delivery of resources is a standard procedure in the industrial production of goods. The reasons for introducing this paradigm and its potential benefits are in large parts applicable for the area of web-based Natural Language Processing Services as well. This contribution focuses on prerequisites and potential outcomes of a Just-In-Time-capable infrastructure of Natural Language Processing services using an example service. The benefits of such an endeavour are sketched with a focus on the ongoing development of large scale service delivery platforms like the European Open Science Cloud or similar projects.**

Keywords–NLP Services; Research Infrastructure; Just-In-Time Delivery; Cluster Computing.

I. Introduction

In industrial production environments, providing resources immediately before they are required in the context of a larger production chain – typically called *Just-in-Time Delivery* (JIT delivery) – is a standard procedure for many decades now. The transfer of this concept into the area of information technology offers a new competitive opportunity that promises significant advancements, such as faster responses, improved quality, flexibility, and reduced storage space [1].

The use of linguistic applications – i.e., tools for preprocessing, annotation, and evaluation of text material – is an integral part for a variety of applications in scientific and commercial contexts. Many of those tools are nowadays available and actively used in service-oriented environments where – often complex – hardware and software configuration is hidden from the user. In the context of large research infrastructures, like CLARIN [2] or DARIAH [3], or cross-domain projects, like the European Open Science Cloud (EOSC) [4], one of the key goals is to facilitate the use of services which are seen as integral and indispensable building blocks of a modern scientific landscape.

These research infrastructure projects can be seen as driving forces for current trends in the dissemination and delivery of tools and services. However in many respects, they are undergoing a similar development as already completed in many commercial areas where delivery and use of services is performed in an industrial scale. Systematic assessment and improvement of quality, measurement of throughput times or other criteria are prerequisites for the use of services even for time-critical applications [5].

One of the potential outcomes and goals of a more "industrialised" infrastructure could be a just-in-time delivery of services, providing the benefits – while requiring comparable prerequisites – already accustomed in the industrial production of goods, like reduced response times or reduction of required storage facilities [6]. However, those topics are hardly addressed in today's text-oriented research infrastructures. Some of the missing preliminary work that is required to offer JIT delivery of linguistic services – like transparency of the process and its sub-processes, deep knowledge about required resources and execution times – are addressed in this contribution.

One of the important challenges in JIT delivery is the applied strategy to address the reliability and predictability of services [7]. In IT infrastructures, utilising fault-tolerant techniques is one of the solutions to improve the reliability of an application. Parallelised implementations using cluster-based processing architectures are technologies that are utilised to decrease run-times and to enable the processing of large scale resources. Furthermore, they provide a helpful means to configure processes in a dynamic manner. This allows suggesting several configurations based on the available resources of the service provider or temporal requirements of the user. Clear information about potential expenses and the estimated delivery time for each configuration gives users a means to select a suitable service (or service chain) or service configuration that fits their needs best.

This also helps the users to have a clear strategy for data storage, duration of data retention, and delivery time. These features have the potential to enhance the user's satisfaction and provide added values that lead to a stronger position in competitive industrialised IT infrastructures.

In this contribution, we present an example of a Natural Language Processing (NLP) service with a focus on its transparency regarding execution times and required resources. As a result, valid resource configurations can be chosen considering available resources and expected delivery times.

The following Section II gives more details about the parallelism of just-in-time delivery of IT services and their industrial counterpart. Section III describes the used methodology and technical approaches. Sections IV and V illustrate and discuss the outcomes and results and are followed by a brief conclusion of this contribution in Section VI.

II. Just-in-time Delivery of IT-Services

Just-in-time delivery (or just-in-time manufacturing) is a management concept that was introduced in the Japanese automotive industry [8] and was adopted for many other areas of production and delivery of goods since. Based on experiences and best practices, catalogues were developed that contain extensive lists of requirements that make the usage of JIT delivery chains manageable and trustworthy.

Established requirements deal with all kinds of aspects in the organisational, legal and technical environment of companies and organisations that are involved in the overall process. At least a subset of those requirements, is directly transferable to activities in IT processes and infrastructures [1], including the more recent deployment, provisioning, and use of services in complex Service-Oriented Architectures (SOAs). This contains procedures and guidelines like the strict use of a "pull-based" system, process management principles with a focus on flow management, adequate throughput, and continuous assessment of quality and fitness of used processes and outcomes. Its obvious benefits have made the underlying policies also a cornerstone of modern agile management principles (c.f. [9]).

There is some research about transferring the JIT concept and its principles to service-oriented environments, like the ones gaining momentum in the area of NLP applications. In the context of such IT services chains, the term *just-in-time* can be understood in different ways. It is often referring to the specific decision for a set (or chain) of services – out of a potentially large inventory of compatible services from different providers – as part of the typical discovery/bind-process *at runtime*, i.e., without a fixed decision for specific providers or even prior knowledge about the current inventory of available services. This is sometimes called "just-in-time integration" of services (for example in IBM's developer documentation [10]).

Many essential requirements for a JIT integration are already handled in existing frameworks – for example CLARIN's WebLicht [11] –, like compatibility-checks of all services regarding their input parameters and generated output, a systematic monitoring of all participating service providers of the federation, or – in parts – even adherence to legal constraints.

A different approach for services-based JIT delivery, focuses on the estimated time of arrival (ETA) of the required results for a specific service chain. This is especially important considering the growing amount of text material that is required to be processed. Most academic providers of NLP services are not able to guarantee acceptable processing times – or the completion of large processing jobs at all – with their current architectures for (very) large data sets in the context of SOAs. However, this kind of functionality is required to reach new user groups and to make them competitive offerings in comparison with other (including commercial) service providers. This aspect is hardly addressed in previous and current projects of the field but gains significance in current attempts to make scientific working environments more reliable and trustworthy with a strong focus on cloud-based solutions (like the European Open Science Cloud EOSC).

A key idea is the incremental creation and adaptation of "performance profiles" for all elements of a provider's service catalogue. This contains the identification of all relevant parameters of a tool and well-founded empirical knowledge about their effects on the runtime of every single NLP task for all kinds of plausible inputs. This requires a processing architecture that is able to dynamically allocate resources for each assigned job while minimising (or even eliminating) the effects of other jobs that are executed in parallel.

In the following, we will describe a concrete example of such a service performance profile depending on the assigned hardware configuration and sketch its benefits.

III. TECHNOLOGIES AND TOOLS

In this section, we explain the chosen technologies and their specific features relevant for the context of this contribution. Afterwards, the implemented NLP tools and utilised resources are described.

A. Technical Approaches

For services where response times are a critical subject, the utilised technology should support technical features like fault-tolerance and high availability. Being fault-tolerant relies on the ability of the system to detect a hardware fault and immediately switch to a redundant hardware component. High availability systems refer to architectures that are able to operate continuously without failure during a specific time period. For this contribution, we have selected Apache Hadoop clusters and the Apache Spark execution engine to address the topic of fault tolerance and high availability. Furthermore, this approach supports the parallelisation of tasks to improve response times significantly.

Apache Hadoop is a popular framework to process large-scale data in a distributed computing environment. Its large ecosystem consists of the Hadoop Kernel, MapReduce, HDFS and some other components [12]. Hadoop Distributed File System (HDFS) as a highly fault-tolerant distributed storage system is able to handle the failure of storage infrastructure without losing data by storing three complete copies of each block of data redundantly on three different nodes [13].

Apache Spark is also a general-purpose cluster computing framework for big data analysis with an advanced in-memory programming model. It uses a multi-threaded model where splitting tasks on several executors improves processing times and fault tolerance. Apache Spark uses Resilient Distributed Dataset (RDD), a data-sharing abstraction, which is designed as fault-tolerant collections and is capable to recover lost data after a failure using the lineage approach: during the construction of an RDD, Spark keeps the graph of all transformations. In the event of a failure, it re-runs all failed operations to rebuild lost results. The RDDs are persisted and executed completely in RAM – In-Memory Databases (IMDB) –, therefore generating and rewriting the recovered data is a fast process [14] [15].

B. NLP Tools and Resources

Using Hadoop-based cluster computing architecture, a variety of typical NLP tools were implemented, including sentence segmentation, pattern-based text cleaning, tokenizing, language identification, and named entity recognition [16]. These tools use Apache Hadoop as their framework, Apache Spark as execution engine and HDFS for storing input data and outputs. These tools are atomic services that can be integrated into any SOA-based annotation environment.

In order to have an accurate estimation of execution times, a variety of benchmarks were carried out for all implemented tools. As an example, the duration of sentence segmentation for datasets of German documents with sizes from 1 to 10 Gigabytes was evaluated using different cluster configurations. The cluster configuration varied in the number of assigned executors (1 to 32 nodes) and allocated memory per executor

(8 or 16 GB). Each test was repeated three times; average execution time over all three runs was used for the following statistics. Figures 1 and 2 show these execution times for sentence segmentation from 1 to 10 GB of input data with different resource configurations.

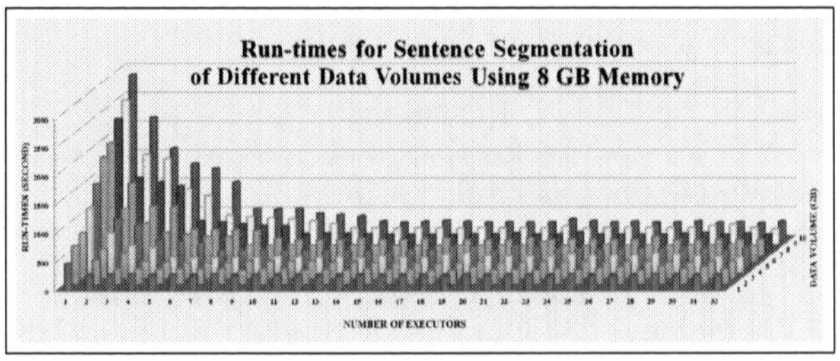

Figure 1. Run-times for segmenting 1 to 10 GB text materials using 1 to 32 executors and 8 GB memory per executor.

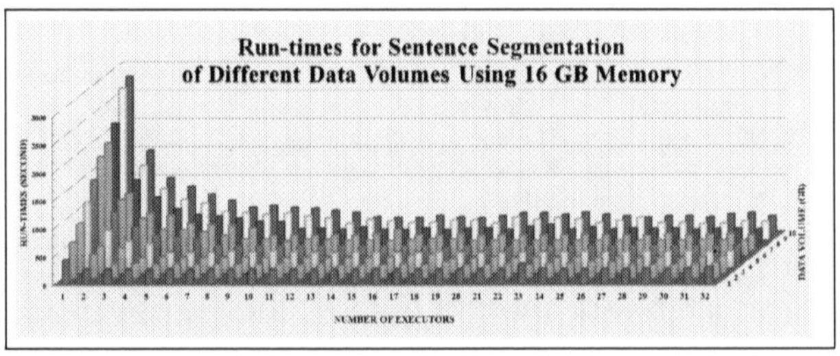

Figure 2. Run-times for segmenting 1 to 10 GB text materials using 1 to 32 executors and 16 GB memory per executor.

These tests were carried out using a cluster provided by the Leipzig University Computing Center [17]. The cluster consists of 90 nodes each with 6 cores and 128 GB RAM. The cluster provides more than 2 PB storage in total and is connected via 10 Gbit per second Ethernet [18].

IV. Results

As Figures 1 and 2 illustrate, run-times vary for different job configurations. As expected, using only a single executor – therefore executing the job without any parallelisation on the cluster – shows the maximum run-time for every data volume. The outcomes of all conducted tests indicate that execution times can be improved with extended hardware resources (i.e. more executors). This improvement complies with the expected behaviour of parallel processing: a sharp decrease in execution time by increasing the assigned resources, followed by a smoother reduction and finally no significant improvement when adding more resources to the job does not improve the speedup anymore. The results show this consistent behaviour for different data volumes using various cluster configurations. Figure 3 gives an overview of run-times for data sets from 1 to 10 GB using 1 to 32 executors and 16 GB RAM per executor.

Figure 4 shows the results for sentence segmentation of 10 GB text material which requires 2860 seconds using 8 GB RAM and 2795 seconds using 16 GB RAM on a single node, where adding a second executor decreases the run-time to 2115 respectively 1480 seconds.

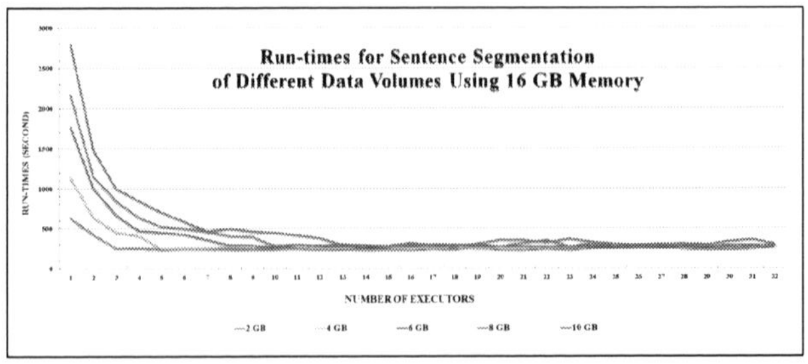

Figure 3. Run-times for different number of executors and data volumes using 16 GB memory per executor

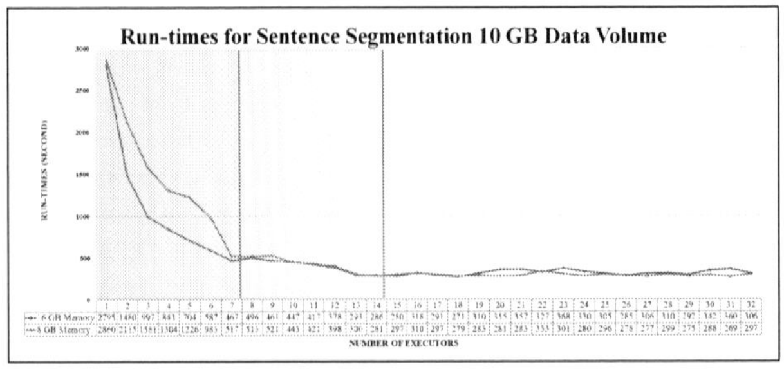

Figure 4. Run-times for different numbers of executors, illustrating different "speedup areas"

The typical trend can be seen again where run-times decrease significantly up to (around) 7 assigned executors, and with no improvements when allocating 14 executors or more.

V. Discussion

Execution times are valuable information that can be utilised for the estimation of times of arrival for annotation jobs in NLP toolchains. Measured execution times give the opportunity to configure the cluster dynamically based on expected response times, available resources and the current load by a varying number of parallel users or jobs. For instance, if there are x free resources available on the cluster and a processing job requires $x+y$ resources, the new job may be scheduled to be executed after finishing the first running job which has allocated at least y resources.

Furthermore, they are also relevant for estimating an "optimal" resource allocation for each individual tool. In the context of this contribution, these resources include the number of executors and the amount of memory which can be assigned to each task. Obviously, the term "optimal" is a very ambiguous one: it depends on the context of which value should be actually optimised. In this context, this may be the overall run-time of a job (i.e. a user-oriented view), the amount of allocated resources (i.e. a cost-oriented view) or a combination of both (by finding some balance between both).

By allocating more executors, execution times can be decreased. At a certain point (which may depend on a variety of parameters), assigning more resources will have no positive effect on execution times anymore. This point can be seen as the optimal configuration for the particular task in respect of optimised run-times, and contains the amount of resources which are required to generate a result in the shortest possible execution time. In this situation, it is also feasible to generate results by assigning fewer resources – with the drawback of extended processing times – but it is obviously not reasonable to assign more resources to the job. As an example, in Figure 4 the fastest configuration for sentence segmentation of 10 GB text data consists of 14 executors with 16 GB RAM per executor where assigning more resources generates more costs without providing faster execution.

The extracted information helps to provide different resource configurations in accordance with the available hardware resources and desired response times for the user's requested service and input material. For instance, if a user wants to segment 10 GB text material in less than 25 minutes, 3 executors with 16 GB RAM or 4 executors with 8GB RAM would be both suitable configurations. In contrast, for a response time of up to 5 minutes, a configuration consisting of at least 14 executors with 8 or 16 GB RAM would suffice. In an environment where accounting of actual expenses is included, the balance between technical or financial costs and acceptable run-times can also be delegated to the user. In such an environment, a user can choose the desired configuration considering estimated run-times and incurred expenses.

The presented diagrams also show that for particular configuration changes resulting improvements of run-time are only marginal. Especially in case of limited available resources or unexpected usage peaks, these configurations do not have to be available anymore as their effect from the user's perspective are small. For instance, in Figure 4 assigning 7 executors with 16 GB RAM generates the expected result in 467 seconds whereas doubling the number of executors leads only to an execution time of 286 seconds (i.e. a 39% run-time reduction).

VI. CONCLUSION

In this contribution, we described some prerequisites for providing JIT delivery in service-oriented research infrastructures using a typical NLP task as an example. We have utilised Apache Spark as execution engine on an Apache Hadoop cluster to allow parallel processing of large text collections and to increase the reliability and predictability of the services. An evaluation of required resources for processing different amounts of text offers information about possible hardware configurations that is useful for estimating delivery times and potential expenses for each individual task.

Naturally, providing and maintaining such resources and tools lead to actual financial costs. In commercial platforms, like Amazon Comprehend [19] or Google Cloud NLP [20] these costs are covered by contracts with costumers based on defined parameters (kind of service, required availability, costs of data storage, CPU cycles, etc.). The selected configuration and execution time can be used as a basis for an accounting system which relies on well-founded expenses for each individual NLP job.

The presented run-times in this abstract can only be a part of a qualified assessment of NLP tasks. Performance profiles require a variety of training cycles to be meaningful and to cover all kinds of input material and their effects on the assessed tool. Furthermore, measuring actual response times for larger toolchains in text-oriented research infrastructures is more complex and needs to take more parameters into account. This is especially relevant for toolchains where multiple service providers are used. Other relevant parameters, like data transfer times between user and service provider or between different services, required format conversions, or similar tasks were not considered here.

ACKNOWLEDGEMENT

Computations for this work were done with resources of Leipzig University Computing Center.

REFERENCES

[1] F. W. McFarlane, Information technology changes the way you compete. Harvard Business Review, Reprint Service, 1984.

[2] E. Hinrichs and S. Krauwer, "The CLARIN Research Infrastructure: Resources and Tools for e-Humanities Scholars," Proceedings of the Ninth International Conference on Language Resources and Evaluation (LREC-2014), May 2014, pp. 1525–1531. [Online]. Available: http://dspace.library.uu.nl/handle/1874/307981

[3] J. Edmond, F. Fischer, M. Mertens, and L. Romary, "The DARIAH ERIC: Redefining Research Infrastructure for the Arts and Humanities in the Digital Age," ERCIM News, no. 111, Oct. 2017. [Online]. Available: https://hal.inria.fr/hal-01588665

[4] EOSC, "EOSC European Open Science Cloud," Online, 2019, Date Accessed: 3 Apr 2019. URL https://www.eosc-portal.eu.

[5] C. Kuras, T. Eckart, U. Quasthoff, and D. Goldhahn, "Automation, management and improvement of text corpus production," in 6th Workshop on the Challenges in the Management of Large Corpora at the 11th Language Resources and Evaluation Conference (LREC 2018), Miyazaki (Japan), 2018.

[6] H. Wildemann, Das Just-in-time-Konzept: Produktion und Zulieferung auf Abruf, 3rd ed. gfmt, 1992.

[7] P. Blais, "How the information revolution is shaping our communities," Planning Commissioners Journal, vol. 24, 1996, pp. 16–20.

[8] T. Ohno, Toyota Production System: Beyond Large-Scale Production. Taylor & Francis, 1988.

[9] P. Heck and A. Zaidman, "Quality criteria for just-in-time requirements: just enough, just-in-time?" in 2015 IEEE Workshop on Just-In-Time Requirements Engineering (JITRE). Los Alamitos, CA, USA: IEEE Computer Society, aug 2015, pp. 1–4. [Online]. Available: https://doi.ieeecomputersociety.org/10.1109/JITRE.2015.7330170

[10] IBM, "Web services architecture overview," Online, 2019, Date Accessed: 3 Apr 2019. URL https://www.ibm.com/developerworks/web/library/w-ovr/.

[11] E. W. Hinrichs, M. Hinrichs, and T. Zastrow, "WebLicht: Web-Based LRT Services for German," in Proceedings of the ACL 2010 System Demonstrations, 2010, pp. 25–29, Date Accessed: 3 Apr 2019. URL http://www.aclweb.org/anthology/P10-4005.

[12] ApacheHadoop, "Apache Hadoop Documentation," Online, 2019, Date Accessed: 3 Apr 2019. URL http://hadoop.apache.org.

[13] H. S. Bhosale and D. P. Gadekar, "A review paper on Big Data and Hadoop," International Journal of Scientific and Research Publications, vol. 4, no. 10, 2014, pp. 1–7.

[14] M. Zaharia, R. S. Xin, P. Wendell, T. Das, M. Armbrust, A. Dave, X. Meng, J. Rosen, S. Venkataraman, M. J. Franklin et al., "Apache spark: a unified engine for big data processing," Communications of the ACM, vol. 59, no. 11, 2016, pp. 56–65.

[15] M. Hamstra and M. Zaharia, Learning Spark: lightning-fast big data analytics. O'Reilly & Associates, 2013.

[16] S. Sahami and T. Eckart, "Spark WebLicht Webservices," Online, 2019, Date Accessed: 4 Apr 2019. URL http://hdl.handle.net/11022/0000-0007-CA50-B.

[17] L.-P. Meyer, J. Frenzel, E. Peukert, R. Jäkel, and S. Kühne, "Big Data Services," in Service Engineering. Springer, 2018, pp. 63–77.

[18] "the galaxy cluster."

[19] Amazon, "Amazon Comprehend - Pricing," Online, 2019, Date Accessed: 4 Apr 2019. URL https://aws.amazon.com/comprehend/pricing/.

[20] Google, "Pricing - Natural Language API - Google Cloud," Online, 2019, Date Accessed: 4 Apr 2019. URL https://cloud.google.com/natural-language/pricing.

International Academy, Research, and Industry Association (IARIA)
412 Derby Way
Wilmington, DE 19810

ISBN 978-1-5108-8609-4

CURRAN ASSOCIATES INC.
proceedings.com

G200 Youth Forum 2017 Conference

Dubai, United Arab Emirates
6 - 10 December 2017

G200
ASSOCIATION